Adventure Cycling

Companion volumes

Adventure Cycling

IN BRITAIN

Tim Hughes

BLANDFORD PRESS

Poole   Dorset

First published 1978 by Blandford Press Ltd.

Link House, West Street
Poole, Dorset BH15 1LL

Copyright © 1978 W. T. Hughes

ISBN 0 7137 0878 6

Set in 10 on 12 pt Baskerville and
printed in Great Britain by Unwin Brothers Limited
a member of the Staples Printing Group
Bound by Robert Hartnoll Limited, Bodmin

Contents

Acknowledgements

My thanks go to all my colleagues of the Cyclists' Touring Club and the Fédération Française de Cyclotourisme who – sometimes un-wittingly – provided me with snippets of information, allowed them-selves to be measured and repeated the action just once more for the cameras. I must also acknowledge the great assistance of my wife, without whom pages 4 and 47 among others might well have been blank, and who kindly lent me two of her bicycles to photograph, to save me the trouble of polishing mine. She also devised some of the day circuits and tours. Miss Hazel Wyatt – who knew nothing about cycle-touring when she started – was of immense help in preparing the manuscript. I am grateful as well to one of my earliest cycling 'tutors', Les Reason, who assisted by lettering the sketch maps. It would be wrong, too, not to recognise my debt to my cycling parents who introduced me to the pastime but neither of whom, sadly, lived to see this book in print. Finally, Chapter 15 is, of course, dedicated to Anne and Audrey and Beryl and Betty and Bubbles and Faith and, oh yes, Heather and Jane and Jennie and Ramona and Tessa . . .

Introduction

Sooner or later, and usually in the most unexpected of contexts, it comes out in conversation that I ride a bicycle for pleasure – and the questions begin. After the inevitable 'How many miles do you do in a day?', the next three are *always*: 'What do you do when you get a puncture? When it rains? When you come to a hill?' One of the aims of this book is to answer these pretty quickly and to get to the real point of it all, which is where we go, with whom, how – and why.

The bicycle has been around in one form or another for nearly a century-and-a-half, and from the first days it was used for travel, for touring, for what was then a great adventure. By a century ago the first organised clubs and national organisations to promote touring by bicycle had been formed. Touring included then, and still does in a cycling context, all forms of cycling for the pleasure of travel and not just the extended journey of days or weeks. By the last decade of the nineteenth century, intrepid lady bicyclists had ridden round the world, while the machine itself had taken on most of the elements of the shape in which it is familiar today.

For a short period, the bicycle was king of the road, darling of high society: in 1891 the largest club in the country was the Cambridge University Bicycle Club. Then came Daimler and Benz and their successors and the bicycle came to be regarded as a more plebeian device: by the time H. G. Wells' Mr Hoopdriver took to the road and pursued The Girl in Grey, even drapers' assistants could aspire to own one. In the first thirty-odd years of the century the bicycle was perhaps one of the major emancipators of the working class and by its means those whose daily toil took them to the coalface, the mill and the foundry could escape for the precious hours of Sunday to a greener and sunnier landscape. 'Cloth cap' image or no, the ready availability

'For a time the bicycle was the darling of high society'.

of the bicycle brought beauty and with it education to people hungry for both.

For the first few years after the Second World War there was a boom in mass cycling, reaching a peak in the early fifties. Then, as more and more people for whom the bicycle had been their sole means of transport and solely a means of transport acquired the money for a car, the numbers of cyclists declined. The first signs of a reversal of the trend came late in the sixties in perhaps the last place one would have expected it – the USA. Worries about the health risks of indolence and of pollution of the surroundings brought to the fore a different type of cyclist, principally middle-class, educated, articulate – and concerned. Hand-in-hand with the recognition that the bicycle was a pleasant means of exercise and a minimal polluter, came the discovery by many that it was an excellent way of exploring and discovering their own and other lands. So we now stand, a hundred years after the foundation in Harrogate of the Bicycle Touring Club as the first touring club – of any kind – in the world, at a point where the numbers of newcomers to our pastime of all ages and from all sources are increasing. It is to them – to you? – that this book is principally addressed.

There is probably no other sporting and recreational activity which covers so wide a range merely by changing the degree of effort involved: running has an entirely different action from walking, and whoever heard of the footballer who dribbled his way to the stadium? This basic identity means that there is a constant interchange between the different types of cyclist. There are many, for example, who take part in competition in the summer and ride for pleasure at other seasons – I have been one of them for quite a few years.

After all, even if a competitive cyclist has an exceptional talent and remains at the top of his powers for a period of, say, ten years, he would be eligible only for three Olympic road titles plus seven amateur World Championship jerseys, or he might aspire to perhaps a dozen or so domestic championships. But anyone, within the limits of his or her ability and inclination can continue to ride a bicycle for pleasure and discovery every day of the year to whatever age they choose.

This, I'm afraid, is one of the dangers of cycling: it can become addictive – perhaps there should be a warning notice on every bicycle sold!

Cycle-touring at its best is utterly free, untrammelled, silent travel. Should one codify and so restrict a sport-cum-pastime in which there should be, by definition, no rules but your own and those of common sense? That is a reasonable question – it has to be understood that wherever I advise a particular way of doing something, that way will be one that I have found by personal experience to work well. In many cases there are pitfalls that may be avoided simply, wrinkles learnt the hard way to be passed on, and quite a number of short cuts to be pointed out. But in almost every case these will be by no means the only, the exclusive way of doing things. There are always choices, counsels of perfection – which I never attain myself! – and ways of getting by at lower cost. Where any skimping would compromise something important, for example safety, I shall say so.

What then should you expect to get out of cycle-touring and why do people become addicted to it? It's a difficult point to discuss without falling to one side or the other of the thin divide between rationalising genuine enjoyment and pretentious – not to say maudlin or cosily priggish – romanticism.

There are those for whom the main object is to visit places and objects in which they are interested – churches, museums, mills, places with historical or literary connexions – and for them the bicycle is, initially, a relatively cheap means of getting there. There are those who feel the urge to explore their own country in detail and to whom the silent, non-polluting nature of the machine appeals. There are some fired by pure curiosity or the talk of friends, and others attracted by what appears to be a congenial form of exercise perhaps with similar company. All these are part of the answer: none has all of it, for there is – perhaps indefinably – more than the sum of these.

Indeed – and this is where the romantic view is difficult to avoid – cycle-touring, alone or in company, should not be merely a voyage of discovery, but one of self-discovery. There are elements of competition – and I would defy even the most avowedly non-competitive cyclist to deny, with absolute truth, that they had not at some time felt a glow of satisfaction on reaching the top of a pass with the world spread at their feet, in getting to the place which seemed so distant at the beginning of the day, even in defying the weather. (Or even all three: the first time I went up the Col du Grand St Bernard, on the Swiss-Italian border, we reached the 2469m (8100ft) summit at the end of a long day under capes in a thunderstorm, and we were elated. A few years later, circumstances brought me to the same spot in a car – and I felt cheated.) There is, then, an enjoyment – without going to the lengths of masochism! – in pitting your strength against obstacles, and a feeling of achievement, of *personal* physical achievement, in conquering

Cycle-touring is obviously not exclusively a male pursuit.

your own chosen Everest or South Pole, by your own unaided efforts –
while admitting a trifle owed to the combined talents of the Michaux
family, John Boyd Dunlop, James Starley, Reynolds Tubes and
Specialités TA.

But it would be entirely wrong to equate personal satisfaction solely
with overcoming adversity. Just as you can never be a total stranger
again to somebody you have shared the work of riding into a headwind
with, or seen bedraggled after a storm, so you can never be again
entirely emotionally remote from anyone who has shared with you
the experience of riding through the dawn. For there are nuances of
exhilaration in open and high spaces, in commanding and ever-
changing skies, in mountain, lake and woodland, in light and shade, in
descent as compared with the triumph of ascent. I don't suppose that
many cycle-tourists would admit it, in so many words, but there is a
feeling almost of spiritual uplift as you turn your wheels towards the
high places, as the valley begins to close in and the road winds higher,
a feeling independent of the individual elements of the scenery.
Equally, and wholly incapable of classification, there is a wealth of

delight in the trivialities and minutiae of cycle travel, for you can deploy all your senses from a bicycle in a way probably impossible in any other pastime. The passing panorama is not merely views, it is a succession of scents, sounds and sensations, all experienced from the vantage point of the saddle. And once you have known these, then they become a base for more sights, sounds and so on, an ever-increasing experience. This is the spirit of cycle-touring: only you can discover it.

The earlier, technical chapters, then, will teach you that the number of miles to be covered in a day may be as many or as few as you feel like, that a puncture is not the greatest disaster that you could ever encounter and what to do if it happens, how to dress appropriately for the rain, to have the right gears for the hills – and not to be too proud to walk. You will have reached your GCE O-Level in Cycle-touring.

In going on in the second part of the book to suggest specific routes I am again aware that they are not the only ones – possibly not even the best, for I cannot know them all – but merely good examples of what you can discover within the boundaries of your own country. They, too, are just a beginning, a nudge in the right direction.

Any qualification from this point on, your A-Level in Adventurous Cycling, say, is a research degree, with every newly-discovered pleasure a fresh chapter for your thesis. And by the time you get to *that* stage you will know that the whole point is to derive as much enjoyment, at the right place and time, from two miles as from twenty-two or a hundred and twenty-two.

Tim Hughes
Spring, 1978

Part One

Cycling and Bicycles

1

The human engine and the bicycle

We shall have to assume that because you have read even as far as this that you have at least some knowledge of the bicycle: you know what it looks like, roughly, and can ride one. Writers of cycling books have not always been able to be sure of this: Lord Bury and G. Lacy Hillier in one of the early books on the subject, the volume *Cycling* in the *Badminton Library of Sports and Pastimes* (see Appendix 2) felt it necessary to provide the most basic instruction. Indeed, at that time our main cities boasted several schools of bicycling. I hope we can start a little beyond this point, and even so you may well find that there are some things you have to unlearn.

As with walking, running, climbing, canoeing or skiing, it is the human engine that provides the power for cycling. This engine is, by the standards of the internal combustion engine or electric motors, derisorily low-powered: a short term peak output for a competitive cyclist in a hill-climb or a sprint is of the order of 1HP (750W), and that sort of effort is maintained only for tens of seconds. A comfortable, continuous output is very much less, perhaps a fifth to a tenth. There is not, therefore, much to spare and it is a tribute to the efficiency of the bicycle that this frail motor is able to carry the cyclist so far with such relative ease.

Part of the secret is that the work of supporting the body is carried out by the machine itself: the legs have only to propel you and not additionally to bear your weight. This is much more effective in the long run than in the short. The top speed of a sprinter over 200m on a bicycle, say 45mph (70kph), is less than twice that of a sprinter on foot. By the time the comparison reaches one hour, we find that two Belgians hold the honours: the cyclist Eddy Merckx with 30·701miles (49·408km) and the runner Gaston Roelants with 12·971miles

FIG. 1.—PREPARING TO MOUNT.

FIG. 2.—MOUNTING, FIRST POSITION : RIGHT FOOT ON RIGHT PEDAL (STATIONARY).

FIG. 3.—MOUNTING, SECOND POSITION : WEIGHT THROWN PARTLY ON HANDLES AND ON RIGHT PEDAL.

FIG. 4.—MOUNTED !

Some very basic instruction from the 1891 edition of the *Badminton Book of Cycling*.

(20·874km). Back in Britain, at 24 hours the best performances on record are Roy Cromack's 507·00miles (815·91km) on the road by bicycle and Wally Hayward's 159·32miles (256·40km) on a track on foot. And when we get to the longest distance for which there is any accurate British comparison, the approximately 872miles (just over 1400km) from Land's End to John o' Groats, the cyclist Dick Poole has a time of 1day 23hr 46mins; the best individual performance recorded on foot, by Malcolm Taylor, is 10days 23hr 53mins.

Nevertheless, there are immense differences between the ease of propelling a well-designed lightweight bicycle which fits you and one which falls outside all these categories. Lightweight is here used as a generic term and does not imply that every component should be pared down to the lightest possible weight. 'One which fits you' is very important. It is probable that the riding position, and hence a large

3

part of the comfort achieved on the machine, plays a greater part than anything else in determining whether or not you give up cycling as 'hard work' before you have reached the point of enjoying its aesthetic charms.

The weight of a cyclist is borne, in varying proportions, by the three – or strictly speaking, I suppose, five or six – points of contact with the machine. These are at the saddle, the handlebars and the pedals. The proportion of the weight taken by each varies with the position adopted and the amount of effort being expended. The racing cyclist at full effort, despite the low position of his hands, is resting relatively lightly on the saddle and probably pulling on the bars. Virtually his whole weight is being taken by his legs and their propulsive contact with the pedals. At the other extreme, a rider free-wheeling gently downhill is likely to put most of his weight on the saddle. The whole art of finding a comfortable position is to place the three contact zones to allow for these variations and we shall see how to do this in Chapter 4.

Many people assume that the point of the downward curved handle-bar bend is to enable the rider to ride bottom-up, nose-down, unseeing, up the tarmac to reach Aberdeen by nightfall. In fact, the purpose is to allow three or four different riding positions to be used, according to the conditions. You might indeed use the 'on the drops' position into a headwind, or in a hurry, since wind resistance is the biggest obstacle to progress on the flat. Unless you are putting in quite a considerable effort, however, too much weight is on the hands.

The normal riding position makes use of the brake levers to give

The four possible riding positions on a modern touring bicycle.

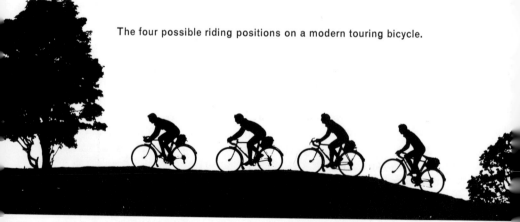

4

additional support and this is generally the most comfortable and convenient for most conditions. The hands are conveniently placed for applying the brakes gently for adjustment of speed if necessary and are at a natural angle, while the overall position is reasonably streamlined but relaxed. Note that in all these positions the arms are bent. A bicycle is relatively unsprung, so that by and large riding with the arms straight transmits road vibration, leading to an ache across the base of the back of the neck, between the tops of the shoulder blades.

The third position, and one which will usually be found very comfortable in very easy conditions where the brakes are unlikely to be needed – above all uphill, where the more upright position gives easier breathing – is to place the hands on the straight part of the bar, one either side of the handlebar stem and about 5 or 6in (12–15cm) apart, again with the elbows bent, backwards and slightly outwards. Change of position between these three while riding lessens fatigue, while the change in attitude of the hands (fore and aft in the first two positions and crosswise in the third) also gives relief to the muscles of the forearm, back of the upper arm and shoulders, as well as to the hands themselves.

The fourth position shown, although strongly condemned by some 'purists', is a perfectly legitimate expedient in certain conditions, provided it is competently carried out. It consists of rising out of the saddle, preferably holding the brake lever hoods, and standing on the pedals, using the weight of the body by transferring it from one pedal to the other as each reaches the top of its rotation. To do this properly, so that neither the body nor the machine waves about all over the place and the bicycle keeps going in a straight line, needs a certain amount of practice and experience. There is, in fact, a natural tendency to take up this position and to get out of the saddle when conditions force the pedalling rate below about 40–45rpm. Although the correct reaction when conditions force the rate down to this level would normally be to change to a lower gear, this may be impracticable if you have been taken by surprise by a sudden change of gradient round a corner, or been baulked, leaving yourself in a higher gear than desirable. Getting out of the saddle – known to the British club cyclist by the unlovely term 'honking', whereas the French liken it to the grace of a ballet dancer on her points and term it *en danseuse* – would seem in these circumstances to be both natural and permissible. I might add that it also relieves the pressure on the seat: the joy of 'honking' for fifty yards over a railway bridge after thirty flat and wind-assisted miles across the Fens has to be experienced to be believed! Even so, if you find it necessary to resort to this style of riding too often, then you are almost certainly using a range of gears which is too large or, less probably, you are grossly wrongly positioned.

Probably, as I have already hinted, the next most important feature to be considered is that of gearing, and once again the precise details will have to be deferred until we have examined the mechanics in the next chapter. The point is that the human engine, although quite flexible and able to offer somewhere near its maximum torque at very low pedalling rates, seems to be happiest when turning the pedals round at a speed of perhaps 70rpm. The speeds for racing are somewhat higher, say in the 90–100rpm range and even faster for short spells, but for steady touring 70 is comfortable. Although it is quite possible in theory to gear a bicycle so that this rhythm could be maintained for a very large range of road speeds, in practice certain factors make it possible to narrow the gearing spread a little. Riding up a moderate hill at walking pace or rather faster, the lower rate of about 50rpm feels quite comfortable. Similarly, when travelling briskly on an easy stretch, at say 20mph (32kph), 90rpm or even higher is by no means uncomfortable. If we assume then that the range of road speeds is to be from 3½mph (5·5kph) to 20mph (32kph) and the pedalling rates from 45 to 100rpm, respectively, the ratios of the highest and lowest gears are somewhere about 2½:1. Personal preferences will also move the ranges up or down a little. Lightly-built but powerful riders are likely to be naturally good at hill-climbing but may feel that their weight does not help so much when going down and could well prefer to use slightly higher gears. The heavier rider would probably make the reverse decision. The general rule (expanded in Chapter 2) is that it is better to have one low gear in reserve than an extra high one, and that being undergeared is, however tedious, far less uncomfortable and damaging than being overgeared.

Personal observation over a number of years has indicated that many women and girls prefer slower pedalling rates than male riders, while at the same time having perhaps less muscular 'push' on hills. At one time I believed it to be a 'fault' in technique to be eradicated but it seems to be a real enough phenomenon: whatever the physiological or psychological factors, many women, even very experienced cyclists, just do not find pedalling fast comfortable and need a wider gear range.

The consideration of both riding position and gearing brings us to the topic of riding style. The generally accepted definition of a 'stylish'

rider is one whose legs rotate smoothly without any jerking or uneven-
ness while the upper body remains to all intents and purposes still
relative to the machine. In addition, as already mentioned, cultivating
the practice of riding with the elbow joints at least a little bent also
aids comfort. In general a smooth style is also an efficient style and less
tiring: most of the outstanding long-distance riders – or for our purpose
riders able to ride comfortably all day – have been notable stylists.

The enemies of good style are generally too high gears, the wrong
saddle position and feet badly placed on the pedals. All the joints of
the leg take part in a smooth pedalling action, and the correct placing
is with the ball of the foot over the inner pedal bearing, allowing ample
flexibility. My personal advice is that as soon as you have the pro-
ficiency to ride a bicycle straight, you should fit the appropriate
length of toeclip (next chapter) and straps. The greater the proportion
of the pedal revolution that you can exert force over, the smoother
your style and the greater your efficiency are likely to be. Clips and
straps help in this – even to the point where you can actually pull up
on a pedal as well as pushing it down. The old style of 'ankling' – that
is to say commencing a pedal stroke at the top with the foot pointing
upwards and rotating the foot about the ankle joint throughout the
stroke until it was pointing down at the lowest point – without recourse
to toeclips – has largely died out, although some of the same action
but less exaggerated is inherent in any smooth pedalling style.

Further questions of riding technique, as they affect safety and
efficiency, will be dealt with in Chapter 5.

Now that we have brought the human engine and the bicycle
together, we have to consider the capabilities of the combination. A
gradual working-up without exceeding your ability is essential. The
great French cycle-tourist Paul de Vivie, who evangelised for the
pastime under the name *Velocio* in the 1920s and 30s, formulated a set
of precepts, the main of which were to stop before you are tired, eat
before you are hungry, drink before you are thirsty and change down
a gear before it gets hard. Fifty years on they remain no less true.
Probably more cyclists have been lost to the pastime, more beautiful
friendships ended before they had really begun, more new marriages
foundered, from the purchase of a tandem and a set of panniers
followed by a holiday or honeymoon in those two very tough counties,
Devon and Cornwall, than from any other cause.

Everybody – even the cocktail party questioners – knows that hills
can make cycling hard, but then they offer the corresponding bonus

7

of the swoop down the other side. Hills and mountains make the countryside attractive and the cycle-tourist has to live with the consequent gradients. The wind is a far more insidious enemy. I have known the dead flat sixteen miles from Cambridge to Ely harder than any continental pass. Cut your coat according to your cloth – with enough left over for patching! Any normal person from an age of about fourteen upwards should be able to manage fifty miles (80km) in a day in moderately undulating country, provided they do not try to do it all in the first two hours. There is a natural rhythm, a combination of your particular strength and pedalling cadence, which will determine your most comfortable cruising speed – probably somewhere between about 9 and 15mph (14–24kph) on the flat. For a start, assume that your capability is at the lower end, add on time for voluntary – and involuntary – stops and you will find that your 50mile (80km) trip may need about six to eight hours for comfort.

Finally, the human engine requires fuel. The advantage that the bicycle confers in supporting the body while the legs propel it, can also tempt and allow the cyclist to go quite a long way further towards exhaustion through lack of food than can, say, a walker without necessarily being aware of it. Blood sugar can be reduced to quite a low level and the resultant shaky feeling with jellied knees and cold sweats is known by club cyclists as 'bonk' or 'hunger knock'; the semantics are uncertain but there is a suggestion of greater actual muscular fatigue inherent in bonk. The technical term is hypoglycaemia and the immediate cure is to take sugar in a readily absorbed form such as honey or glucose, together with a short rest.

What you eat is largely a matter of your own tastes, little and often being better than a lot at long intervals, and moist things generally more palatable than dry. Cycling on a very full stomach is very little more comfortable than riding on a very empty one, and for this reason most of us tend to take a light midday meal, with the morning broken up perhaps by morning coffee and the afternoon by some tea, and leave the main meal until after the majority or all of the day's miles. There is no doubt that cycling stimulates the appetite, and food and drink – after cycle equipment – seem to be the most spoken-of topics in the average club. You should not be worried that you require more – and probably more 'stodgy' – food while riding than on a sedentary day.

It is on the question of thirst and drink that differences in metabolism become most marked. Sweating is a body temperature-regulating

Food and drink play a large part in the cycle-tourist's life.

mechanism and varies very much with the individual, clothing, the weather and humidity. It is possible, on a very hot summer day, to find that it is subjectively cooler riding at a moderate pace than standing still. This is because the sweat evaporates in the airstream as it is formed and so carries out its function of cooling the body very efficiently. The moisture and the salts dissipated have to be made up, however, and the cyclist is soon aware of a thirst which demands to be quenched. Water and natural fruit juices, avoiding things too sweet which can become cloying, are perhaps the best on the road.

Now for the bicycle itself.

2

The bicycle

Quite a few years ago, there appeared in one of the cycling magazines a competition to design the 'ideal touring bicycle'. The result was rather in the vein of that committee-designed horse which bore a remarkable resemblance to a camel. Even so, there does exist some sort of general agreement on what is, or is not, suitable. This consensus of views is probably much closer now than it ever has been in the past and I think the bicycle illustrated here would be pretty well universally acceptable.

You will see that it is in overall appearance not unlike a road-racing machine, but with mudguards and carrier, and there are good reasons for this. If a Tour de France rider spends hours in the saddle, day after day, then so does the cycle-tourist but the latter's equipment must be more durable and self-contained, and gears lower.

The parts of the bicycle

We shall go through the major components of the bicycle and their choice in this chapter on the assumption that you are buying a top-class lightweight made to measure from one of the small makers specialising in this type of work. Most experienced cyclists would order a frame and choose and assemble the rest themselves – it depends on your competence and experience whether you can do this, and on whether you find it thrilling to see the completed machine grow under your own hands: it is better to have the builder assemble it if you are in any doubt. The suggestions that follow are in that case ideas which you would talk over with the maker, adjusting them to your requirements. Cultivating a good dealer and builder is worthwhile – a few minutes of demonstration can save hours of trouble later. This way of buying a bicycle is unlikely to be cheap, so that the Chapter 3 will cover ways of adapting an existing machine, with some hints on buying secondhand. It is unfair to expect a builder or dealer to spend a lot of time on giving you advice and also to offer the ultimate in discount prices.

The frame

The frame is the heart of the bicycle and is the main thing which decides whether the machine is going to fit you. As you will see from

A modern touring bicycle.

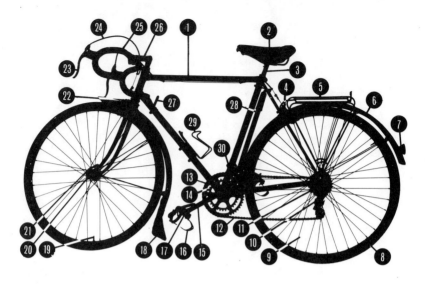

The parts of the bicycle: 1 frame, see next figure; 2 saddle; 3 seat pillar; 4 rear brake; 5 bag carrier; 6 rear mudguard; 7 reflector; 8 rear wheel tyre and rim; 9 spoke; 10 rear gear; 11 freewheel block mounted on rear hub; 12 chain; 13 outer chainring; 14 inner chainring; 15 crank; 16 toeclip with toestrap; 17 pedal; 18 mudflap; 19 tyre valve; 20 front hub; 21 front hub quick-release lever; 22 front brake mechanism; 23 brake lever; 24 brake cable; 25 handlebar bend; 26 handlebar stem; 27 gear lever; 28 pump; 29 bottle cage; 30 front gear mechanism.

the illustration, the frame size mentioned in catalogues and specifications is the length of the tube known as the 'seat tube', the one leading from the 'bottom bracket' where the chainwheel is fitted, up towards the saddle. British frames usually progress in $\frac{1}{2}$in steps – 21, 21$\frac{1}{2}$, 22 and so on – although some British makers now work to metric measurements.

There is a relationship between the correct frame size and various body measurements, which has been expressed in a variety of ways by different sources. Most of these formulae have covered the 'normal' range of frame sizes – say 20$\frac{1}{2}$ to 23in – but since I hope this book may be of use to younger riders who need frames smaller than this, I have shown in graph form the frame size which goes with a given full inside leg measurement – from the crutch to the ground, without shoes – for a wide range of sizes. Generally speaking, foot and shoe size and thigh length vary pretty much in line with this inside leg measurement: if you know that you have large or small feet for your height or a long

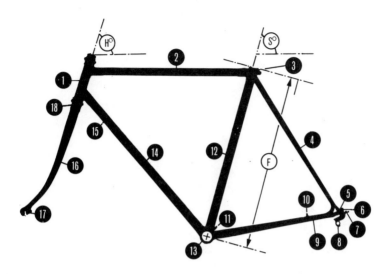

The parts of the frame: 1 head tube; 2 top tube; 3 seat cluster (seat lug and clamp bolt); 4 seat stay; 5 rear fork end; 6 mudguard eye; 7 rear axle stop adjuster; 8 rear gear hanger; 9 seat stay; 10 rear gear cable stop; 11 tunnel for gear control cable wires; 12 seat tube; 13 bottom bracket shell; 14 down tube; 15 gear lever stop; 16 front fork blade; 17 front fork end incorporating mudguard eye. F is the quoted size of the frame. H° and S° are the quoted head and seat angles, respectively.

or short thigh in relation to your total leg length you may want to adjust your choice by about ½in either way.

If you move around much in cycling circles, or read the cycling press, you will hear quite a lot of talk about frame angles: the illustration shows, as a matter of record, how they are specified. Although frame angles affect steering, comfort and 'liveliness' of the bicycle, they are also one of the valuable variables that the frame builder has at his disposal in making sure that a frame is not only the right size *vertically* but also *horizontally*. By manipulating particularly the seat angle, one can ensure that the forward reach reasonably matches the rider. This is a common fault with small mass-produced frames which the younger rider might well buy: some are just 'cut-down' versions of big ones and the junior rider for whom, say, a 19½in frame might be suitable finds that it stretches him too far fore-and-aft. Better manufacturers do not make this error: if you ask for a touring frame to fit you, you won't go far wrong.

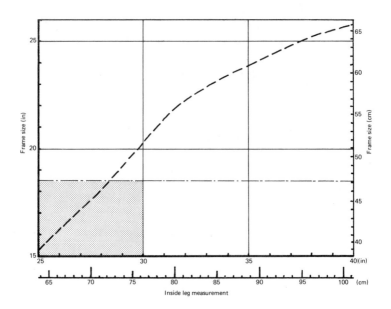

The selection of frame size from inside leg length measurement. The frame sizes are those measured by the British system as shown on page 13: note that frames specified in metric measurements may be measured according to the Continental or American systems (see text). The shaded area covers frame sizes below the approximate limit for use with 26in wheels, about 18½in (45cm).

The best frames are constructed from seamless drawn tubing of special alloy steel, the most famous of which is Reynolds 531, either brazed into 'lugs' at the points at which the tubes join, or so-called 'bronze-welded', where the joints are made and strengthened by a smooth fillet of brazing alloy. Unusual shapes may only be possible as a 'welded' frame (see Chapter 3). The high strength of the alloy steels enables the tubes to be made quite thin and it is from this that the lightness of the frame derives. You should therefore remember – even if the price doesn't bring it home to you – that a lightweight hand-built frame is a piece of precision engineering and doesn't take kindly to being knocked about (literally) or similarly abused.

It is usually worth having certain items brazed on when the frame is built in order to avoid having to use clips later. The minimum ones are a gear cable stop on the right-hand 'chainstay', gear-cable stops or 'tunnels' at the bottom bracket for both front (if used) and rear

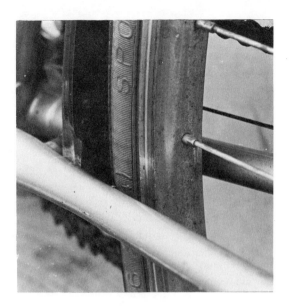

For touring use, particularly off the beaten track, wide clearances between the wheel and the frame and the wheel and mudguard are essential.

gears, brake-cable stops on the top tube for the rear brake cable and possibly, if centre-pull brakes (see 'Brakes', Chapter 2) are used, a rear 'hanger' behind the seat stays to hold the cable end. In view of the variety of pump lengths and possible positions it is on balance probably better not to have brazed-on pump fittings. The same goes for bottle 'cages'. For maximum strength and aesthetics, mudguard eyes should be incorporated into the fork ends (into which the wheels fit) and now that gear fittings to frames appear to have been standardised around the Campagnolo standard 10mm fitting, a right-hand rear fork end incorporating the gear bracket is also reasonable.

Your frame builder will need to discuss the length of crank you intend to use and your shoe size, so that he can allow adequate clearances at the right points. Crank lengths available, related to inside leg length are shown on page 27.

I have said nothing so far about frames for female riders – for the simple reason that most initiated lady riders use the same style of 'diamond' frame as the one generally thought of as a man's. The 'open' type of frame is generally less resistant to the twisting stresses it receives in use than the conventional diamond frame and this whippiness is accentuated when the bicycle is loaded. If, for reasons of your own – and this may also apply to those with back troubles who find difficulty in getting on an ordinary frame – you prefer an open frame, some lightweight builders will supply a more rigid design in which instead of a single tube running from the steering head to part way down the seat tube, a pair of thinner parallel tubes runs right through from the head to the rear fork end, bridged for stiffness at several points.

The saddle

By far the most intimate contact you will have with your bicycle will be with the saddle. A saddle which suits you is a thing to be treasured and hung on to: even hard-boiled Continental professionals frequently have a favourite saddle which they retain at all costs.

The general causes of saddle discomfort are two: chafing, caused by the saddle being too wide or having spread where it goes between the

Many riders treasure an old saddle once it has worn to their contour: note the concave shape from front to rear. An adjustable seat pillar of this type permits accurate adjustment of the angle of the saddle.

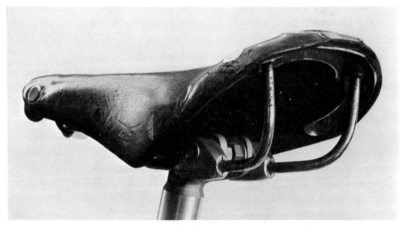

rider's legs, and bruising due to poor support. Despite folklore, the most comfortable type of saddle in the long run is the plain unsprung type mounted on two stout wires. Modern designs have a curved rear cantle plate which is relatively wide and then taper rapidly forward towards the peak. Seen from the side they are gently concave, and in fact when you are really accustomed to a saddle, the feeling is much more one of sitting *in* it than *on* it. The weight of the body is taken by the ischial promontories – two small bones that you can feel if you sit on your hands. A saddle with a curved cantle plate can accommodate a wide range of separations of these bones, the position of which varies quite a lot between individuals, and between males and females.

Leather has always been the traditional material for saddles, but a new leather saddle requires a period of 'breaking in', which may be quite prolonged – possibly some thousands of miles. There are many pet methods of achieving the necessary balance of properties; most of them involve oiling the underneath of the saddle with neats-foot or castor oil and working the surface with objects as diverse as rolling-pins and milk-bottles or the saddle may be bought ready treated. There is alleged to be a craftsman in the Gironde, in France, who makes liberal use of a red wine! Oil treatments, however, can quite easily make an unsightly mess of touring clothes. The name synonymous with quality in leather saddles the world over is Brooks, and their current top model, the Brooks Professional, should accommodate most requirements. It has no loops for holding a bag, however, and bolt-on ones have to be used.

Since the mid-sixties or so, and despite a lot of initial distrust, plastic – usually nylon – saddles have been gaining ground. They can be made with a resilience very close to the ideal and are available plain or with various types of covering, the most popular being suede, with or without a thin cushion of plastic foam beneath. Pioneers in this field and still the suppliers of the largest range are the Italian Unica Nitor, although there are now many others. Examine them carefully, for some makes are *very* hard and unlike a leather saddle they will not soften appreciably with use.

The saddle is fitted to a seat pillar (or 'saddle pin') either by a clip – which can be fitted in four ways (in front of or behind the seat pillar, above or below the saddle wires) giving a wide range of adjustment – or to the top of a specially shaped pillar which is adjustable for angle. The saddle should initially be fitted with its top horizontal: see Chapter 4.

Handlebars and stem

The most popular, and indeed the most practical, shape of handlebar bend is one of the varieties named after the Belgian prewar rider Sylvère Maes. The characteristics of the Maes bend are a squarish shape, a relatively modest drop, usually just over 5in (13cm), about 4in (10cm) forward reach, and a long straight horizontal transverse portion. They are generally about 15–16in (38–40cm) wide. The top and bottom of the forward-aligned parts have a nearly similar inclination, while the straight cross-portion also allows a comfortable grip, satisfying the criteria for providing the desirable choice of position. Handlebar bends are made by a number of manufacturers, GB are the principal ones in Britain, and the standard material is a polished aluminium alloy. The diameter seems now to be standardised on $\frac{15}{16}$in (23·8mm) with the centre portion bulged or with a ferrule to bring it out to about 1in (25·4mm) where it is gripped by the forward part of the handlebar stem. Steel ones may differ; check for compatibility.

Handlebar stems have taken on a smoother look in recent years and nearly every manufacturer (GB again the principal British one, Cinelli, Mavic, Ava, TTT, Pearl, Shimano, Sakae from abroad) now produces one similar to that illustrated. The lower part fits quite closely into the 'fork column' of the frame. To tighten and lock the stem in position, a bolt pulls a steel cone upwards inside the stem and expands the bottom part either side of the slots outwards to grip the inside of the fork column. Most of the better quality handlebar stems now have a

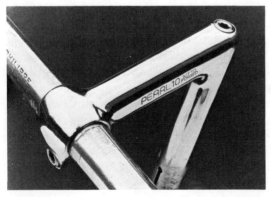

Modern aluminium alloy handlebar stems have neat allen-key fittings for both handlebar clamp (*left*) and the expander bolt. The length of the extension (here 10cm) is measured from the expander bolt to the centre of the handlebar.

recessed top and the expander bolt is tightened by means of an allen key, making an extremely neat fitting. The material is again an aluminium alloy, preferably forged.

The forward extension of the stem – from the centre line of the expander bolt to the centre line of the handlebar bend – is nearly always nowadays quoted in metric measurements and a range from 20 to 150mm is fairly readily available, with most being in the 70–120mm range. The actual choice of length depends upon riding position: see Chapter 4.

Brakes

Brakes are literally vital, for life itself. Lightweight bicycles use the wire-operated rim-acting type, where a multiple laid-up inner wire cable moves inside an outer coiled wire tube, the latter usually plastic-coated. Where brazed-on brake cable stops are used then the inner wire between the stops is left bare, reducing friction to a slight extent.

There are two principal types of brake, again usually made in a forged aluminium alloy. The first, known as the 'side-pull', has a type of scissor action to pull the two brake blocks in to grip the rim. There are many makes. Although they are quite effective there can be problems in centring the cheaper brakes of this kind so that neither brake block touches the rim when the brake is not being used. The expensive Campagnolo model, it should be added, has a special patented lock washer to ensure the maintenance of centring. The second type is known as the 'centre-pull', and in all its current forms the single wire from the brake lever is clamped to a small triangular shaped cable guide. The two arms carrying the brake blocks are independent in bearing and springing, and a straddle wire passes from the end of one arm to the other via the triangular guide. The net effect when the brake is operated is to pull both blocks inwards with a considerable leverage. On the centre-pull the centring is accomplished by a separate adjustment to a plate which carries the two brake arm pivots. Centre-pull brakes are generally more lightly sprung and, despite a slight feeling of sponginess, are more effective than all but the most expensive side pulls: the price ratio is about 6:1! The principal makes available here are Mafac and Weinmann: the Mafac Racer – the original brake of this type – offers rather more adjustment if wheels of different type are to be used from time to time. An alternative

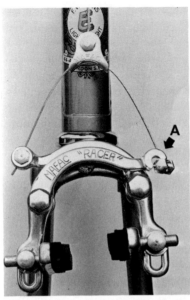

The first, and still one of the most popular, of the modern generation of centre-pull brakes. To allow wheel removal the cable is rapidly disengaged at A.

A medium weight wired-on tyre of the type suitable for touring is the Michelin Sports shown here: this is available in both 26 and 27in sizes.

version of the Mafac, the Criterium model, is fitted to brazed-on pivots on the frame: this does not allow a change of mind on wheel size later.

Nearly all the brake levers are similar in concept, and most are, or can be, fitted with moulded rubber sleeves on the hood part to make comfortable hand rests when the second and fourth of the two positions on page 4 are used. The most positive handlebar fixing appears to be the Mafac, whereas the Italian Universal is one of the most comfortably shaped levers in the medium price range.

Tyres and wheels

Two different types of tyre are in use in this country, although only the second of them is made here. The less common is the lighter type used mainly for racing and known as a 'tubular', or popularly 'tub'.

Tubulars are, not surprisingly, tubular in cross-section, with the very light canvas part – technically known as the 'pocket' – sewn up along the base. A very thin latex inner tube is fitted inside and can only be reached by undoing the base stitching. Since the stitching can itself only be approached by removing a strongly-stuck base protection tape, repair of these tyres is slow although the whole tyre can be changed very quickly. In view of the need to carry spares (two or three would be prudent), the fact that replacements – in Britain – are only available from specialist dealers, the high pressures to which they have to be inflated when extra loads are carried if chafing at the rim is not to occur, and their general fragility, it is my considered opinion that they are not to be recommended for touring purposes. You may well hear stories of riders covering 6000km from Norway to Gibraltar on 7oz tyres without a single puncture – but for every one of these there are countless numbers who keep quiet about the evenings spent in hotel bedrooms repairing and sewing-up their spares. For racing, fine – that's what they're designed for: for touring, no.

Nevertheless, the tourist does not want to ride around on the heaviest of equipment and a reasonable compromise is the 'open-sided' (or rather amber-walled) sports tyre such as the Michelin Sports or High Speed. These tyres fall into the familiar category of 'wired-on' tyres. The outer cover of the tyre has a steel wire built into its edges, which seat onto surfaces on the rim, a rubber rim tape covers the top of the spoke heads, and a separate inner tube is fitted. The question to be determined here is the size of wheel to be used.

The most-used size on lightweight machines in this country is $27 \times 1\frac{1}{4}$in (ISO 32–630): see Appendix 4 for a full listing and explanation of terms. The only disadvantages of $27 \times 1\frac{1}{4}$in tyres are that on many frames, the clearances between the tyre and the mudguard are very close, leading to clogging-up in muddy conditions, and in addition they can look a little out of proportion on small frames – say those smaller than $21\frac{1}{2}$in. For those eventually planning to travel abroad, they have no European equivalent.

The second most popular size is $26 \times 1\frac{1}{4}$in (ISO 32–597), which again has no European equivalent. Types of rim available (below) are limited. On the other hand, whereas the range of covers in $27 \times 1\frac{1}{4}$in is limited to very light down to moderately light ones, such as the Michelin types cited, the range in $26 \times 1\frac{1}{4}$in is from moderately light (Michelin Sports) to heavy. The less popular $26 \times 1\frac{3}{8}$in size, usually fitted to heavier bicycles, is directly equivalent to the European

The two types of valve generally used on British bicycles, the Presta or 'high pressure' (*left*) as fitted to most lightweights, and the older Woods type. They need different rim drillings, and the Presta type requires a pump connector or adaptor drilled deeply enough to clear the plunger. The knurled locknut, arrowed, has to be unscrewed before inflating or deflating.

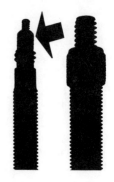

650A size; the cyclist who expects eventually to do a great deal of European travel could do worse than have a pair of 26 × 1⅜in or 590 × 22mm width wheels as a standby or for general use. The British 26 × 1½in size – usually fitted to roadster cycles is the equivalent of the European 650B, a size more used abroad than 650A. The larger cross-section of 1⅜in or 1½in tyres may theoretically be slightly less 'lively', but appropriately inflated the extra drag is unlikely to be detected.

The life of tyres can be considerably extended by buying them well before they are needed and allowing them to 'mature' for some months in darkness and at normal room temperatures.

Inner tubes are of two types, butyl (black) and natural rubber (red). The butyl tubes, which are now by far the commonest, retain their pressure, when unpunctured, almost indefinitely but they are slightly less 'lively' and take longer to repair. Valves are usually of one of two types, the Woods – usually fitted to heavier machines – which is the 9mm diameter type with valve rubber or replacement inserts, while the type most commonly used on lightweight cycles is the Presta or 'high-pressure'. This type has a narrower (6mm) body with a small screw-down plunger: they require a suitable 'high-pressure' pump connector or fitting, one with enough bored-out depth to accommodate the plunger. The car-type Schräder, common in the USA, is not generally used for lightweight cycles made in this country, although some imported 'sports' (semi-lightweight) models are fitted with them. Although inner tubes are made to fit specific sizes of outer cover, in practice and with care, different sizes can be used in emergency – e.g. 27in tubes in 26in tyres although the reverse is more difficult. For normal use tyres should be inflated to about 70psi (say 5kg/cm^2) – but see Chapter 14. Small pressure gauges to check Presta valve-fitted tyres are available, although the flexibility of cycle tyres is enough for an experienced thumb to assess pressure pretty accurately.

Wheels consist of (basically) three components – rim, spokes and hub. Aluminium alloy rims are generally preferable, although rather more fragile than the alternative – chromium-plated steel. Alloy rims give better braking, particularly in the wet, and they are both lighter and more resistant to corrosion. However, for very strenuous off-the-beaten-track use some experienced riders prefer a steel rim for its sheer strength. It is not a once-for-all decision: wheels are about the easiest component of the bicycle to change. There is a wider range of makes of alloy rim available in Britain in 27 × 1¼in – Weinmann, Fiamme, Mavic for example – than in 26 × 1¼in, where Weinmann appear to be the only current suppliers. Both sizes are available in steel, either the Dutch van Schothorst or the French AFA Rigida.

The standard British spoking is 32 in the front wheel and 40 in the rear; the European practice is to have both wheels 36-spoked. (24 and 28 are used in various combinations for racing purposes, but rims for wired-on tyres are not made with these drillings.) It is doubtful whether the choice makes any appreciable difference to the tourist, and since the supply of 32/40 hubs and rims is rather more sporadic than the 36/36, any rider starting from scratch would probably do better to choose the latter.

All of today's best hubs are machined from aluminium alloy forgings; the commonest makes are Campagnolo, Zeus, Maillard and Shimano. Two methods of fixing the hub into the frame are used, either a solid hub axle held into the frame with nuts with integral serrated washers (known as 'track nuts', obligatory for track racing), or 'quick-release', in which a cam-action device acting on a skewer through a hollow axle clamps the hub into the frame in a single movement. The solid axle is cheaper, possibly stronger, and has no practical disadvantage unless there is a frequent need to remove wheels, say for fitting a cycle to a car roof-rack or when travelling by air. The overall width of hubs is now effectively standardised at about 100mm (front) and 120mm (rear), the latter accommodating a five-speed freewheel block. Rear hubs are available with screw-threads on one side only – to take a multiple freewheel – or with threading both ends to allow a spare sprocket to be used on the other side. Many experienced cycle-tourists prefer to have the extra threading and sprocket to fall back on if the main freewheel develops a fault – which, if it does, it will do just at the

A modern small-flange quick-release hub. This 32-spoke wheel is built 'three-cross': each spoke crosses three others. Note, when replacing spokes (Chapter 8) that the spoke heads are alternately inside and outside the hub flange.

wrong moment. There is no real point in specifying large-flange hubs for touring, although you may find difficulty in getting small-flange solid-axle hubs. The small-flange hub will give a slightly more resilient wheel and a more comfortable ride. This characteristic is also affected by the method of wheel-building. As each spoke is traced from the hub to the rim it crosses other spokes on the way: the larger the number of crossings the more resilient the wheel, the smaller the more rigid. Both racing and touring cyclists require a compromise. For touring, building with three crossings (32-spoke wheel and possibly 36-spoke small-flanged) and four crossings (36 or 40 spokes) is advisable. Two or less, or hybrid radial and tangential mixtures, may have speed advantages but also transmit more road vibration. The practice of tying with fine tinned copper wire and soldering at the spoke intersection furthest from the hub, as is frequently done for track racing or time-trials, is not to be recommended for touring where a spoke may have to be replaced at the roadside. Thicker spokes seem to be the norm nowadays and most hubs and rims are drilled to take

One of the most popular touring chainsets is made up by using TA aluminium alloy rings – here in a triple 28–40–48 combination – with either TA or as here Stronglight 5-pin fitting cotterless cranks.

14-gauge spokes; better quality spokes are 'butted' – ends thicker than the centre, and 14/16 gauge is the most commonly used combination. Probably the best type for touring wheels are the zinc-plated so-called 'rustless' ones. Chromium plated ones look very attractive initially but are less resistant to corrosion.

Cranks, chainwheel and pedals

The transmission section of the bicycle comprises the cranks and their axle, the chainwheel (usually made up of separate rings bolted to the cranks), the pedals, the chain, the gear mechanism(s), and the rear sprockets. I assume here that you are considering a bicycle with multiple derailleur (chain) gearing: some of the perhaps unexpected advantages of using a single fixed gear or freewheel will be dealt with in Chapter 14.

Cranks, as it now appears does nearly everything else on the bicycle, come in two types, depending on the way in which they are fixed to the bottom-bracket axle. The lighter and more expensive are made of aluminium alloy and use a special axle with tapered square ends. They are held in position by bolts screwing into tapped holes in the ends of the axle. Most types have their own individual fitting and special tools are required – and supplied – for each. The chainrings are bolted to the cranks in a variety of ways, although there appears to be some standardisation. The most versatile is the 5-pin fixing used by the French manufacturers Stronglight and TA and also on some types of steel cottered crank (below) including one by the British firm Nicklin. The tourist needs to have available very small front chainrings – the 5-pin fixing allows this, when used together with TA Cyclotouriste rings. Note that with all types of chainset the appropriate length bottom-bracket axle for the number of chainrings and the type of crank in use must be employed to ensure that the chain runs in as nearly a straight line as possible: see the manufacturer's data.

Less than a fifth of the cost are steel cranks with a cotter-pin fitting. The 'cotter-pin' – in this connexion, though not in general engineering terminology – is a tapered mild-steel plug, threaded at one end, and which, when tapped home and with a nut tightened on the threaded portion, holds the cranks firm on the axle. This is the commonest fitting on all types of bicycle in this country. The advantages are cheapness and universal availability; the disadvantages that it requires a certain level of skill and practice to fit properly and that it is inherently less concentric than the cotterless squared-end fitting – important when front gear mechanisms are used. The British company Nicklin make these cranks in a variety of fittings including the 5-pin N54, which may be used with the TA Cyclotouriste rings, and the N34 3-bolt fixing (formerly Williams C34) which allows the use of its own style of ring down to 32T. For 'cottered' chainwheels the 3-bolt fixing on which the rings may be removed over the crank has some advantage; it may even so be necessary to remove the right pedal.

Cranks are available in a variety of lengths, and it is possible to make a similar, although less precise, correlation between inside leg length and crank length in the way that we did for frame size. Foot size and thigh to inside leg ratios, may alter choice slightly. Alloy cotterless cranks are generally available in lengths of 175mm (nominally 7in), 170mm (6¾in) and 165mm (6½in), less frequently in other sizes. Steel cranks from Nicklin are available in 6½ and 5½in sizes in the N54 5-pin and in 6½in in the N34 fitting. Other shorter lengths are

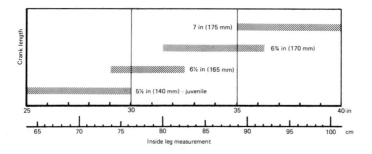

The relationship between crank length and inside leg measurement. This is rather less critical than the frame size and ranges are indicated.

only available as juvenile chainsets with fixed rings although, with skilled DIY, conversion is possible.

The worldwide standard chain for derailleur gear use is $\frac{1}{2} \times \frac{3}{32}$in ($12 \cdot 7 \times 2 \cdot 38$mm) and care should be taken to avoid inadvertently fitting the wider $\frac{1}{2} \times \frac{1}{8}$in size used for single-gear or hub-gear machines, or obtaining rings or sprockets intended for that size. The chain is cut to length using a special tool properly termed a bearing-pin extractor (but commonly known as a chain-link remover), and then the two ends joined using the same tool. The 'spring-link' used with the wider chains is not used with derailleur gears.

Pedals are again one of your personal contacts with the machine and need to be chosen with some care. Price is generally an indication of the engineering quality of construction. Only all-metal pedals are considered here, as it is assumed that toeclips and straps are eventually to be fitted. Check, when wearing the shoes to be worn for cycling, that there is enough width of pedal to support the foot and still allow clearance between the foot and the crank, with room for a strap. If there are such things as national characteristics, the possession of broad feet is a British one, and many of the best pedals, such as the Italian Campagnolo Strada model have a design of frame such that the outer end of the plate can tend to dig into larger feet. The only answer is to try them out. Most of the better pedals are made of aluminium alloy – or even titanium, at a price – but the British-made Chater-Lea, which seems to arrive on the market in small and none-too-frequent batches, has smooth stainless steel side-plates which accommodate wider feet

27

easily. The Barelli – also British made – is available with interchangeable side plates. Check that the pedals have proper ball-bearings and are adjustable and capable of being lubricated; some cheap-and-nasty ones have plain unadjustable bearings.

Pedals screw into the ends of the cranks, the right-hand one with a right-hand thread, the left-hand with a left-hand thread. There is a standard thread for British use, $\frac{9}{16}$in × 20TPI. Never attempt to force a pedal into a thread it doesn't want to fit in; check that the pedal is at right-angles to the crank, that it is indeed a right-hand pedal that you are trying to fit to a right-hand crank, or left to left! Some pedals are made with longer threads (about 13mm as against the usual 9mm) for use with alloy cranks: note that they are too long for Campagnolo and similar cranks and also protrude when used with steel cranks.

Toeclips bolt onto the front plate of the pedal (when, in the case of single-sided pedals which can be used only one way up, the pedal is the right way round); some have specially placed holes, and the most expensive tapped bosses and special fixing bolts. The size of toeclip to be used depends on shoe size: the table gives the appropriate length for given British and European *cycling* shoe sizes. The almost universally used make of clip is the French AFA Christophe and all sizes from other manufacturers correspond with the Christophe sizes. The clip determines the fore-and-aft positioning of the foot, but it has a second function, that of supporting the strap which holds the foot onto

The pedal assembly showing the fitting of the toeclip and strap.

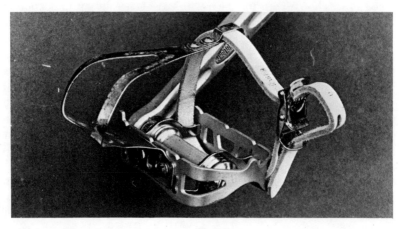

28

Toeclip sizes related to shoes (cycling shoes are assumed)

| Clip designation | Shoe size | |
(AFA Christophe)†	British	Continental
D (dames) or short	up to 5	up to 38
Normal or medium	$5\frac{1}{2}$	39
	6	
	$6\frac{1}{2}$	40
	7	41
	8	42
Special or long	9	43
	$9\frac{1}{2}$	44
	10	
	$10\frac{1}{2}$*	45*
	11*	46*

† These designations are generally used by other manufacturers too.

* These sizes may require a packing piece of metal strip or plywood between the clip and the front pedal plate, as may shoes of smaller size not designed for cycling. These should, like cycling shoes, have a narrow 'turned' welt.

the pedal. These special 'toe-straps' have a quick-release buckle which allows a wide range of close adjustment. It is essential if the straps are to be used as toe-straps – and they have a lot of other uses for the tourist as well – that this type of buckle is fitted so that a single flick of the finger releases the strap when necessary.

Gears and gearing

I have already mentioned that if the cyclist is to cover a wide range of terrain with ease then a range of gears with a ratio of about $2\frac{1}{2}$:1 between the highest and lowest is desirable. We will now see how this can be achieved.

Gear ratios are still generally expressed in Britain and the USA in inches – not logically, as the distance covered per pedal revolution (as used, in metric units, in Europe and known as the 'gear development') but as the diameter of wheel which it would have been necessary to fit to the old high Ordinary Bicycle ('Penny-farthing') to achieve the same effect! There's tradition for you – but it persists, probably because the figures are convenient to remember.

The 'gear', then, is the diameter of this hypothetical wheel: it may be calculated by multiplying the number of teeth on the chainring by

Big chainring and small sprocket (*left*) = big gear; small chainring and big sprocket = low gear.

the diameter of the actual wheel and dividing by the number of teeth on the rear sprocket – a simple but tedious calculation, which explains the popularity of gear tables. Alternatively, particularly in racing circles, a gear may be called, say, '42 × 17' – (chainwheel and sprocket sizes) 27in wheels being assumed. It is of course necessary to have different tables for different wheel sizes. The three tables given here are for 27in wheels, 26in or 650 wheels, and for 24in or 600 wheels (fitted to the larger type of juvenile bicycle). I have restricted the tables somewhat from those usually published to include only those gears and chainring sizes likely to be of use in touring, bearing in mind the minimum and maximum sizes of chainring and freewheel sprockets commonly available. All values are rounded off to the nearest inch, since wheel diameters are nominal.

16T is normally the largest top (small) sprocket that can easily be obtained on a standard freewheel block and 28T the commonest bottom (large) one, although 30, 31, 32 or even 34T are available for some. Not all gear mechanisms can cope with such big sprockets, though. I am assuming throughout that you will be using a five-speed freewheel, in combination with either a single or double chainring. While it is quite easy to cover the full range of gears we shall consider with a five-speed freewheel and a single ring, there are two signal disadvantages, the first that the gaps between the gears are large, giving rather a jerk to the muscular system when you change, and second that if the chainring is aligned with the centre sprocket, then it is being pulled out of alignment on the extreme top and bottom sprockets, resulting in some power loss, noise and chain and sprocket wear. By using the inner chainring of a double ring with the bottom

The meaning of chainline. With the derailleur gear on the largest, bottom gear sprocket (*left*) and the smallest, top gear sprocket (*centre*) the chain is quite appreciably out of line. Correct lining-up of the rear sprocket and chainring using spacers is essential with a single fixed gear – see Chapter 14 – as shown (*right*).

four sprockets and the outer with the top four, then a closer-spaced range of eight usable gears is obtained with less out-of-line running. Many European cycle-tourists – particularly the French – go even further and use a triple chainwheel on the same basis, but this practice has not spread very far in this country as yet. Six-speed freewheels are available and are extensively used for road racing but the greater weight on the rear wheel of a loaded touring bicycle – even more a tandem – can cause axle bending or breakage, so they are best avoided in this context.

Gear table for 27in wheels. Selected values between 80 and 30.

Rear sprocket	Chainring (front)															
	50	49	48	47	46	45	44	42	40	38	36	34	32	30	28	26
13										79	75	71	67	62	58	54
14									77	73	69	66	62	58	54	50
15							79	76	72	68	65	61	58	54	50	47
16				79	78	76	74	71	68	64	61	57	54	51	47	44
17	79	78	76	75	73	72	70	67	64	60	57	54	51	48	45	41
18	75	74	72	71	69	68	66	63	60	57	54	51	48	45	42	39
19	71	70	68	67	65	64	63	60	57	54	51	48	46	43	40	37
20	68	66	65	63	62	61	59	57	54	51	49	46	43	41	38	35
21	64	63	62	60	59	58	57	54	51	49	46	44	41	39	36	33
22	61	60	59	58	57	55	54	52	49	47	44	42	39	37	34	32
23	59	58	56	55	54	53	52	49	47	45	42	40	38	35	33	31
24	56	55	54	53	52	51	50	47	45	43	41	38	36	33	31	29
25	54	53	52	51	50	49	48	45	43	41	39	37	35	32	30	28
26	52	51	50	49	48	47	46	44	42	40	37	35	33	31	29	27
27	50	49	48	47	46	45	44	42	40	38	36	34	32	30	28	26
28	48	47	46	45	44	43	42	41	39	37	35	33	31	29	27	25
29	47	46	45	44	43	42	41	39	37	36	34	32	30	28	26	24
30	45	44	43	42	41	40	40	38	36	34	32	31	29	27	25	23
31	44	43	42	41	40	39	38	37	35	33	31	30	28	26	24	23
32	42	41	41	40	39	38	37	35	34	32	30	29	27	25	24	22
34	40	39	38	37	37	36	35	33	32	30	29	27	25	24	22	21

Gear table for 26in (or 650) wheels. Selected values between 80 and 30

Rear sprocket		Chainring (front)														
	50	49	48	47	46	45	44	42	40	38	36	34	32	30	28	26
13									80	76	72	68	64	60	56	52
14								78	74	71	67	63	59	56	52	48
15					80	78	76	73	69	66	62	59	56	52	49	45
16		80	78	76	75	73	72	68	65	62	59	55	52	49	46	42
17	76	75	73	72	70	69	67	64	61	58	55	52	49	46	43	40
18	72	71	69	68	66	65	64	61	58	55	52	49	46	43	40	38
19	68	67	66	64	63	62	60	58	55	52	49	47	44	41	38	36
20	65	64	62	61	60	59	57	55	52	49	47	44	42	39	36	34
21	62	61	59	58	57	56	55	52	50	47	45	42	40	37	35	32
22	59	58	57	56	54	53	52	50	47	45	43	40	38	36	33	31
23	57	55	54	53	52	51	50	48	45	43	41	38	36	34	32	29
24	54	53	52	51	50	49	48	46	43	41	39	37	35	33	30	28
25	52	51	50	49	48	47	46	44	42	40	37	35	33	31	29	27
26	50	49	48	47	46	45	44	42	40	38	36	34	32	30	28	26
27	48	47	46	45	44	43	42	40	39	37	35	33	31	29	27	25
28	46	46	45	44	43	42	41	39	37	35	33	32	30	28	26	24
29	45	44	43	42	41	40	39	38	36	34	32	31	29	27	25	23
30	43	42	42	41	40	39	38	36	35	33	31	30	28	26	24	23
31	42	41	40	39	39	38	37	35	34	32	30	29	27	25	24	22
32	41	40	39	38	37	37	36	39	33	31	29	28	26	24	23	21
34	38	37	37	36	35	34	34	32	31	29	28	26	24	23	21	20

Gear table for 24in (or 600) wheels. Selected values between 70 and 25

Rear sprocket	50	49	48	47	46	45	44	42	40	38	36	34	32	30	28	26
13									74	70	66	63	59	55	52	48
14							75	72	69	65	62	58	55	51	48	45
15				75	74	72	70	67	64	61	58	54	51	48	45	42
16	75	74	72	71	69	68	66	63	60	57	54	51	48	45	42	39
17	71	69	68	66	65	64	62	59	56	54	51	48	45	42	40	37
18	67	65	64	63	61	60	59	56	53	51	48	45	43	40	37	35
19	63	62	61	59	58	57	56	53	51	48	45	43	40	38	35	33
20	60	59	58	56	55	54	53	50	48	46	43	41	38	36	34	31
21	57	56	55	54	53	51	50	48	46	43	41	39	37	34	32	30
22	55	53	52	51	50	49	48	46	44	41	39	37	35	33	31	28
23	52	51	50	49	48	47	46	44	42	40	38	35	33	31	29	27
24	50	49	48	47	46	45	44	42	40	38	36	34	32	30	28	26
25	48	47	46	45	44	43	42	40	38	36	35	33	31	29	27	25
26	46	45	44	43	42	42	41	39	37	35	33	31	30	28	26	24
27	44	44	43	42	41	40	39	37	36	34	32	30	28	27	25	23
28	43	42	41	40	39	39	38	36	34	33	31	29	27	26	24	22
29	41	41	40	39	38	37	36	35	33	31	30	28	26	25	23	22
30	40	39	38	38	37	36	35	34	32	30	29	27	26	24	22	21
31	39	38	37	36	36	35	34	33	31	29	28	26	25	23	22	20
32	38	37	36	35	35	34	33	32	30	29	27	26	24	23	21	20
34	35	35	34	33	32	32	31	30	28	27	25	24	23	21	20	18

34

A cycle-tourist riding gently along a flat road with negligible wind and pedalling at his most comfortable rate – say 70rpm as we discussed before – would find a gear of 60 to 65in about right. In very easy conditions, say with a considerable wind behind, a 75in gear pedalled reasonably nimbly at 95rpm can take you along at nearly 22mph (34kph). Faster than that downhill you can freewheel! I have never found a gear much above this to be of appreciable practical use when touring. I use – and everybody else uses – considerably bigger ones for racing but even when they have been available I have not really found any use for them on tours ranging from the Fens to the Alps and County Cork to the Baltic. When it comes to low gears, it is very different. If we accept 75in as a reasonable top gear, then a $2\frac{1}{2}:1$ ratio brings us to 30in as the bottom one. If you are going to ride up some of Britain's steeper hills at about walking pace, then a 30in gear will enable you to do so at about 45rpm. You can gear lower than this but with two disadvantages: the first, mentioned earlier, is that the subjective effect of riding a very low gear at normal rpm up a long hill is dispiriting, while the fact that the legs meet with some resistance on a slightly higher gear seems, to the befuddled brain, to be wholly in order; the second is that, on a laden bicycle (not a tandem) it is quite possible unless care is exercised to lift the front wheel off the ground by putting in a sudden effort on such a low gear. I have taken account of this in the gear tables by marking the gears below 30in (25in for 24in wheels with $5\frac{1}{2}$in cranks). This is not to say they are not usable – but they need care.

Notes to gear tables:

1 Gears below the zigzag line, lower right of each table, may present problems – see text.

2 Many common rear gear mechanisms do not work satisfactorily on sprockets larger than 28T, hence the broken line at this point.

3 Gears above the zigzag line, 24in wheel table – top left, are not recommended for young riders.

4 If you should for some reason need to know the distance travelled per pedal revolution (the 'gear development'), *divide* the gear in the table by 12·5 for an answer in metres, or by 3·8 for an answer in feet. These are accurate to 1–2%. Conversely if you are confronted by a continental gear table in metres, *multiply* by 12·5 to give the gears, English-style, in inches.

5 Gears for other wheel sizes $= \dfrac{\text{wheel diameter (in)} \times \text{chainwheel teeth}}{\text{rear sprocket teeth}}$.

Within the various limits then, I would suggest, with a double chainring and 27in wheels:

	16	18	20	23	26
46	78	69	62	54	(48)
30	(51)	45	41	35	31

or if a single chainring is preferred:

	14	16	19	23	30
38	73	64	54	45	34

With 26in or 650 wheels, similarly:

	16	18	20	23	26
48	78	69	62	54	(48)
32	(52)	46	42	36	32

or:

	14	16	19	23	30
40	74	65	55	45	35

The gears in brackets are not generally usable, particularly the small ring/small sprocket combination. For a younger rider with 24in or 600 wheels and 5½in cranks – which offer less leverage and hence need lower gears – the following would be a suitable range with a single chainring:

	13	15	18	22	30
38	70	61	51	41	30

or:

	13	15	18	22	30
36	66	58	48	39	29

The young are generally nimbler pedallers than their elders, and should be encouraged to remain so!

There is not a large choice of makes of multiple freewheel, particularly wide-ratio ones. The Italian Regina is the most frequently used, with the Franco-Italian Simplex fairly close. A number of Japanese types – Shimano and Sun Tour for example – offer very large bottom sprockets and have built up a considerable reputation in the USA, where it is considered a slight on one's dignity not to be able to ride up everything in sight. The bottom four sprockets on the Maillard, Shimano and Sun Tour are slip-on splined types, with the top one screwed on as a locking device. Most of the others have a combination of right- and left-hand threads and diameters. All freewheels require special tools – usually specific to that make – to remove them undamaged from the hub.

Gear mechanisms have the task of shifting the chain from sprocket to sprocket (rear) and from chainring to chainring (front). There is quite a choice of rear gears – and a very wide range of prices. All modern types use a distorting parallelogram system to move the 'cage' containing the chain tensioning sprockets inwards and outwards. The first to use this was the Italian company Campagnolo, while at the other end of the price range the Simplex SX 110T gear makes intelligent use of plastics to produce a light, inexpensive and effective mechanism. Most of the recent developments in gear design have come from Japan, whose manufacturers have changed the plane of operation of the distorting parallelogram so that the chain follows more closely the different diameters of the sprockets. The total capacity (the number of teeth difference between the largest and smallest rear sprockets *plus* the difference between the chainwheels) for the gear ranges recommended is about 24–26 with double rings (although the extremes are not used it must be possible to engage them inadvertently without damaging the mechanism) and 16–17 with the single ring. These, and the largest sprocket of 26 with the double chainring systems, are within the range of pretty well all the gears on the market. Some mechanisms may not be too happy with 30T bottom sprockets and the actual chain length may be critical. The most effective front changers also have a parallelogram action, although the other types work adequately. The extent of movement of the gear mechanism inwards and outwards is regulated by screw-adjusted stops. The adjustment of the bottom-gear stop on the rear gear to prevent the mechanism fouling the spokes is particularly critical: the instructions with the gear should be studied with care.

Most gears sold as front/rear sets have a double lever, the left-hand one controlling the front mechanism – and the right-hand one the rear. The double down-tube lever is preferable to and a good deal less complicated than the handlebar-end control: the lever boss should be fitted about 4in (100mm) down the tube from the head.

Mudguards and carriers

No touring bicycle in the British Isles is complete without mudguards. It is foolhardy to embark on any sort of lengthy ride without being prepared for wet weather. If top continental professional riders can fit them to their winter and early spring training bikes as a matter of course, I don't see that there's any loss of face for a tourist, who is always after the odd bit of extra comfort, to do the same. The best for normal use are the lightweight plastic ones. This is one field in which British products are pre-eminent (something to do with our weather?), Bluemels being a world-famous name. The mudguards are secured by $\frac{1}{8}$in (3mm) wire stays to the eyes built into the fork ends; the attachments are adjustable at the other end and protruding excess lengths of mudguard stay should be neatly sawn off with a fine-tooth hacksaw.

There is, I feel, only one pattern of bag carrier worth considering for the prospective cycle-tourist. This is the basically triangular pattern made by several manufacturers which is fitted at the top end to the front or rear brake bolt as appropriate and at the bottom to the fork-end mudguard eye. This gives an adequately rigid support for a saddle-bag at the rear and for light panniers at the front. Nearly all other types of clip-on or bolt-on device are relatively ineffective when it comes to bearing any real load, with the exception of two elegant types to support a handlebar bag. The plastic-covered patterns of carrier are apparently more weatherproof than the plated versions.

Summing up

These then are the main components of the bicycle: if you had bought the best at each stage from a bespoke builder, you would by this point be most of a bicycle the richer – and some hundreds of pounds the poorer. Chapter 3 looks at some ways of cutting the cost, and Chapter 4 gives the finishing touches – including the all-important topic of positioning.

3

Cutting the cost

Adapting an existing bicycle

Of course, you can use any bicycle for touring: a ten-year-old earned himself an English Schools Cycling Association award a year or two ago for reaching Cape Wrath, the top left-hand corner of Scotland and at the end of a very remote and hard road, on a Raleigh Chopper. Even so, it will be easier if you can adapt the bicycle to make it as near to a 'proper' touring one as you can. And it must naturally be the right size to begin with.

The simplest type to convert is the sports or semi-lightweight type: the sort that already has cable brakes but may have a mattress saddle, heavy wheels and comparable fittings. If you have an 'about-town' small-wheeler or a really heavy roadster with rod-operated brakes, you would probably do better to look for something secondhand than to try to undertake or have done all the work that would be needed.

There are some sports-type bicycles which you can use for touring with very little modification at all and which are not too expensive. Among these are, made in Britain, models from the Falcon range and, in imports, models from the Peugeot and Motobecane ranges. These are some of the very few off-the-peg models with appropriate gears. The deficiencies you are most likely to encounter among others are that the gear ranges are too high and too close, saddles are probably unsuitable or lower quality ones, the machine may lack components such as mudguards and carrier, while pedals and handlebars may not be right. All these are quite easy to change and, of course, you can do these modifications in stages, making the most important changes first and leaving others until later.

Gears

First and foremost, the gear ratios – almost certainly too high – should be brought down to the sort of range advised in the last chapter. Here is where you can use the gear tables on pages 32–34.

Bearing in mind that the largest top sprocket easily come by is 16T (or 18T with Regina) and that 28T is the largest bottom one that the type of gear mechanism you already have will probably cope with, it may be necessary to change both the chainwheel and the freewheel block. If the chainwheel is of a type with a fixed ring – not bolted on – this will mean a new right-hand crank, say a Nicklin N34 three-bolt fixing or N54 five-pin, *of the same length as the left-hand one* or possibly a pair of cranks. Don't throw any of the old bits away – they will be useful in the winter. Then, from the gear table, choose a freewheel range to give you some low gears as close as possible to the sets quoted on page 36 and get your dealer to fit them. If necessary, have a new chain fitted at this stage as well: an old chain does not run well on new sprockets, or vice versa.

The bicycle may be fitted with a single gear, in which case it will almost certainly have a ½ × ⅛in (12·7 × 3·18mm) chain, chainwheel and freewheel. The rear wheel hub will be unlikely to be suitable for a multiple freewheel, so it will be necessary either to have the rear wheel rebuilt with a hub designed for a gear or to buy a complete new rear wheel, and to change the chainwheel. Choose gears as before, and buy a reliable but relatively inexpensive gear mechanism.

These two Simplex gears, front and rear (SX110T), are inexpensive and very suitable for modifying a bicycle at low cost. They make extensive use of plastic.

If the machine is fitted with a hub gear you have two choices: modify the gear range to bring it down to something useful, or replace it with a derailleur system. In the case of the latter, proceed as for replacing a single gear. A number of mainly older riders, however, use hub gears quite happily for touring, and the deficiency on a cycle supplied with one is once again likely to be that the whole range is too high. The standard type of Sturmey-Archer three-speed* has the ordinary gear as shown by the gear tables on pages 32–34 for the chainwheel and sprocket size as its *middle* gear; top is 1·33 times greater, while bottom is 0·75 times smaller. The range of sprockets available for these gears is strictly limited, usually 14 to 20T and more commonly 18T. To avoid recourse to calculators and log tables, if a 26in wheel is fitted, I can reveal that this will give a middle gear of 66 or 69 with the usual 46 or 48T chainwheels respectively, with top a horrifying 88 or 92, and bottom a still high 50 or 52. To give yourself a usable touring range – although, don't forget, the jumps between gears will still be very big – the *middle* gear needs to be about 50. The top will then be about 66 and usable as your normal gear on the flat, 50 the next, and bottom 38. To get a 50in middle gear you will need, with an 18T sprocket and 26in wheels a 34T chainring, or with a 20T a 38T, so that you will almost certainly have to change the chainset as above.

Wheels

The cheaper 'sports' bicycle is likely to have wide steel rims on steel hubs, although the more expensive types will have alloy rims on better hubs. It might be worth replacing these when you change the gear ratios, preferably by others of the same diameter, 26in for 26in, etc. in order to avoid problems with brake adjustment. A cheaper frame may not be designed to take the standard width of lightweight hub and may require the fork ends to be pushed gently apart to get them in –

* Sturmey-Archer used to make a whole range of three and four-speed gears of different spacing of ratios, but only the three-speed wide ratio or five speed (to special order) are now available. (If you have one of these older four-speed gears, the commonest one, the FW, gives ratios of 1·27:1·00:0·79:0·67. On the scheme we have been using, a direct drive of 52in – with a chainwheel double the sprocket size – will give a range of 66, 52, 41 and 35. The five-speed S5 has in addition an extra high gear of 78 – the gear designation is marked on the outside of the hub. Information on other types – FM-four medium, FC-four close, AM-three medium, AC and ASC-three close and three close without freewheel, respectively, should be available from the manufacturers. Some of these are now collectors' items.)

inconvenient but provided the movement is not too great, it is no real problem. The slot in the front fork may not take a quick-release hub which has a larger diameter axle: it can be *carefully and symmetrically* filed out.

Saddle
Changing the saddle is simple: just fit the replacement saddle (Chapter 2) to the seat pillar in place of the old one. The top, thinner bit of the pillar is of standard diameter, although several different diameters are used for the part which fits into the frame. When in doubt, take along the old part – recommended practice when replacing any component.

Pedals
Rubber pedals do not allow the fitting of clips and straps. British pedal threads are standard, so they may merely be unscrewed – and replaced (right-hand pedal, right-hand thread and vice versa!) (see Chapter 2).

Brakes
These are another item, like the saddle, where it is foolish and even dangerous to make false economies. If the bicycle has good aluminium alloy side-pull or centre-pull brakes, such as Weinmann, GB or Mafac, then they will be quite satisfactory without change. The cheaper steel ones fitted to some bicycles may not be effective: if you are in any way dissatisfied with the brakes, fit a good pair of new ones.

Handlebars
The advice on positioning in Chapters 1 and 4 may be impossible to achieve with the handlebars fitted to the bicycle. The diameter of the bottom part of the handlebar stem is standard so that a new stem and bends may be fitted directly as a replacement. However, before choosing the length of the new extension, read Chapter 4.

Mudguards, carriers, etc.
If these components are not already on the bicycle, then the types advocated in Chapter 2 should be fitted.

Buying secondhand

An alternative to adapting a bicycle is to look out for a good secondhand one. These are available through some dealers, through advertisements in local papers and *Exchange and Mart,* etc. and through advertisements in the cycling press (Appendix 2).

If you buy a secondhand machine you must differentiate between essentially expendable items, components which may easily be replaced and those that you will be stuck with once you have bought the bicycle.

Expendable items which have to be replaced on any bicycle from time to time are, in order of frequency, brake blocks, tyres, chain, freewheel sprockets, various bearings (hub, bottom bracket, head set, pedals), brake cables and perhaps pedals themselves. Their condition may be indicative of the treatment the bicycle has had and may influence how much you decide to pay, but the fact that they are worn is not of itself a bar to buying it.

Easily replaced items include those we have listed in dealing with adapting an existing machine. Wheels may not be what you want. Racing wheels have a secondhand value themselves, or you can have wired-on rims rebuilt on the same hubs. If you have to change the chainrings to get a touring range of gears, check that the chainwheel set will allow you to fit small rings. Some racing types such as Campagnolo or Zeus do not allow this. Check carefully the straightness of alloy cranks and the degree of wear of the pedal threads.

Basically, what will decide the suitability of the machine is the frame. Ask yourself the following questions:

'Is it the right size?' This is fundamental.

'If it is a racing frame, has it clearances for mudguards and eyes on the fork ends to allow you to fit them?' Beware of very close-clearance short-wheelbase time-trial frames. Check clearance for mudguards – is it feasible perhaps to fit 26in wheels with mudguards and is there enough adjustment on the brakes for this? Do the pedals plus toeclips clear the front wheel when the steering head is turned – making allowance for mudguards?

'Are the bearings standard?' 'Unofficially' imported foreign frames may have, for instance, French bottom bracket fittings (right-hand thread both sides). British-built frames will be all right, but don't forget that replacements for an expensive headset, particularly Campagnolo, will be equally so, and most other types cannot be used.

'What is the general condition?' Re-enamelling is quite expensive, so overall condition is important. Replacing a dented or cracked tube, followed necessarily by re-enamelling, is similarly costly. If the bicycle has been involved in a collision, the frame and forks may be distorted. Run the finger gently along the underside of the top and down tubes just behind the head tube: any frontal collision is perceptible as a slight rippling on the smooth profile of the tube and can often only be felt and not seen. The front forks may be slightly bent back. View the bicycle from the rear with the wheels in and ensure that both wheels are in the same plane. Any sign that they are at an angle to each other suggests that the frame is twisted: another check of the same point is to stretch a string from front to rear about a third of the way up from the ground to the hub. If the whole is perfectly in track, it should be possible to make the string just touch the rims at four points, two on each wheel. A very sensitive test is to attempt to ride the machine 'hands-off' – it should go straight. Other tell-tale signs of crash damage are abrasions on the ends of pedals, bent cranks and scores or abrasions on brake levers.

Cycles for the family

It seems appropriate to introduce this topic at this point for several reasons. First, my own experience as a family cyclist suggests that having everything multiplied by five – or whatever – means that cost is one of the most important factors. Second, many specialised family cycling items appear to be obtainable only on the secondhand market, and in some cases only if you are already a member of the family-cycling Mafia and have something to offer in exchange! Many items are of use to a given family for no more than a year or two, so there is a steady traffic and recirculation of special items.

Children can enjoy, and demonstrate their enjoyment of, cycling from a very early age, from the now-rare sidecar and trailer, through inactivity on the seat on the rear of a parent's bicycle, then on a child-back or adapted tandem to a bicycle of their own.

It is the choice of a bicycle for the young rider that calls for further comment. The graph of frame size against inside leg length on page 14 has been deliberately extended to include sizes compatible with a child of about eight or so. Although it is preferable to follow the precepts of good positioning, for a small child the ability easily to put a foot down on the ground is paramount. Normally, with an adult, this is automatic if the bicycle is competently designed. This does not always

Children can derive pleasure from cycling – and show it – from a very early age.

One, two, three . . . and three ways of carrying them. Not common nowadays – the sidecar: most of those now in use are home-made, but this one used a then commercially-available Watsonian body on a home-made rigid chassis. The first graduation from the sidecar stage is to a seat. All change, and move up one – the oldest now has a place on the rear of a specially constructed childback tandem. The front half is adult-sized, the rear 16in (40cm), so that a child from about five or six can ride it, using short cranks.

Both in sidecars and on seats the child must be strapped firmly in and protection fitted to keep small hands and feet away from wheels or any mechanism. The sidecar hood gave quite adequate protection in the wet: in the boot go the sordid paraphernalia of young children. The sidecar plus seat outfit taught me more about the use of gears, in a space of a few weeks, than I had learned in the previous twenty years!

One of the most satisfactory child seats made was the prewar Ashby (page 46) with a resilient wickerwork back and leg-guards on a steel frame. Naturally the basketwork wears out and this particular one had been rebuilt by a blind craftsman using the original as a model. Most carrying of children on bicycles involves some degree of do-it-yourself or specialised building and the examples shown on these pages are given as ideas from which to work.

Another solution to putting a child on the back of a tandem is to use a junior pedalling attachment on an adult-sized tandem (*left*). The attachment can be moved to a lower position as the child grows and the chain between the junior chainset and the tandem rear bottom bracket shortened. These attachments are still made: see Appendix 3.

apply to bicycles made for small children, and the positioning rules are a little less easy to apply.

Early in our family cycling history, as our oldest child approached the age of seven, we had made by a local specialist builder a proper lightweight frame to the smallest size that appears possible with 26in wheels, namely 18½in (47cm), with a low bottom bracket intended for use with 5½in (140mm) cranks and as short a top tube as the wheel and crank size would permit. It was necessary to incorporate a sloping top tube in the design – a curved one would have had a similar effect. The construction was necessarily bronze-welded, since the frame angles were not within the range covered by any standard lug set. But – and this is the point – since this frame was built as a normal lightweight, its cost was comparable with any handbuilt frame of the same type. It was only the fact that it had about a dozen years of prospective usefulness for three children that made it, to us, an economic proposition.

Below this size, or if it is not possible to go to such lengths, there are small bicycles using smaller wheels. Points to check when buying a machine of this type are that standard components are used as far as possible throughout. This applies particularly to hubs (otherwise multiple freewheels cannot be fitted), to diameters of seat pillars and, more important, handlebar stems. Many juvenile machines, usually smaller than this, use odd sizes.

I have not mentioned tandems and tricycles other than in the context of family cycling since I feel that neither is really a machine for the relative beginner. In particular – as stated in the text – many novices have been sadly disillusioned by the sluggishness of a tandem on hills. Nevertheless, they can allow not only the young but also the handicapped to enjoy the *feel* and open air freedom of cycle-touring. There are long-standing contacts between some cycling clubs and blind schools and a recently-registered charity Tandems for the Blind (current address available from the Charity Commissioners) has been set up to promote such contacts and to provide suitable machines. People with an impaired sense of balance have successfully ridden on tandems, too. There are also companies specialising in building tricycles both for sporting and recreational use and another which includes specialised machines for riders with various physical disabilities among its products. Addresses are given in Appendix Three.

4

The finishing touches

Finding the basic riding position

Together with gearing, the basic position on the bicycle is what governs the comfort of riding. We have now reached the stage of being able to establish your positioning on the bicycle.

We have already seen how frame size depends on inside leg measurement. The curve on page 14 is based on allowing both a practical and aesthetically acceptable length of seat pillar to protrude above the frame when the right position has been achieved. In positioning on a bicycle, as in so many other things, if it looks right and comfortable, then it is likely that it *is* right and comfortable: the converse is even likelier to be true.

Of the three basic triangulation points at which the body contacts the bicycle, one is irrevocably fixed. That is the position of the bottom bracket around which the pedals revolve. Crank length has already been decided, as – largely – has foot position, so any adjustments must be made to the other two, saddle and handlebar. Of these, the saddle placing is the first to be determined.

A much-quoted figure in coaching circles is that known as the 'Loughborough Formula', derived from ergometer efficiency studies at the College of Technology there. This work arrived at the empirical figure of 1·09 as the ratio between *a* the distance from the top of the saddle to the pedal axis with the crank in its lower position as a prolongation of the seat tube (effectively maximum leg extension) and *b* the inside leg length, for maximum muscular efficiency under laboratory conditions. This, however, gives a rather too high a position for comfort during sustained moderate effort – the ergometer studies

50

Even when a properly positioned rider is doing something far from relaxed his position still looks comfortable: multiple champion Ian Hallam MBE fights to bridge a vital gap in an early-season road race.

Finding the right saddle position. With the heel of the shoe on the upturned pedal and the crank in line with the seat tube (*left*) the leg should be straight but not stretched. The check should be carried out using a cycling shoe or similar with no more than a thin heel. The second check (*right*) is carried out with the cranks horizontal and the foot in its proper position in the toeclip. The hinge of the forward knee should be on or just behind the centre line of the pedal spindle.

last only for a matter of minutes as a rule – and for our purposes a ratio between 1·05 and 1·07 is more likely to be satisfactory. Now comes the fiddling part of the adjustment. This is best carried out with someone else as helper, measurer and observer. First, sit on the saddle wearing the clothing you will cycle in and cycling shoes. Place the *heel* on the pedal; the leg should be just straight but not stretched at its most extended point, where the crank is in line with and below the seat tube. Then, with the cranks horizontal and the foot in its proper position in the toeclip, the position of the hinge of the forward knee joint in relation to the pedal axis should be noted. It should be at this stage as nearly as possible vertically above the pedal axle: move the saddle backwards or forwards as necessary, until it is. This will upset the vertical adjustment, so put the saddle *up* by about $\frac{1}{6}$ of the distance you move the saddle *forwards*, or *down* by $\frac{1}{6}$ of the amount you move it back. Then do a final check with the heel-on-pedal routine. That is

Finding the right handlebar position. The often-quoted method of placing the handlebar bend level with the tip of the fingers of the extended hand with the elbow against the saddle peak takes no account of varying upper body length (*left*). The system (*right*), in which the handlebar bend position is such that the elbow just brushes the kneecap with the crank in line with the down tube and the hands on the bottom of the bar, makes some allowance for this.

the basic saddle position: you may later wish to move it back ½in (say 15mm) or so, but never move it any further forwards. Any change in your position on a bicycle feels odd at first, so give yourself say 50 to 100 miles of use (not necessarily continuous!) before making any alteration. Check that all the adjustments are tight, then put a strip of adhesive plastic insulating or similar tape round the seat pillar just touching the top of the frame seat lug. You will thus be able to tell the extent of any later adjustment.

The final variable point to be fixed now is the handlebar, in both the vertical and horizontal dimensions. Having determined the saddle position, the usually quoted method is to place the elbow so that its back just touches the peak of the saddle and to stretch the forearm and hand forward, parallel to the top tube of the bicycle: the tips of the fingers should just touch the handlebar bend. This takes account neither of the position of the peak of the saddle relative to the sat-on

The symmetrical placing of the brake levers may easily be checked by placing a straight-edge across them and comparing its line with the straight top of the handlebar.

part nor of the personal ratios of arm-to-trunk length, so it should be considered only a basis. Another method of establishing handlebar stem length proposed by a French cyclist with long experience in fitting young riders to their bicycles, and which allows to some extent for these variables is illustrated. The top of the handlebar bend may be positioned according to choice – and according to overall height and arm-to-trunk length – from just below level with the saddle to about $1\frac{3}{4}$-in below (40-50mm). Unfortunately, all this differential calculus brings in the well-known Catch 22: you have to have a handlebar stem before you can determine the correct length of handlebar stem. . . . The bends are clamped into the stem so that the lower grip slopes down to the rear a little, 5° – at the most 10° – to the horizontal.

One detail of the position remains: where the brake levers are to go. This position has to be a compromise between having them far enough down the handlebar bend for the brake to be easily applied from the 'drop' position and having them far enough up to be comfortable to rest the hand on in general riding. An acceptable average for normal

54

sized hands is with the centre line of the brake lever hood about 1½in (35mm) above the halfway point of the handlebar bend; this makes the top of the hood around 15° to the horizontal.

Taping and plugging the bars

The universally accepted covering for the handlebar bend is a cloth tape such as Tressorex or Allez. Plastic tapes are slippery and tend to become very uncomfortable in hot weather, and the more comfortable feel and surer grip of a cotton twill tape made for the purpose outweigh its disadvantages – that it becomes soiled and eventually wears; replacement once or twice a year is reasonable. Pad the grip with a strip of polyurethane foam of about ½in (say 15mm) thickness and some 1in (25mm) wide, compressed and taped firmly to the top of the grip with a plastic electrical insulating tape. The final cloth tape is then wound on top of this, each turn roughly half overlapping the rest, with more overlap on the curves. I have always found it more satisfactory to wind the tape in the opposite direction to that often suggested: I begin at the end of the bar and work up to the brake lever. The tape is then cut with a diagonal tapering cut and taping resumed just above the brake lever and continued to a point about 3in (say 8cm) from the handlebar stem, thus covering all the parts of the bar to be held at any time. The two cut ends of the tape, at the lever and the top, are neatly held in place by means of a narrow strip of matching or contrasting plastic insulating tape. The natural direction of friction of the hands then tends to smooth down the overlaps of the turns of tape, rather than curl them up. As a refinement, wind the tape on one side of the bar clockwise, the other anticlockwise. Whatever colour they begin, tapes almost all end up black, which isn't a bad colour to start. Other deeper colours, such as red, if they match the general *décor* of the machine do not discolour too badly. The white favoured by top racing men is frequently replaced before every race or race stage! Washable (non-adhesive) handlebar tapes are now becoming available with 'suede' or smooth finish. A possible alternative is twill carpet-binding tape. Both must be fitted over a sticky insulating tape.

Handlebar ends must be plugged as an elementary safety precaution. The most satisfactory in fitting are made of plastic and have a screw-in 'expander'. Rubber plugs, if they can be persuaded to stay in firmly, offer even more protection against perforated knees.

Fitting cables

The brake and gear cables can now be fitted. It is a matter of choice whether the left lever is used to operate the front brake and the right the rear (which is the choice of a significant proportion of experienced cyclists) or the opposite (which is the choice of most British manufacturers). The preference seems to have no correlation with right- or left-handedness of the rider. On balance, for British use when the right hand may have to signal a change of direction or change gear while braking, the former seems preferable.

The cables should follow the shortest path consistent with allowing a smooth curve and also with placing the hands on the bars. Both should curve to the same height when the front wheel is pointing straight ahead and the rear one should be long enough for there to be no strain even if the bars are turned inadvertently as far as they will go. With handlebar stems longer than about 40mm the cables should pass behind the bars. When cutting the outer casing to length, make sure that the last strand has not been crimped in. The inner wires should preferably be cut to length after fitting, so that no more than about ½in (say 10mm) protrudes beyond the brake cable clamp. Clean cutting is aided if the wire is soldered over a length of about 1in (25mm) where the cut is to be made. The inner wires should be greased before being fitted.

Gear cables should similarly follow the shortest smooth path. If a bottom bracket guide or tunnel is used, then the only length of outer casing will be from the chainstay stop for the rear gear to the gear itself. The casing should be long enough to allow the cable to enter the gear mechanism at right angles in all gear arm positions but no longer.

.

Pumps

There are four basic places for the pump, and several eccentric ones; all have their disadvantages. None is very convenient when the machine has to be picked up and carried, but on balance, if there's room, my preference is behind the seat tube. It can be held there by a single screw-on peg at the top with the bottom resting on the chain stays; this is also the most secure position. Pumps are of plastic or alloy and come in lengths of (nominally) 12, 15, 17 and 18in. The longest

56

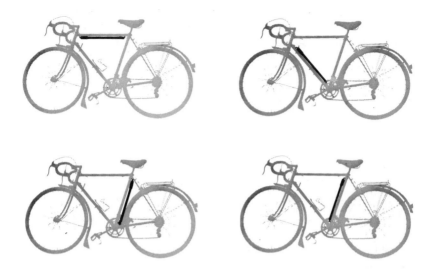

The four basic positions in which the pump may be fitted.

A neat and light bottle cage, here the Italian Emmepi, is the most practical and simplest way of carrying a drink.

that you can fit is the most efficient. Connectors are of two types, the familiar rubber flexible tube – which must have a deep-drilled end for the Presta valve – or a metal push-on device which is heavier but more effective. This latter also fits into the crook of the frame and avoids the need for a bottom pump peg. The Italian Saba range and the latest Bluemel models nestle in front of the seat tube without pump pegs.

Bottles and cages

It is not only in hot weather that you get thirsty cycling and the most convenient way to carry liquid is in a bottle designed for the task, carried in a carrier or 'bottle-cage' fitted to the frame. The most elegant cages are the simple aluminium alloy or heavily chromed steel wire ones such as the Italian Emmepi or French TA, which are fitted

Mudflap essential! Fording the River Alne, Northumberland.

either to brazed-on bosses on the frame or by means of two bolt-on clips, preferably on the down tube. There are several suitable makes of plastic bottle complete with lid – including Campagnolo and TA, at surprisingly low prices considering the names they bear!

Mudflaps

These are a small but vital item. Most plastic mudguards and some aluminium alloy ones when sold have a flexible plastic flap fitted to the front one with the intention of cutting down the spray hitting the rider's feet, the pedals, the bottom bracket and the transmission generally. These flaps are vulnerable and nearly always have to be replaced long before the mudguard wears out or becomes damaged. The most effective material that I have encountered for the purpose is a section of lorry tyre inner tube – 2-3mm rubber. The replacement flap should be cut using the old one as a pattern for width but made longer, until it is only perhaps an inch or two (30–50mm) off the ground, to be really effective. It may be fitted by reriveting or bolting with 2BA (or 5mm) bolts, in the original position or on the inside of the mudguard just below it.

Maintenance

It is not the purpose of this book to deal in detail with maintenance (see, however, Chapter 8). There are already one or two excellent and inexpensive books on the topic and to repeat the advice here would double the length of this one. They are listed in Appendix 2. Some large manufacturers – notably Raleigh who give out a 40-page booklet – supply quite detailed instructions with new machines sold, while a lightweight builder will give advice. There is no substitute for learning by experience or direct tuition; cultivate your dealer and join a local club or CTC section.

5

Road conduct
and riding technique

The Law

After prolonged representations by the Cyclists' Touring Club – in the case which really established the CTC as the cyclist's champion – the Local Government Act of 1888 declared cycles to be 'carriages', thereby thwarting attempts by some local councils to make piecemeal regulations affecting cyclists' general use of the road. The bicycle's status was established and is subject to national legislation. As a cyclist you are, then, technically in charge of a vehicle, but – despite Mr Bumble's protestation – the law is not an ass all the time, so that the cyclist is reasonably enough subject to obligations and restrictions roughly midway between those of the motorist and pedestrian.

As the law now stands, you *must*:

● Before setting out, ensure that your cycle has efficient brakes. Two independent braking systems are required on a bicycle with wheels larger than 18in in diameter, one acting on each wheel. For the purposes of this Act, a fixed wheel (direct drive without freewheel) counts at present as a braking system.

● When riding your bicycle, and even when wheeling it, observe traffic signs and signals – *including one-way directions and no right/left/ U-turn indications* – and the directions of a police officer or traffic warden controlling traffic. You must also stop when required to do so by a school crossing patrol or police officer in uniform.

● Give way to ambulances, fire engines or police vehicles with sirens sounding and blue lights flashing.

● Whether wheeling or riding the bicycle, give precedence to pedestrians on 'zebra' or push-button controlled 'pelican' crossings.

● When riding after dark (defined as half-an-hour after local sunset time to half-an-hour before local sunrise time), carry a front lamp showing a white light, a rear lamp bearing the British Standards Institution mark and the number 'BS 3648' and showing a red light, and an approved rear reflector, such as one marked 'BS AU40 LI'. The red warnings must be attached to the machine on the centre line or offside, not more than 20in (50·8cm) from the rearmost part of the bicycle, and at a height from the ground of not more than 3ft 6in (106·7cm) nor less than 15in (38·1cm). These lamps are required to be visible 'from a reasonable distance'. (These details of placing of lights apply to bicycles and tricycles with wheels greater than 18in in diameter; there are slightly different requirements for those with smaller wheels or with sidecars.)

You *may not*:

● Ride recklessly or at a speed or in a manner which is dangerous to the public, nor without due care and attention, nor without reasonable consideration for other persons using the road. (The splendid old offence of 'riding furiously' was, sadly, taken out of the Statute Book a few years ago: I knew one cyclist who committed all sorts of folly in vain hope of being booked on this magnificent-sounding charge!).

● Ride under the influence of drink or a drug. There is no statutory limit on blood alcohol concentration for the cyclist, nor any compulsion to submit to a test, but such figures have been quoted as evidence of impairment of faculties.

● Hold onto a motor vehicle or trailer in motion on any road.

● Carry a passenger unless your machine is 'constructed or adapted for the carriage of more than one person'.

● Stop, except in an emergency to avoid an accident, on a pedestrian crossing, or leave your cycle where waiting is prohibited, or leave it on any road in such a way that it is likely to cause danger to other road users. Neither may you 'by negligence or misbehaviour interrupt the free passage of any road user or vehicle'.

The meaning of road signs must be memorised.

● Wilfully ride on a 'footpath by the side of any road made or set apart for the use of foot-passengers' – that is, on what everybody except the law and highway engineers calls the 'pavement'.

● Ride along a road designated as a motorway or on a road or path covered by a valid order prohibiting cycling and showing the appropriate signs.

You *may:*

● After dark without lamps wheel your bicycle while on foot as near as possible to the left-hand edge of the carriageway, or stop in a similar position temporarily with lamps unlit while mounted to comply with traffic signals etc.

● Ride in marked bus lanes where they flow with the normal direction of traffic and, where indicated, on certain 'contra-flow' lanes.

● Ride on a bridleway or prescribed long-distance cross-country route with the obligation to give way when necessary to walkers and riders. The position on country footpaths is obscure: there is certainly neither blanket permission nor proscription and commonsense and courtesy should be observed.

The Highway Code

The Code has not the force of law, but breaches of it may be quoted as supporting evidence for charges, particularly in the ill-defined regions of recklessness, carelessness, danger or obstruction. The Highway Code exhorts you:

● To make sure that your cycle is in good condition before you ride it.

● Before starting off or turning right or left or pulling up, to glance behind to see that the manoeuvre is safe, and signal your intention.

● Not to ride more than two abreast and to ride in single file on busy narrow roads.

● Before turning right on a busy road to check that it may not be safer to pull into the left and wait for a gap in the traffic in both directions before crossing.

● While riding, always to hold the handlebar and keep your feet on the pedals, not to hold onto another vehicle or cyclist, not to ride close behind another vehicle, not to carry anything which may affect your balance nor to lead an animal.

● To use a 'suitable' cycle path beside the road, if there is one.

The cyclist and other traffic

The bicycle is relatively fragile and its rider vulnerable by comparison with motor vehicles. This is why, in part, the suggested routes in this book and the type of road chosen by experienced cyclists are on roads carrying little motor traffic (the other main reason for avoiding traffic is noise and smell). The only method is to ride defensively: know your rights, be prepared to take them up – but above all be prepared to give way rather than collide with anything.

This does not imply that you should be anti-motorist on principle. In any group of people – motorists, cyclists, fishmongers or graduates of the University of St Andrews – there will be the competent, those who are from time to time forgetful, the intolerant and those who appear to have no clue at all. Riding defensively involves hoping that all fall into the first category while being quite prepared for them to be in any of the other three.

The main hazards arise when some change of direction is involved, at junctions or roundabouts, and where there is a considerable speed differential between other vehicles and the cyclist.

The first essential at a junction is for you yourself to know where you are going and to be in the appropriate place – in the correct lane,

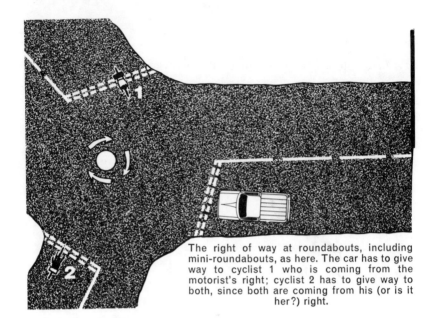

The right of way at roundabouts, including mini-roundabouts, as here. The car has to give way to cyclist 1 who is coming from the motorist's right; cyclist 2 has to give way to both, since both are coming from his (or is it her?) right.

particularly if arrowed. If you are caught unawares, take the left turn until you can conveniently stop and sort yourself out. Do not obstruct the junction while you decide. Signal your intention decisively, *after looking behind* and go through with it – once you are assured that other drivers involved have seen you. Many claim not to have seen a cyclist when challenged: according to their recollection, a true statement. There may be nothing wrong with their physiological optics, but somewhere in the complex information-processing route from the optic nerve to the brain a computer-type sub-routine has 'filtered out' the retinal image of the cyclist, as something slow and unimportant to be ignored. You must be prepared to make yourself and your intentions conspicuous enough to countermand that sub-routine.

Roundabouts can be particularly tricky: about a third of all road users seem unaware of the rule that traffic coming from the right has precedence. Some are confused and some just follow an extension of Newton's First Law of Motion and assume that the heavier vehicle has right of way, unanswerable by the cyclist in practice. At roundabouts, *know* when you have right of way – but for goodness sake know just as readily when to concede defeat.

In heavy traffic or a slow-moving line, it is tempting to exploit the bicycle's manoeuvrability and small width to filter past other vehicles. Be careful in this: concealed pedestrians may be crossing between vehicles. You should also avoid placing yourself to the left of a car – or even more a heavy vehicle – which intends to turn left and whose driver may not have seen you. Remember, too, that – justifiably or not – some long vehicles and cars with caravans or trailers have to make quite wide sweeps to get round tight bends, so avoid being in the swept space.

In point of fact, in fairly heavy but moving traffic, the bicycle is very often travelling at about the same speed as the rest and so moves as part of the general stream with little worry – except for the concentrated stench of petrol and diesel exhaust fumes. Particularly on well-regulated routes, where crossings are controlled by series of linked traffic lights, the hazards of this type of riding are quite small.

When the speed differential factor comes into play, the cyclist is affected not so much by the physical vehicle as by the disturbance it creates in the surrounding air. A fast-moving motor vehicle, particularly a coach or lorry, has an aerial 'wash' as illustrated in the sketch.

A diagrammatic representation of the air flow round a large vehicle which affects the cyclist as he is being overtaken. The wave at a, whose position will vary with the speed and size and shape of the vehicle, tends to push the cyclist to the left, while the turbulence at b tends to push the cyclist to the right, which can be tricky if another vehicle is following. The 'traffic-induced wind' effect shown stippled can extend some way behind the vehicle, certainly up to 50m.

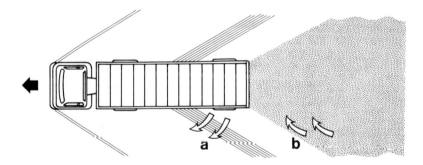

The necessary reactions to hold a straight line must be cultivated. Take advantage of every possible source of information – unusual sounds, reflections in shop windows, reactions of drivers approaching you – to ensure that you know at all times the relative position of

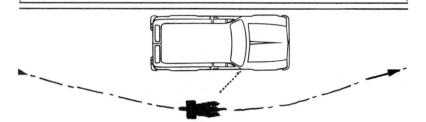

In passing a stationary car allow, if at all possible, and if there is anybody in it, enough room to pass a suddenly-opened door. The manoeuvre should be a smooth curve, not a sharp swing out-and-in, and any looking behind and signalling should be complete before moving out at all.

yourself and other traffic. Most drivers are reasonable and considerate people; once again you must use every scrap of warning you can glean to advise you of the approach of one of the other sort. The ability to glance over either shoulder without deviating from a straight line must be learned and practised.

One other vehicular hazard is the parked car. Either it is another obstacle to be got round – and again you should follow as straight a line as possible, not swinging out just before reaching it – or it may present an even more tricky problem, the suddenly opened door. It is an offence for a driver to open 'any car door so as to cause injury or danger to anyone' – but it happens. There are tell-tale signs which warn you that this is liable to occur: a car drawing to a halt and the driver fumbling with a seat belt, a stationary car with someone moving in the driving seat, any subtle movement. If there is room, pass at least a door's width clear; if not, play safe and wait.

In traffic, the cyclist is generally constrained to use the extreme left of the road, almost the gutter. Unfortunately, this is the very part of the road into which all kinds of debris – beer cans, bottles, shed bits of car trim and broken windscreens.– are swept by the tyres of passing cars. This edge may well be the result of widening as an afterthought and lack the strong foundation of the rest of the road, as well as being the natural habitat of gully grates (drain covers to the rest of us), and the urban or suburban cyclist may soon find himself undertaking a sort of obstacle ride. Cultivate the art of selecting a riding line, avoiding as many obstacles as possible, and sticking to it. Do not weave, but practise momentarily easing yourself clear of the saddle when going over bumps such as drains.

Courtesy

It is trite but true that when you are on a bicycle, you are immediately identifiable as a cyclist and are therefore an ambassador of the pastime to the outside world. You should ensure that your own road conduct and behaviour – including observance of road signs and the law – are beyond reproach. If somebody else – another cyclist, a pedestrian, a rider or a motorist – does you an unsolicited kindness, acknowledge it with thanks. Common courtesy and good manners need not stop at the tarmac's edge. Finally, one of the most friendly – perhaps more sentimental – aspects of cycling is the time-honoured way in which one cyclist greets another, known or unknown, on passing on the road. It's a tradition worth preserving.

Riding technique

Right at the beginning, I suggested that there might be a few things to unlearn, and it is now that you may have to unlearn them.

Getting on
Even as I suggested that the 1890s pictures on page 3 would not be needed today, I had second thoughts. The correct and safe way to get on a bicycle remains that shown in the woodcuts. You should, as the young lady shows, put your leg through the open frame or over the top tube of the diamond one – forwards or backwards, Western Roll or Fosbury Flop, is immaterial – and put the right foot in its proper place on the right pedal. You should *not* scoot along with the left foot on the left pedal and throw your leg over when you have enough speed: this is unstable, unaesthetic and not particularly good for the bicycle. Having checked that the road behind is clear, accelerate by pushing down with the right foot and bringing the left one onto its pedal. The art of picking up the left pedal when using toeclips is more easily acquired than described. The weight of the clip and strap should ensure that the pedal is always upside down when you put your foot on it. A light backwards movement of the foot turns the pedal up so that the front inch or two of the left shoe goes into the gap between the toeclip and strap and the proper surface of the pedal. A deft wriggle forwards of the foot and it is in the right place. It is essential that you master this until it becomes second nature – as it rapidly will – by practising on a

suitable quiet stretch of flat surface. It is desirable to be able to do it with equal facility with either foot. Toestraps should be moderately tight but not too much so: before stopping flip the quick-release buckles loose.

Riding

The rudiments of actually riding the machine are easily picked up, but some refinements are worth noting. The most important perhaps involve braking and this merits a separate section below.

A properly-designed machine and one which is in track should be almost self-steering. Riding 'hands off' is a very sensitive test of the alignment of a bicycle's wheels and the converse is true: if the line is right it almost steers itself. A slight leaning of the bicycle into the corner aids this and steering is then virtually automatic. You should cultivate the practice of raising the pedal which is on the inside of the corner, on the side leaning in, to increase the ground clearance on that side – always assuming you are using a freewheel. Ninety-nine times out of a hundred it will make no difference, but on the hundredth it may avoid grounding the pedal on the inside – a most unpleasant and potentially dangerous happening.

The bicycle is less stable when it is cornering, with sideways forces acting on it, than when it is travelling in a straight line, so that it is best to avoid actions, such as braking, which put further forces on the tyres at the same time. Similarly, slippery surfaces make themselves much more objectionable when you are cornering, while surmounting small obstructions is also more difficult at an acute angle. Potential hazards of this type, notably railway lines at level crossings, raised road markings, low kerbs at laybys and entrances and so on, should be crossed as nearly as possible at right angles, especially when it is wet.

The risk of puncturing can be reduced by careful riding methods. You should be ready to avoid glass from broken bottles, car lamps, etc. – windscreen glass is less sharp – by spotting its tell-tale glint well ahead of you. Perhaps the most prolific cause of punctures in country lanes is from hedgerow clippings, mainly hawthorn. Be wary when riding along a road which shows signs of recent hedge-trimming and be ready to stop if you hear the characteristic 'tick-tick' noise each wheel revolution which indicates that something is sticking into the tyre. Early action can often remove the thorn before it has had time to pierce the inner tube. If it already has, and you can hear air escaping, it is better, paradoxically, to leave it in: a thorn often partially plugs the hole it has made, leaving the tyre going down relatively slowly – quite often long enough to ride some miles between each pumping-up.

Stopping

It is the *front* brake that does the stopping. The effect of decelerating is to throw the effective line of action of the body's weight forward, so that more of the weight acts on the front wheel. However, a violent application of the front brake can move the direction in which the rider's weight acts so far forward that he or she goes right over the top – gentleness is the first, middle and last word of all riding techniques. On slippery surfaces – say a just-wet road after a long dry spell, oil patches, leaves, loose gravel, metal road furniture, level-crossing rails – the insufficiently gentle application of either brake can induce a skid. With the rear brake this is quite possible even on a dry smooth road, and the machine slews either from side to side or away entirely to one side. Do the same with the front brake, particularly on a corner combined with any of these hazards, and a front-wheel skid could put you on the ground. Gentleness is not only the first word etc.: it is everything. You *must* cultivate the art of summing up the road ahead and braking before bends or hazards.

The rear brake is not, however, a mere ornament. In emergency you may have to use both: an undignified right-angle skid is preferable to a collision. The instinctive reaction when applying the brakes hard is to tense yourself against the deceleration and push the body slightly backwards, and this fortunately tends to help prevent back-wheel skidding. Its main purpose, though, is not to decelerate but to keep speed steady on downhill stretches where this may be desirable and to supplement the front brake when necessary. On a long descent, the rims heat up and may even melt off any patches on the inner tube: both brakes have to be used to distribute the heat dissipation between the wheels. A flat front tyre caused by this can leave the bicycle very difficult to control. Cycle rim brakes do not suffer, however, from 'fade' in the motor-car sense.

Remember that brakes are much less effective in the wet – stopping distances can be many times greater than with dry rims. It is wise to dry off the rims by applying the brake long before it is needed. The heating helps to remove the thin water film from the rim surface. You should be particularly careful of this if you are using chromium-plated steel rims which are very bad in this respect.

Using the gears

For the beginner, the derailleur gear provides some problems, leading to noises which French cycling humorist Jacques Faizant has described as reminiscent of a van overloaded with a consignment of loose teaspoons cannoning into the front of an old-fashioned ironmongers.

Derailleur gears cannot be changed when stationary, despite the contrary belief of small children when you leave your bicycle outside a café. The whole system of derailleur gearing comes into the *brutal-mais-ça-marche* category by breaking all manner of engineering rules but nevertheless functioning. First problem is that there are no definite indicated markings or click-settings for the rear gear's five positions. The top and bottom are limited by the gear adjustment stops, but intermediate ones have to be found, like toeclips, by feel. The chain has to be moving at a reasonable speed, so do not try to change down (that is, onto a larger rear sprocket) below about 50rpm; do not leave changing too late on a hill, therefore. Ease the *pressure* on the pedals momentarily, particularly when changing down, while still turning them at the same speed. The lever should be moved briskly slightly beyond the position required and then flicked back to the right place – where the chain neither clanks against the next larger sprocket, nor rides up and tries to change to the smaller one, a different grating noise. You will soon become familiar with the two out-of-gear noises and know which way to move. All modern rear gears move back to change down, forwards to change up. With practice changes can be made almost silently.

The front changer has only two basic positions, one for each ring. It may, however, be necessary to 'trim' the adjustment slightly on either front ring after you change the rear gear to compensate for the different chain line. Naturally, it is much easier for the chain to drop from the large ring down to the small one, giving a lower gear, than to climb up. This gives you a useful second chance if caught out by an unexpected hill or if baulked. By remaining on the big ring for the four top gears and only then changing to the small one you have this emergency drop from the large to small ring in hand over most of the range. On the way back up again, the reverse change is probably best carried out when the chain is still on the lower sprockets of the rear gear and you are pedalling briskly. Depending on the type of front changer you may have to move the lever forwards or backwards to change down. Although it is normal to operate the rear gear lever with the right hand and the front one with the left (not both at once!)

it is worth learning to move either lever with either hand if necessary.

The correct way to tackle hills, then, is to use the rear and front gears to maintain a reasonable pedalling rate – which may be a little slower uphill – by changing down early enough. If you are in too low a gear you can always change up, but rarely the reverse.

Finally, learn to change down for junctions or before stopping, so that you will be in the right gear for moving smoothly away. I have to admit that I learned more of the necessity for this in the first few weeks with a child in a sidecar than in the previous twenty-five years!

Training

It may seem odd to discuss training in a non-competitive pastime like this, but there is no doubt that a certain degree of fitness makes cycle-touring more enjoyable. (I know cyclists who would claim that they race for the rest of the year only to make their Alpine tours seem easier!) It would be folly to set out on a long tour without any previous miles, and a steady programme of building up both fitness and familiarity with the bicycle and its controls is well worthwhile. The easiest way is to use the bicycle – for however short a distance – in some way every day, for a trip to the shops or work or a few miles in the evening. Start out with weekend rides of perhaps 20–30 miles (30–50km), stopping when you feel like it, and gradually build up by a few miles each week. These rides, too, are the time to sort out your techniques and details of your riding position.

The best school, however, and one which I shall have more to say about next is with a group of like-minded enthusiasts. There you will find advice (most of it conflicting!) and company. Appendix 1 tells you about cycling organisations.

Riding with a group

Both road conduct and riding technique have to be modified when you ride with other people. Ideally, you should become so used to each other's riding patterns that the group can move as one. A certain discipline is essential. The maximum comfortable size of group is about ten, and the riders should be able to move at a prearranged signal (most clubs have their own 'language') from the maximum double file

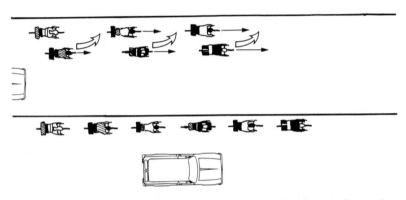

The basic sequence of manoeuvres in moving from double to single file to allow a car to pass on a narrow road. The riders accelerate to the extent of the straight arrows, the members of the outer file at the same time moving into the gaps created. When singling out to meet a vehicle, the front members of the inner file should accelerate and the rear ones slow down to allow the outside file into the gaps. It is easier to move into a gap created by acceleration, since it is in front of you and you can see it, than to move into one behind you created by braking.

to single when circumstances demand. It is desirable that one person should be in charge of the route to be followed while the group is on the road, and this leader should ensure that manoeuvres at junctions etc. are performed in a way which permits everybody to carry them out together. This does not free the individual rider from making sure that it is safe and sane to carry out his or her part of the manoeuvre. This requires some practice, probably the most difficult circumstance being turning right off a fairly busy road, with the necessity to filter to the centre. The basic necessities of looking round and clear signalling cannot be overemphasised.

You should be aware of what is going on around you: a well-drilled and experienced group can ride quite close together, perhaps a foot (say 30cm) apart, but it is essential to learn which are the predictable back wheels to follow. Riding in a group can be easier, since everybody is sheltered except for the front pair. If you are further back, be prepared for the pace to drop quite suddenly when you turn a corner into the wind, even although you may not feel the increased resistance yourself. The Highway Code stipulation 'never more than two abreast' should be adhered to. The road-racing, continuously-changing echelon to give the most shelter and the fastest progress is not practicable on the average road in a touring group.

Finally, on hills or into the wind, watch the rider who is about to ride out of the saddle – 'honking' – since it is very probable that his, or her, bicycle will move, apparently, backwards as the rider moves forward, to maintain the position of the centre of gravity. By the same token, you should be careful not to endanger anybody yourself.

There are considerable rewards and advantages in riding in company, in sharing your cycle-touring experiences, and for me – at least – this is one of the most attractive sides of the pastime. Make sure that it is also one of the safest, for you and for others.

Some of the most pleasurable cycling is with a group of fellow-enthusiasts but group riding demands both discipline and self-discipline.

6

Clothing and the weather

In this chapter we look into equipping the rider, into clothing for normal and abnormal conditions. All the recommendations apply equally to male and female riders: the photographs throughout the book illustrate most of the points.

Clothing

Opinions on suitable clothing are nearly as diverse as those on bicycle components, and just as susceptible to changes of fashion as any other clothes. All that I can do is describe what is practical and leave you to superimpose your own personal tastes.

Naturally, you will require different clothing for summer and winter riding; in spring and autumn you may require both types. Most riders would choose some type of shorts for the summer and some form of long trouser for the winter, combined with a variety of shirts, pullovers and jackets.

For summer use, a pair of light shorts, preferably made for cycling, in a material such as terylene-worsted, other wool-synthetic mixtures or possibly cotton drill or denim, are suitable. They should fit reasonably closely while allowing the legs to move freely for pedalling, should not ride up between the legs and cause chafing, and should not have heavy seams anywhere where they might come between you and the saddle – one of the most frequent and less easily spotted causes of saddle-soreness. What you wear under them is up to you, with the same seam-free proviso. Many cycle-tourists take a leaf – if that is the right word

Nylon windproof anoraks can be useful when it is cold but are generally not suited to strenuous riding.

– out of the racing cyclist's book and wear next to the skin a pair of chamois-lined wool or wool-synthetic racing shorts. These are un-doubtedly the most comfortable cycling wear (and they also offer great warmth and comfort in winter use) and fit very snugly to the body and legs. It is probably best to buy, at least for summer use, a pair described as 'track' shorts, which have shorter legs. A more serious disadvantage to the tourist who is away from home for some days is washing and drying them. To retain its softness the chamois-leather insert needs to be washed very gently and carefully with a toilet soap and dried slowly and naturally, which it may not do overnight in a typical British summer. You can use two pairs alternately, and many people do. On tour probably the best treatment for the leather is to dust it liberally with a talcum powder before use. Easier washing chamois-substitutes are becoming available. Check that the waist elastic of the racing shorts is not too tight: they should be snug enough fitting for elastic to be almost unnecessary. Some tourists emulate the racing cyclist by wearing only these shorts (which are always black), others prefer to use them beneath touring shorts.

On the top half, a light shirt, or T-shirt, supplemented as desired by thin pullovers, is probably the most practical. Again, some prefer to use the type of racing jersey used in road events, often with rear pockets, and this too is a matter of taste. There is no point in aping the racing cyclist just to look fast – but there is no doubt that where comfort comes into it, as with the shorts, racing experience has a deal to offer.

Generally speaking, if you find that you have a tendency to sweat heavily, it is better to wear one, two or even more pullovers – and this goes for the winter, too – rather than any form of jacket. The moisture can get out through several layers of wool, whereas it cannot through the less permeable jacket material – usually a proofed cotton. Against this the wool is less windproof and it may be necessary to carry a light unlined nylon anorak for long downhill stretches – or to use the old racing dodge of putting a double layer of newspaper between the two outer jerseys before a long descent. The amount you sweat also depends of course on the amount of effort you are putting into riding; you should never, therefore, attempt to ride uphill for any distance while wearing impermeable plastic anoraks. Quilted plastic jackets and plastic cagoules, admirable for standing around in in exposed places, are not suitable for cycling. A suitable compromise between jacket and pullover and having some of the advantages of both is the wool or acrylic tracksuit top, which should be of the close-fitting type designed for cycling.

In summer the only other items of clothing are for the feet and, possible, the hands. Most riders use cotton or nylon ankle socks, or in hot weather go sockless – which you do is a matter of choice. In warm wet weather it is certainly more comfortable to put on a pair of dry socks after riding sockless in the rain than to be landed with wearing sodden ones. Colour is I suppose a matter of choice, but the standard and smartest colour is white. Most riders wear nothing on the hands in summer, but for those with especially sensitive skins or who tend to get sore hands, I would recommend another racing item, the 'track mitt'. These are soft leather fingerless mittens with a crocheted string back for coolness. They are available in several sizes and should fit very closely indeed, like a second skin. If you can get them off without pulling them inside-out, they are too big.

For winter and colder weather, some covering for the legs is essential – and here I cross swords with some older riders who swear by shorts all the year round. It is not generally on the bicycle itself that you get cold, but after a very few moments of inactivity. The most practical trousers are of wool tweed or again wool-terylene or acrylic mixture, worn with long wool socks. They are a close-fitting type with a slight extra fullness at the knee, and with an elastic or Velcro fitting below. Full-length, close fitting trousers in the same material with a long zip from the ankle to just below the knee are sold as 'training trousers'. In summer, on cool evenings or for long descents, the lower half of a tracksuit can be slipped on over shorts and ankle socks. The tracksuit bottom, even more than the top, *must* be one designed for cycling and be skin-tight in fitting to keep clear of the chain and the ends of the cranks. Tracksuits designed for athletics are not suitable. Neither are jeans, since cotton denim is relatively stiff, a poor heat insulator and, worst, absorbs a lot of water when wet.

For normal winter or cool weather a single pair of adequately long wool socks is enough. These should be of such a length to come up to just below the knee joint.

In winter and the wet some kind of headgear is desirable, although preferences and tolerances apparently vary. Probably the most popular is the knitted woollen hat – which offers quite a bit of warmth across the forehead and is surprisingly resistant to rain. Riders with glasses may need something with a peak to keep the rain (or sun) off and the choice is between woollen or cloth caps. I shall cover specific rainwear below.

Another field in which tolerance to cold seems to vary widely is the hands. Some people seem to be able to ride barehanded while others at the same moment are wondering where their second pair of gloves has got to. Once more we seek an impossible compromise – a glove which will be perfectly windproof but at the same time not make the hands sweat. Probably the best is again to use several layers, with woollen fingered gloves as the inside one, and woollen thumb-plus-four-fingers-together mittens outside. Thick leather gauntlets and plastic impermeable gloves are unsatisfactory. It is essential in every case that you should be able to operate brakes and gears with gloves on (see also Chapter 14).

Apart from socks I have not mentioned colour. Cyclists, in addition to coming in all shapes and sizes, appear to favour all kinds of colour, from sombre browns and lovats to some quite garish combinations, such as purple and yellow. This is largely a matter of choice, though you should have some regard to general visibility. That is, however, a much more important point in the dark (Chapter 14) and the rain (below).

Shoes

There is no better footwear for cycling than cycling shoes – an obvious statement, needing some qualification. Most cycling shoes are designed for racing, and for the sort of riding we have in mind something slightly different may be needed. Typical racing shoes, nearly always black, are made of thin calf leather and look rather like a running shoe without spikes, and with a very thin heel. The type preferable for touring, where some walking may be involved, has most of the characteristics of the other, possibly a little more stoutly built but still light, but with a reasonable, say $\frac{1}{4}$–$\frac{3}{8}$in (6–10mm), heel. They are available with perforated uppers for ventilation – in hot weather – or un-perforated, which is preferable for the winter. Some have steel or nylon stiffeners in the sole which spread the pedal load. Most have leather or smooth composition soles, and it may be advantageous for touring use to fit stick-on rubber soles straight away, before use. (Note by the way that changing your shoes can alter your effective saddle height and hence your position, often by a surprising degree.) The shoes should be a quite snug, close fit. If you plan, as I hope you will, all-year-round riding it is well worth while having a summer and a winter pair, the latter slightly larger to take account of thicker socks or two pairs; try *all* shoes on with the appropriate socks before buying. There are two English makers from traditional cobbling country – Northamptonshire – who make an excellent range of touring as well as

Cycling shoes are made of thin leather, cut low at the ankle, and with a shallow heel. Touring shoes generally have more heel than racing ones, as here, and a stouter sole. Shoes with perforated uppers can be more comfortable in hot weather.

racing shoes – Pete Salisbury and Reynolds. Some lighter types of ordinary shoe, provided they have narrow welts ('turned' shoes) can also be used.

Further possible additions are shoeplates. These are metal, or less commonly plastic, plates which are screwed or nailed to the sole of the shoe and have slots in them to engage the rear plate of the pedal, so holding the foot firmly in position. Their use is almost invariable in racing, since they allow the pedal to be pushed forward or pulled backwards at the top and bottom of the stroke. The main point in their favour for general riding, is avoiding clip pressure on the big toe and wear on the front end of the shoe. They are certainly an aid while actually riding, but there is no doubt that, if any degree of walking or riding on rough tracks is contemplated, they can be a liability. A group of shoe-plated cyclists in Worcester Cathedral also makes a remarkable noise! It is necessary to be very much more careful of the degree of tightness of your toestraps when using plates, loosening them when needed by flipping the quick-release buckle. You must be

79

absolutely competent in the use of clips and straps with smooth shoes before trying shoeplates. They are certainly not items for novices. The plates are fitted so that the foot is in the proper place with the end of the shoe just clear of the clip. The most satisfactory way of fixing them is to bolt them from the inside of the shoe using 6BA (or 3mm metric) countersunk bolts and nuts. If you always use the same type of plate, new ones can be directly replaced in exactly the same position.

Wet weather

One of the first enquiries I mentioned was what one did if it rained. I forbore at that stage to tell the truth. The real answer is: get wet. There is no way of keeping *entirely* dry on a bicycle, but there are several ways of keeping the level down to merely moist. Anything which is entirely impermeable to moisture from the outside is at the present state of technology equally impermeable to moisture from the inside. Since the most commonly worn – and indeed the most satisfactory – rain protection, the all-embracing cape, effectively cuts down the normal circulation of air round the rider's body, the atmosphere under the cape soon becomes that of a tropical forest, often with some of its mysterious smells. In reasonably warm conditions wear at least one layer *less* under a cape, and replace it once the rain has stopped. In this way you compensate for the lack of air circulation and sweat less.

The cape should be large enough to cover you completely with the hands in the forward position on the brake levers. Cape sizes are quoted by arbitrary description ('large', etc.), or by length, or less frequently now by skirt diameter. Try one in the actual riding position before buying, to make sure that it is big enough. Capes are made nowadays in two weights of plastic material. The lighter is a translucent embossed pvc type of material, or less commonly nylon, is quite suitable for summer use, is of low bulk and very light in weight. The sturdier is a fibre-reinforced pvc, which is more suited to winter use. They come in a variety of colours and should be chosen with visibility on a rainy day in mind. The fluorescent orange ones show up very well on a grey day but much less in the dark. All in all, the most visible colour over the range of night and day circumstances is a bright yellow: yellow on black offers the highest visual contrast. *Never* buy a black cape.

Light plastic anoraks offer some protection against showers, but are

The favoured rainwear is the all-enveloping cape which covers not only the rider but the handlebars. This group seems to favour woollen hats but a variety of headgear is described in the text. There appears to be no rational explanation for the cyclists' smiles, given that it is on a steep hill in November and they are walking because their feet were cold.

not generally very effective in heavy or prolonged rain. They – and 'racing capes' which are similar in pattern – also pick up a great deal of internal condensation. Their real advantage, which is why I advocate them for long downhill runs, is that they have much less wind resistance than the all-enveloping cape, which needs care in high winds.

Headgear in the rain can either be nothing, the woollen hats already mentioned, or the time-honoured sou'wester – which must have its back part placed so that it drains *outside* the cape!

In general, other fittings such as spats and leggings are more trouble than they are worth, while nylon over-trousers as used for climbing or walking are both dangerously baggy and uncomfortable. Better a good mudflap and spare socks.

7

Bags, baggage and beds

Carrying it all

There is no set list of the things you need to take on tour or for a simple ride. It is possible to set out with the irreducible minimum of tools plus a toothbrush and a spare pullover – and a bulging wallet. Alternatively, you can load up with all your requirements, a lot of food, a tent and a £5 note for emergencies: for a day ride you can easily take everything you need. But whatever course you decide on, you will have to have some sort of a cycle bag to carry it in. For if there is one rigid rule to be observed in cycle-touring, it is that you should never carry things on your back – with the possible exception of a camera and, for short distances, a small bag with food or other small items for immediate use.

It would be as well to clear this last item out of the way from the very beginning. Such a bag may indeed be very handy for carrying oddments but it is *not* the thing for carrying all your touring needs. The cycle-tourist is likely to find them of use for packing in short-term oddments such as easily damaged fruit between the shop and the lunchtime picnic or evening stop. They are also handy for carrying personal valuables such as cash, cards, passport, tickets, and so on, when you may require to produce these or if you want to remove them *en bloc* when leaving the bicycle to walk round a town or site of interest. Even in these two cases, the bag is best carried while on the bicycle by looping the strap round the saddle and holding it down on top of the saddlebag by means of a couple of elastic straps.

The best way to carry anything is in a bag firmly attached to the

The four basic positions in which bags may be fitted: as a rear saddlebag, as rear panniers, as front panniers fitted to a special carrier, and as a handlebar bag, usually used with a small support fitted to the front brake.

machine. (Try comparing carrying a sack of potatoes and wheeling it in a barrow if you're dubious!) A loaded bag anywhere affects the handling of the bicycle and this is kept to a minimum if the load is not too great (obviously), low down and within the wheelbase. Each of the four bag positions has its advantages and disadvantages.

Two major British manufacturers of cycle bags, Carradice and Karrimor, both produce excellent models of basically similar type in cotton duck and proofed nylon. The traditional waterproof black cotton duck is tried and tested and is certainly to be recommended for the beginner. (It is definitely waterproof: we once had to bale out the bag of a young cyclist who had allowed her bicycle to fall over in a ford!) The main enemy of bags is abrasion, particularly as a result (unavoidable) of leaning the bicycle against walls, etc. Natural materials wear, fibre by minute fibre, whereas the thicker individual fibres of nylon melt microscopically when abraded. The nylon material has proved quite satisfactory for mountaineering bags, where the wear pattern is different, but nylon cycle bags have perhaps not been on the market long enough yet to be unconditionally recommended, if only because they have so far been used mainly by careful, experienced riders. Some of the all-plastic zip-type fasteners are also suspect for prolonged practical use. The nylon bags are a little over half the weight of the others and about 50% more expensive.

The saddlebag is traditionally most used in Britain. Two straps hold it to the saddle; a third fixes it to the seat pillar or carrier. The largest size is recommended: the Carradice Camper, 14 × 9 × 7½in (35·5 × 23 × 19cm), a total capacity of 950 cubic inches (15·6 litres) plus two fair-sized end pockets; or the Karrimor Dalesman, 15 × 8½ × 7in (38 × 21·5 × 18cm), 890 cubic inches (14·6 litres), plus again two end pockets. Both are available in versions with a long top flap bringing up the capacity to about 1200 cubic inches (20 litres). It should be possible to pack into one of these bags everything you need for a week or more's bed-and-breakfast, hotel or youth hostelling tour: only camping demands appreciably more capacity than this. Equally, it should easily carry all you need for a day or weekend. These saddlebags have loops on top for carrying a rolled-up cape. The large side pockets are particularly useful for carrying items which you may want to get at, such as tools and maps, without disturbing the main contents. The main disadvantage of the saddlebag is that it carries the weight high up, has to be firmly strapped to prevent its swinging and may not fit too easily below the saddle. There are smaller models, such as the Carradice Low-Saddle, but with a capacity about one-third less.

The handlebar bag is most used in continental Europe, although both Carradice and Karrimor now also make versions. The most widely used version abroad is the brown canvas TA model, with dimensions of 9½ × 8 × 6in (24 × 20 × 15cm), 450 cubic inches (7·4 litres), and no less than five small pockets, with a further transparent pocket to take a map on the top flap. The handlebar bag again has the disadvantage of carrying the weight high up, but it is of course smaller, and is very handy for getting at, riding or momentarily stopped. Its principal drawback is that if strapped to the straight top portion of the bar, it prevents the use of one comfortable riding position. Experienced continental users advocate making up a parallel wooden or aluminium alloy bar with a cross member bolting to the handlebar extension handlebar clamp bolt, to space the bag from the bars. TA, and others, make an extremely neat support for the base of the bag, fitting to the pivot and fixing bolts of a centre-pull brake. A handlebar bag makes a good supplement, and longitudinal weight balance, for a saddlebag. The British versions are intended to be rapidly detachable for use as shoulder bags.

Large pannier bags may be necessary when you are camping but are otherwise in my opinion best avoided. They have to be well back on the carrier to avoid fouling the heels and are so outside the wheel-

Left Probably the most popular British saddlebag – the Carradice Camper in black cotton duck. A bag of this size needs to be supported, at least on most frames of average size, by a substantial carrier of the type shown. *Right* Another Carradice product: small panniers which may be used on either front or rear carriers, although they are described as front panniers. They are particularly convenient on a small bicycle or child-backed tandem where there is not enough clearance below the saddle for a saddlebag.

base of the machine, making handling unpredictable. They keep the weight low down, but get a certain amount of spray and mud from the wheels. Smaller panniers are made for use with a front carrier, the Carradice version (in black duck) being a very handy $8\frac{1}{2} \times 8\frac{1}{4} \times 4\frac{1}{2}$in ($21 \cdot 5 \times 21 \times 11 \cdot 5$cm) each; total capacity is 630 cubic inches ($10 \cdot 3$ litres). These complement a rear saddlebag very well and are also useful when a child seat is fitted. I have used two pairs of these small panniers on a child-back tandem; with a thin nylon 'stuff sack' with light bulky items strapped to the top of the rear carrier, the 1250 cubic inches ($20 \cdot 5$ litres) holds enough for both occupants for a week's tour.

These nylon stuff sacks are very useful, either for the purpose mentioned, or as inner bags in saddlebags. Note however, that most are not completely waterproof.

What – and what not – to take

Respectively, 'not too much' and 'nothing unnecessary'. Obviously, there are essentials: tools for basic repairs plus some form of first-aid kit (Appendix 4), and then – according to the length of trip and the accommodation – what can usefully be divided into wearing things, washing things, sleeping things and eating things. The ideal is to use everything you take – except your cape, tool kit and first-aid outfit.

A certain minimum of spare clothing is essential and varies with the season, but it is in this section that it is easiest to take too much. For a day trip, an extra pullover for a cool evening plus gloves may be enough in summer, with possibly some leg covering as well. In autumn or spring, it may be necessary to have a little more, although you will start out in the cool of the morning and gradually shed layers as the day warms up, only to put them on again later. In this case, don't forget the space in which to put them. In winter, you will need more extra clothing for possible unscheduled stops – since it's much warmer riding than stopped – and perhaps a spare pair of socks and gloves in case one set gets wet. As the journey you plan becomes longer, so you will need rather more: there will be occasions when you can wash and dry underwear overnight, but it is as well to have spare sets of these, shirts or polos, plus say two extra pairs of socks, together with a change of lightweight trousers (or skirt, to choice) for wear in the evening. Clothes will be your bulkiest luggage, although probably not the heaviest: they should fill about two-thirds of the saddlebag space.

Washing things include soap, towel, razor, toothbrush and tooth-paste to taste, and should be large enough to last the trip but not much more. It is convenient to carry the whole washing equipment in one of the saddlebag side-pockets so it should be able to pack into that space. A small tin filled with detergent is useful for clothes washing.

Sleeping things are very much a matter of personal taste, but should be chosen for small bulk. The whole question of requirements for sleeping is turned inside out if you are camping. Lightweight camping is a very specialised occupation, too much so to be covered here, particularly since very sound and detailed advice is available from other sources; see Appendix 1.

What you take for eating depends entirely on how you intend to sustain yourself. While it is possible to buy meals in most towns and many villages in Britain, and snacks such as ploughman's lunches in many pubs (often only on weekdays, though), you will have to consider picnicking at some stage – certainly if you get off the beaten track. You will need a sharp knife for bread cutting, always best done on the spot rather than carrying prepared sandwiches, a further knife for other cutting and spreading, perhaps a lightweight cup and, depending on the epicurean level to which you aspire, a tin-opener, a bottle-opener or a corkscrew. Some – and this is a particular tradition in Scotland – like to carry a small paraffin pressure stove (such as a $\frac{1}{2}$-pint Primus) or the lighter and more convenient gas stove (e.g. Camping Gaz S200) and brew up (Scots: 'drum-up') a hot drink; this means utensils *plus* matches or a lighter. Although dearer to run, the gas stoves are cheaper to buy, quicker to start and avoid the risk of getting smelly paraffin over everything.

The check-list in Appendix 4 has two purposes as a reminder: first, what you may have forgotten; second, what you can leave out.

Accommodation

Where the cyclist can stay and buy meals depends entirely on the depth of the individual's purse. The cheapest is with relatives or friends; many first tours have been dictated by the location of strate-gically-placed aunts and second cousins. Next – once more leaving aside camping, where there is an element of capital spending – come youth hostels, of which there is a chain of about 250 in England and Wales, and a further 80 in Scotland under a separate administration (details in Appendix 1). They occupy a range of buildings from remote con-verted farm cottages to National Trust-owned castles, and from a converted barge to town houses. Prices are relatively moderate. All-in-all they provide an excellent introductory range of halts, particularly for young cycle-tourists. The coverage of the country is generally good although there are some rather large gaps in places. There are in addition a few private establishments run on similar lines. Advance booking is desirable at popular holiday weekends, such as Christmas, New Year, Easter, May Day, Late Spring, and Late August, in England and Wales, and New Year, May Day and Early August in Scotland, and essential during summer holiday periods and at nearly all times in very popular areas such as the Lake District, Peak District and Devon and Cornwall.

Next up the scale come private 'Bed and Breakfast' houses. The least expensive of these come in fact very near to youth hostel prices.

A true-to-life cycling picture. For CTC members the annual *Handbook* lists places where cyclists are welcomed.

Next are small private hotels and finally the larger ones. These are listed in the CTC *Handbook* and various guides issued by regional tourist boards and by local authorities. Tourist information offices – marked by a stylised *i* symbol – are becoming common in towns and cities which expect considerable numbers of visitors, as well as in national, forest and country parks.

Most accommodation, except hostels, is cheaper and sometimes easier to find for two people than one. Although I have ridden perhaps two-thirds of my total mileage alone, as I have already indicated cycle-touring is for me essentially a sociable pastime. All the little pleasures of a day's ride are increased by sharing them with someone else; most of the troubles lessened. Probably the most convenient group is of four people: accommodation is not too difficult to find, four people are pretty well as manoeuvrable as one on the road, and you have three people to talk to with little extra encumbrance.

Although the very word 'touring' suggests a vaguely circular route, it is quite possible to have a very enjoyable cycling holiday from one or more fixed centres. Self-catering holidays at rented cottages are very popular generally and lend themselves very well to this type of cycling, particularly if the area is well-chosen to offer a variety of countryside and – ideally – a fair number of routes out. Many people successfully divide a fortnight's holiday between two differing centres, each offering its own choice of country. This sort of cycle-touring – largely because only a small proportion of the total baggage has to be taken out each day – lends itself very well to family cycling.

Getting there

It is not everybody who has the time to be able to ride to their chosen area from their very door: for many some help from public transport or private is useful. Bicycles may be carried by most trains – following the 'indefinite' extension of a 1977 experiment – simply by buying a passenger ticket for the rider, labelling the bicycle and putting it in the guard's van. Exceptions are the '125' and Pullman trains where half-fare is payable. The free carriage followed nearly a century of lobbying by the CTC and other cycling bodies.

Bicycles may also be taken by air, for a nominal charge or free within the appropriate baggage allowance, depending on the airline. You may have to remove the pedals and front wheel (tying it to the frame) and turn the handlebars to make the machine as compact as possible – check when booking (see Appendix 1).

Most foot ferries and all internal car ferries in Britain will take bicycles, and again conditions and fares vary. CTC members will find the latest available information in the Club's *Handbook*.

Particularly if more than two wish to travel together or if there is no suitable train or air service, it may be convenient to travel by car with the bicycles on a roof rack. This may be of the usual luggage-carrying kind, in which case most people carry the machines upside down but vertical, fixed to the cross-members of the rack with toestraps at the saddle and the handlebars – on or near the brake levers. Care should be taken that the fixing of the rack and bicycles is secure, and that the recommended weight limits for the rack and the car roof are not exceeded. The saddle and handlebar tape may need protection with pieces of plastic foam. Avoid straining brake cables. Alternatively, a special cycle-carrying rack may be fitted (see Appendix 3): these generally carry the bicycles vertical and right way up, with the front wheels removed and the forks bolted to special cross-pieces. The rear wheels fit into cradles or slots, again preferably secured there by toestraps.

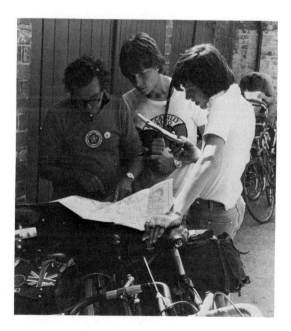

8

Basic self-sufficiency

Because you will be travelling some way from assistance or refreshment, it is essential that you should know what to do in the case of the commoner mishaps, and how to prevent some of them.

Tools and spares

As your cycling experience increases, you will find that you seem, almost imperceptibly, to accumulate tools. There is, however, an irreducible minimum that you must start with. These are the basis of your travelling toolkit, and the type of thing you should have with you even for the shortest of journeys. They are: spare inner tube (not necessarily new, possibly repaired, but definitely airtight), tyre levers, spanner ($\frac{5}{16}$ and $\frac{3}{8}$in BSF) to fit front and rear hub nuts, respectively, unless you have quick-release hubs, puncture outfit comprising patches, canvas, sandpaper and rubber solution, spare lamp bulbs if you're travelling after dark, and the ever-useful small 35mm film tin of Swarfega.

As you go further afield, there are more things it is desirable to carry, a few more tools, but mostly spares. These are illustrated and listed in Appendix 4. It is probably wise for tandem riders to carry in addition a spare rear hub axle of adequate length. Since tandem-length gear and brake cables are not readily obtainable, I generally carry a small length of solder and a little flux paste to allow resoldering cable nipples if necessary: this can be done over any indoor or outdoor gas stove, or even on an electric radiant ring. Solo handlebar control gear

One of the specialised small tools which makes a difficult job easy – the Cyclo Rivoli chain bearing-pin extractor. It is one of the few tools to be supplied with specific instructions for its use.

inner wires are long enough for tandem use with down-tube controls and in emergency, with a spoke nipple threaded on, as a rear brake cable. In this case substitute a proper cable as soon as possible.

Other oddments, not strictly spares, can be very useful. First are spare toestraps, say two pairs, which can be used for almost everything from strapping the bike onto a car roof-rack – or when travelling by train to stop it falling over – to jury-rigging a broken carrier, plus strapping on the extra pullover, long loaf or cucumber. A couple of fabric-covered elastic straps with hooked ends are useful too. Next is a roll of plastic insulating tape, for securing cables, or as a possible emergency extra (waterproof) layer for a badly cut tyre; a needle and strong linen thread – for tyre outer cover, bag or even shoe repairs; a length of thin, say 18SWG, iron wire for broken mudguards etc.; several pieces of paper towel or handkerchief; and a small leak-proof container of oil for lubrication. (Many a tin discarded by the motorist or motorcyclist as empty will be found to contain quite enough for a bicycle chain or hub.) By far the best material for tyre repairs is a section of a worn-out light tubular tyre (Catch 22 . . . I advised against tubulars!); otherwise small pieces of denim are quite effective.

Roadside repairs – and preventing their causes

The picture sequences show how to carry out the commonest roadside repairs, but it is of course best to avoid them as far as you can by means of a few simple 'pre take-off' checks:

1

2

3

4

5

6

7

Puncture repair. First pump the tyre up and see if you can hear where the air is coming from: if you can find the puncture in this way you may only have to lever off a section of tyre and avoid removing the wheel from the bicycle. Otherwise, and if you want to change the inner tube, you will have to remove the wheel. Then let the tyre down completely and remove the knurled valve locking ring (1). Push the spoon end of the first tyre lever gently under the tyre wire, either near the puncture if you have found it, or otherwise near the valve (2). (Arguments rather like the Lilliputians' one about which end of the egg to crack rage between those who start taking the tyre off and finishing putting it on *at* the valve and those who carry out the operation starting and finishing *opposite* it. I favour the former: it's possibly no more than a habit, although I could give theoretical justifications. But I won't.) Hook the notch in the first lever round a convenient spoke. Then insert the second about 7cm (say 3in) away from it (3) and repeat with the third if necessary until a long enough length is over the edge of the rim for you to be able to remove the rest by hand. At this stage (and in fact any time you have the tyre off for any reason) feel carefully round the inside of the outer cover (4) to check whether anything sharp is sticking through – if there is, remove it, and note the position if you haven't already found the puncture. Return to the tube. Pump it up lightly, say ten pump strokes. Listen carefully round it or hold it very close to the sensitive surface of the upper lip to try to find the hole by sound or touch. Alternatively immerse the tube in water, moving it round and look for the tell-tale stream of bubbles (5). Dry the tube thoroughly if necessary and clean the area round the hole with sandpaper (6). Then apply a coat of rubber solution to the cleaned area and spread it to cover an area rather greater than the patch you intend to use (7): you rarely need to use the large patches for thorn or flint holes. On black butyl rubber tubes allow this coat to dry and then apply a second coat and allow that to dry; red natural rubber tubes need only one coat. Select

94

your patch and remove its protective foil backing to expose the adhesive side (8). Press the patch firmly into position, taking particular care to press down the edges (9). Remove the backing paper by pinching the patch so that the paper tears across the middle (10); you can then take it off from the centre with no risk of lifting the patch edges. If you use the feather-edge Bridgport 'Cure-c-Cure' patent patches you can repair holes quite close to other earlier patches (11). As a refinement you can lightly dust the tube with french chalk, then inflate it slightly, say four pump strokes. Put the valve through the hole in the rim and nestle the tube into the outer cover (12). Begin to replace the outer cover (in my system opposite the valve) by rolling it with the thumbs (13) (not pulling it from the other side, which can end up ripping your fingernails). Continue to roll on both sides until there is say a 20cm (8in) length left bridging the valve. Depending on the tightness of the cover you may have to deflate the tube completely at this point and roll the tyre wire right down into the well of the rim all round the length you have already replaced. Then roll on the last section in the same way (14). Push the valve up to make sure that the hexagonal nut which holds it into the tube is above the tyre wire. Replace the outer knurled locknut and pump the tyre up. If the tyre is quite a tight fit on the rim you can probably go straight ahead and pump it right up. If not stop after about, say, fifteen strokes and check that the cover is on straight and if necessary correct it by pulling it up so that the lines of the moulding are the same distance above the rim all the way round then finish pumping up. You have mended your puncture! The tube repair section (5–11) can of course be omitted if you merely change the tube but it's just as important to check that whatever caused the original puncture is no longer in the tyre. And *never* use the tyre levers to replace the tube: it is quite easy to do it by hand if you follow the advice to roll it on from the front rather than trying to pull it on from behind.

8

9

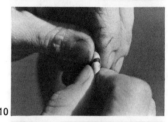

10

11

12

13

14

Roadside spoke replacement. Spokes nearly always break at the head where it goes through the hub flange. Unscrew the broken spoke as shown (if necessary stop and think which way is unscrewing: it is possible if you screw it the wrong way to pierce the rim tape and inner tube!) and then pass the replacement through the hub flange (remembering that heads of alternate spokes are on opposite sides) and screw the original nipple onto it as shown using the nipple key. The spare spokes should be short enough not to protrude through the spoke nipple on the inside.

Tyres before setting out, or after returning, check that the outer cover is not too worn, has no sidewall cuts to be patched, and that small flints, thorns etc. are no longer stuck in any of the inevitable small cuts in the tread.

Cables these fail either after a very short time through faulty soldering (relatively rare) or after long use by fraying. Any cable which shows any sign of fraying at the lever or grates when the brake is applied or gears changed should be immediately replaced. Take out inner wires and clean and regrease at intervals.

Brake blocks replace blocks, or if in doubt, both block and shoe, when the studs on the block are worn away. Clean out any grit or metal swarf from the braking surface. Check that no part of the block touches the tyre.

Spokes not much that you can do, I'm afraid, except to check that they are all intact and reasonably tight, and that the wheel is true.

Freewheels European freewheels have 21 internal ratchet teeth and two sprung pawls which engage them. If both pawls are working, a complete revolution backwards of the freewheel should produce 42 clicks, or each half-turn 21. If you make a pencil mark on the freewheel body and on the top sprocket at the starting point, then it is quite easy to check. If only one pawl is working, then you will get only 21 clicks

1

2

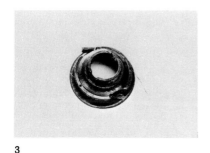

3

4

5

Freewheel pawl spring replacement. The operations shown here would normally be carried out with the freewheel fitted to the hub; in addition the three outer sprockets have been removed for greater clarity. First the locking ring and combined front bearing of the freewheel should be tapped undone with a soft punch: the 75mm nail shown here (1) is quite adequate and portable and any handy fairly heavy object can be used to tap it round. Note that this ring has a left-hand thread. The removal of this ring exposes the front row of balls (2): turn the wheel over carefully, holding the freewheel together and empty the front balls onto a sheet of paper. Then gently lower the sprocket part of the block away from the centre. This exposes the pawls and their wire springs (3). Spare springs can be fitted or a strand from an old brake cable manipulated with pliers into the right shape and length: note that some newer freewheels have a different type of spring. The springs fit behind the pawls, pushing them outwards. To reassemble, hold the pawls in with a length of thin thread (4) and, still pulling the ends of the thread tight, lower the centre piece with the immobilised pawls into the sprocket section with the rear bearing balls in position (5). Turn the wheel over carefully, replace the front bearing balls and the locking ring-cum-bearing. Finally remove the thread.

per revolution. If neither pawl is working, it freewheels in both directions – which is what you want to avoid on the road, so replace the spring on the idle pawl (see the picture sequence). This check is most easily made by hand with the wheel out.

Bolts   should be checked for tightness, particularly chainring bolts, mudguard bolts, toeclip bolts, carrier fittings, brake lever fittings, brake fittings.

Chain   remove by physical brushing or scraping as much as possible of the oil-mud compound in which it is covered. Then brush it clean with paraffin, applied with an old toothbrush. Removing the chain and soaking in petrol or paraffin although often advocated is *not* a good idea since it dissolves out the internal lubricant added by the manufacturer. This usually remains in good condition throughout the life of the chain and is difficult to replace effectively. Oil the sliding surface of the sideplate pairs and the rollers with a fairly heavy oil.

Gear mechanism   as for the chain, remove oily dirt, brush clean and lubricate. Oil pivots of the parallelogram, otherwise leave well alone.

Lights   check that bulbs and batteries (if used) are in working order.

Toeclips and straps   check that neither is so worn that it is likely to break. Toeclips usually break eventually just at the sharp bend in front of the pedal or at the similar bend beneath the toe – one side goes first, so look for cracks.

Major bearings   check that these are correctly adjusted and lubricated.

Major disasters

The remedies here are drastic and designed only to get you home or to some source of help.

Badly buckled wheel   a wheel damaged in a fall or a rut or pothole, can often be made true enough to run between the forks by levering it back towards the right shape in a gate, fence or drain, or by laying it on the road and standing on the appropriate bits. It will still be fairly concentric but may wave from side to side alarmingly. Be very careful in using brakes.

Broken fork blade or crown   very rare nowadays in normal use and there is virtually nothing you can do except walk. It is dangerous in the extreme to attempt to ride a machine with any part of the front fork broken.

Broken fork column   usually leaves the machine dangerously unridable *unless* the break is at the top threaded portion, in which case it *may* be possible to bridge the break by putting the handlebar stem as far down as it will go into the fork column. This requires extreme care.

Broken frame tube or stay   a broken top or down tube (also very rare) will generally make the machine unridable. A broken seat tube may allow you to freewheel gingerly, but cause everything to jam up when you apply pressure; the same goes for a broken chain or seat stay. You may be able to walk part and 'scoot', hobby-horse style, or freewheel. It may be helpful to lower the saddle.

Broken handlebar extension   leaves the machine unridable.

Broken handlebar bend   can be ridden, although not legally unless the unbroken side carries the front brake lever and you have a fixed wheel. Depending on the distance you have to cover, it may be worth swapping the front brake cable to the side remaining and riding in a gingerly fashion.

Freewheel freewheeling both ways   see p. 97, or try the following. Walk if necessary to a point where you can freewheel for a distance. Then, with the chain set to give you a reasonable gear for the rest of your journey, try pedalling once you have got up to a moderate speed – centrifugal force *may* push the pawls out against the ratchet. Once you have made one of them engage, then keep pedalling, against the force of the brake if necessary, and do not attempt to freewheel at any point. Or, of course, if you have one, use the spare single freewheel on the other side of the hub.

Freewheel jammed   try riding very carefully. Any attempt at freewheeling or any lagging behind the road speed of the bicycle will wrap the gear mechanism up in the chain; or you can shorten the chain to bypass the gear.

Bent or broken rear gear   Shorten the chain so that it will bypass the gear mechanism: use on one sprocket to give you a single gear (see Chapter 14). It is nearly always easier to straighten a twisted gear at home with the proper tools.

Broken seat pillar you may be able to jam a piece of wood to hold the two bits together, clamping the join by the frame seat bolt or, alternatively, lower the saddle and use what's left. This may leave you problems in getting the broken bit out.

Broken saddle frame or clip 'honk' – also applicable to the preceding!

Broken carrier you can strap it up or fashion one from a piece of wood as illustrated.

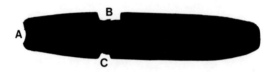

A makeshift saddlebag support can be fashioned from a piece of wood. The curved end A fits against the rear of the seat tube of the frame (it may be necessary to move the pump), notches B and C fit against the seat stays, resting on the brake bridge. Notch B is bigger to clear the brake mechanism – a side-pull one in this case.

Food

We mentioned in Chapter 1, the need for the cyclist to keep his or her blood sugar level up by regular feeding, preferably little and often. Generally, something to eat every three hours or so is reasonable. It is worth carrying with you, particularly when you are relatively new to the game, some spare energy-giving food so that you can stave off hunger rapidly. Among these are bars of chocolate, bananas, fruit malt loaf, and the very popular Kendal Mint Cake. A picnic lunch should be a reasonable mixture of appetising foods to your taste. We have always found it more convenient to carry a loaf, or part of one, and to cut slices as necessary rather than to prepare sandwiches – I suspect the sandwich of hiding the paucity of what's inside! Followed by biscuits and fruit, even bread and cheese makes quite a satisfying meal.

Since sweat is by no means pure water but a solution of various salts, drinking water or fruit juices alone may not be enough to slake thirst when it is very hot. The main solid lost is common salt – sodium chloride – and this may be replaced by adding a little salt to a fruit drink. Too high a concentration makes things worse: a flat coffee-spoonful per litre (0·2%) is reasonable. Salt is not the only compound lost, however, and proprietary drinks, designed for competition, are available to restore the other cations, principally potassium. It is equally possible to make up a home-made mixture to the following recipe:

Unsweetened citrous fruit juice		
(orange, lemon, grapefruit)		250ml
Unsweetened apple, grape or similar juice		250ml
Water		500ml
Honey	up to	100g
(*or* Dextrose)	up to	40g
Salt (sodium chloride)		2g
Potassium gluconate		1·5g

The honey or glucose level can be decreased if the mixture proves too sweet. An alternative which I have found palatable, hot or cold, for competition and touring is:

Water	1000ml
Honey	50g
Salt (sodium chloride)	2g
Potassium gluconate	1·5g
Peppermint essence	12 drops

In less hot weather, both drinks without the added salts are refreshing. You should avoid excessively chilled drinks at all times.

Part Two
The Cyclist's Britain

9

The anatomy of Britain

By the standards of America, Asia and Africa – and even of continental Europe – Britain is a small country, yet it has a range of scenery practically unrivalled. True, our mountains scarcely get up to 1250m – even Ben Nevis is only 1343m (4406ft) – but to see that great bulk rearing up from sea level is to see a sight nearly unknown in Europe outside Norway – or Ireland. If our highest road is scarcely over 600m (2000ft or so), then the climb from the sea loch at Kishorn to the summit of the Bealach-na-Ba is as daunting in prospect and as exhilarating in the achievement as any other within a thousand miles.

Highland and lowland Britain

It is convenient to divide Britain into two parts and the map opposite does so by showing in black all land over 250m (820ft). This coincides mainly with northern and western Britain – with most of Scotland and Wales, and large tracts of northern England – together with a large part of the county of Devon. This division is also very close to the geological division between areas of hard rocks, constituting the high ground, and softer deposits. It also represents the divide between agricultural and industrial Britain on the one hand, in the lower areas, and moorland Britain, either wasteland, in the agricultural sense – but of great scenic value as far as we are concerned – or given over to hill sheep farming, on the other. It also marks, consequently, the boundary between populated Britain and the rest. Finally, and don't be deterred by this, it also falls fairly close to the 1000mm (40in) isohyet (annual

Highland and lowland Britain – land over 250m (800ft) in black.

rainfall contour) with the higher ground definitely on the rainier side.

The geological distinction makes the biggest impact on the type of country, so that it is convenient to consider the regions on a roughly geological basis. We start from the south-east, not to show a bias but simply because it is there that the newest deposits in the geological sequence occur. Our travel northwards and westwards is largely a journey back in geological time through country of increasing grandeur.

The chalk hills and the London Basin

The chalk is the youngest of the rocks which lie in ridges, running roughly south-west to north-east across England. In most parts it forms an escarpment – an abrupt edge – facing north-west with long gentle slopes to the south-east. The main ridge runs from Dorset in the south-west, forming the principal Dorset uplands, the great open space of Salisbury Plain, the Hampshire and Berkshire Downs and then the Chiltern Hills, tapering away to diffuse undulations in Suffolk and Norfolk. Beyond the sea inlet of the Wash the chalk surfaces once more as the open uplands of the Lincolnshire Wolds, continuing north of the River Humber as the Yorkshire Wolds, finally petering out just north of Bridlington. South of London, more recent geological movements have forced the formerly level strata up into a great dome, the top of which has long since been eroded away, so that the chalk forms two ridges, the North and South Downs. Because of the tilt of the rocks there are quite steep slopes on both sides of the Downs. The main characteristics of the chalklands are that they are well-drained, often grass-covered or agricultural, uplands with steep-sided dry valleys, with other lower valleys carrying clear streams. In places the chalk is capped with other deposits, such as clays, sands and gravels, which change the vegetation, giving, for example, the heavily-wooded Chilterns and the heath Brecklands of Suffolk a different character. There is a pronounced 'grain' to the countryside and the cyclist would be wrong to assume that because the highest points on the chalk ridge are only about 250–280m (850–950ft) that it is easy country. Ridge roads are relatively flat, but to cross the Chilterns or Dorset across the grain involves the cyclist in a rapid succession of steep climbs, many steeper than 1-in-7 (14%) and equally sharp descents.

The chalk is overlain to the east over most of the London area and the counties of Essex, Suffolk and Norfolk by clays and sandy deposits. The slope of the chalk itself is lower and the relief less marked. Outside the very extensive built-up region the area is mostly cultivated with some heathland in sandy areas. The human race has had a hand in changing the scenery both in the past, in forming the Norfolk Broads, and at the present day with extensive afforestation of the Brecklands. Don't dismiss East Anglia as flat and uninteresting: it is an area of vast open space and perhaps of tamed landscape, but also of unexpected undulation, particularly in northern Essex and southern Suffolk, and near the north Norfolk coast. All three counties have interesting broad, lazy river valleys.

Where the chalk and the harder of the other rocks meet the coast they give rise to cliffs of varying height; most notable are those of the South and North Downs, including Beachy Head, but once more the north Norfolk coast can offer some surprises.

One final, practical point: embedded in the chalk are nodules of flint used, among other things, as a road surface dressing. Now, the mineralogical structure of flint is very close to that of a glass, so the small flint particles can be very sharp. It may surprise the cyclist from the north or Midlands to find how penetrating these near-microscopic particles, often only 1–2mm, can be – particularly in wet weather. It may well be considered prudent to use *heavier* tyres in this part of the world, particularly off the major roads and in winter, than in others.

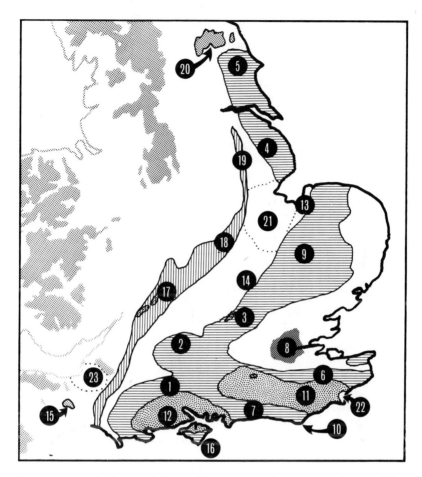

South and east England: 1 Salisbury Plain; 2 Berkshire Downs; 3 Chiltern Hills;
4 Lincolnshire Wolds; 5 Yorkshire Wolds; 6 North Downs; 7 South Downs;
8 London; 9 Breckland; 10 Beachy Head; 11 The Weald; 12 New Forest;
13 Sandringham; 14 Woburn; 15 Blackdown Hills; 16 Isle of Wight; 17 Cotswolds; 18 Northamptonshire; 19 Lincoln; 20 North York Moors; 21 The Fens;
22 Romney Marsh; 23 Sedgemoor. Horizontal shading chalk; stipple sandy
areas; vertical shading oolite, mainly limestone.

The sand country and the Isle of Wight

The sand and clay areas of the Weald of Kent and Sussex, and the New Forest, together with the belt of gently consolidated lower Greensand give rise to some distinctive and attractive scenery. The pattern of inward-facing ridges of the chalk

Downs is continued by the Weald, and in fact the highest point in south-east England, Leith Hill in Surrey, 294m (965ft), is on the Greensand. This is a heavily wooded area, with oaks and chestnuts among the hardwoods and extensive pine forests, some recent and man-made, as well. There are in addition large tracts of bracken-covered heath. The cultivated parts bear out the description of Kent as 'The Garden of England' with its extensive orchards, hopfields and market gardening.

Similar remarks apply to the Greensand ridge north and west of the main chalk ridge. Where this reaches the surface, as around Woburn in Bedfordshire and Sandringham in Norfolk, these relatively small areas with pine and birch form delectable pockets well worth a day's exploration. Its outcrop in the south-west, the Blackdown Hills south of Taunton, is similar but more extensive. The more recent sand of the Reading beds, in north Hampshire, west Surrey and southern Berkshire, too, produces a region – where it is neither built on nor annexed for army training – of heath and, largely, pine forest, together with general agriculture.

The New Forest is a quite distinctive area, more open than the other sand landscapes, with rolling undulations, extensive open views giving way to copses and enclosures, some of hardwoods, principally oak, and others of pine. The area becomes very crowded during the main holiday season and well repays a visit in spring or autumn.

The Isle of Wight is a microcosm of the mainland areas we have covered so far, with the geological strata crammed into a small space. The forces which have stood the rocks almost on edge have left also some very steep slopes: the island has a very pronounced east-west

grain and it is possible to travel in these directions on almost level roads. But from north to south . . . There is some quite striking cliff scenery – culminating at the west in the Needles and in the south at St Catherine's Point – and a number of ridge tracks. Like the New Forest, the island becomes very crowded in the main holiday season.

The southern limestone ridge

The second of the great south-west to north-east ridges is that of the Oolitic Limestone, with its best-known manifestation the golden-villaged Cotswold Hills. The ridge lies generally 30–40km (20–25 miles) north-west of the chalk. Relatively narrow there, the Cotswolds proper may be considered to start at about Bradford-on-Avon in Wiltshire. The ridge is sharply dissected by river valleys, with some very steep climbs out of them, particularly in the Stroud area of southern Gloucestershire. At its highest point, 330m (1083ft), at Cleeve Common above Cheltenham, the escarpment stands some 280m (over 900ft) above the Severn valley, with steep climbs to the ridge, some over 1-in-5 (20%). To the south and east lies what is the most typically Cotswold country: fields enclosed between stone walls, warmer coloured stone and soil than the more severe mountain limestone of the north, and closely grouped attractive villages of the same stone often in valleys with small, clear streams. Formerly – with Suffolk – sheep country, the cultivation is now more mixed and there are quite large pockets of beech and other hardwoods. The principal attractive villages and small towns – Bourton-on-the-Water, Broadway, Winchcombe, Burford, Chipping Campden, Bibury, Castle Combe – tend to become very crowded at holiday times, but there is a wealth of small, unfrequented and very rolling roads. It is not an area to attempt to hurry through.

The height of the hills decreases as we move north-east, although Edge Hill, site of the famous battle and just in Warwickshire, still dominates the valley below. As we reach Northamptonshire, an iron-rich ironstone of slightly greater age forms the main ridge and the colour of the stone changes to a deep reddish brown. Iron-ore is won in great open-cast workings near Banbury and around the iron and steel town of Corby.

The ridge begins to turn north-wards in what was the former county of Rutland, around Oakham and Uppingham, and begins to lose the heavy iron colour. The maximum height is around 150m (500ft) and it is an extremely pleasant cycling area with a fair amount of woodland and undulation. The ridge narrows as it passes into Lincolnshire, until by the gap in which Lincoln lies it is only some 5km (3 miles) wide and no more than 50m (less than 200ft) above the very flat Trent valley. Even with so small a differ-ence, the great cathedral at Lincoln, perched on this ridge at the top of a steep cobbled street dominates the country for many miles.

The ridge virtually disappears at the Humber, re-emerging some 50km (30 miles) further on to form first the Howardian Hills (named after Castle Howard and the Howard family) and then the spectacular North Yorkshire Moors, an exten-sive area of high moor, some 60km (nearly 40 miles) across at its widest, dissected by deep, mostly south-flowing river valleys. Reach-ing 433m (1422ft) at its highest point, this is true heather-coloured and, in places, very bleak and im-pressive moor. The north-eastern part, known as the Cleveland Hills, looks down onto the valley of the Tees. Gone now is the golden colour of the Cotswolds for the limestone is replaced by darker and greyer shales, ironstones and grit-stones. The valleys house small villages and reach the coast, notably at Whitby, Runswick Bay and Robin Hood's Bay, between spectacular cliffs. Quite a lot of the lower parts of the Moors have been forested, principally to the south and east. The area offers some very attractive cycling, particularly in the spring and autumn, with a number of upland tracks, and some im-posing antiquities such as Rievaulx Abbey. It also has some of the steepest marked hills in the country (I have seen one sign claiming 1-in-$3\frac{1}{2}$ (28% – or an angle of 16°!)), combined with some of the most exhilarating descents.

The fenlands and marshlands

There are a few areas which are almost completely flat, which does not make them ideal cycling country, contrary to popular myth, but they certainly offer a different type of cycling. Here you are always aware of the low plane of the landscape completely subservient to the dome of the sky. But it doesn't stop there, for you are at the complete mercy of the wind, too – whether it is against or behind.

The main area is that of the Fens themselves, covering a large part of Cambridgeshire and Lincolnshire, with some of western Norfolk. The height above sea level rarely ex-ceeds 5m (say 15ft), apart from such former islands as Ely, whose cathedral is visible for some 35km (20-odd miles). There are quite large areas surrounding Ely which lie actually below sea level – man-made lands drained from earlier marsh which has sunk in the pro-cess. Very little of the primaeval fen remains but a part is preserved at Wicken Sedge Fen, near Soham. The Fens are now intensively cultivated with their spectacularly fertile black soil, which strong winds are liable to pile up as great black drifts towards the end of winter. Much of the drainage of this area and of its extension northwards to the plain of York was originally carried out by the Dutch engineer Vermuyden and many of the Fenland towns, such as King's Lynn, Wisbech, Spalding and Boston have a Dutch air about them. Indeed, until the recent county boundary reorganisation, this part of Lincolnshire was called Holland. Many of the roads are straight for long distances, often following the artificial drainage waterways, and some feet above the sunken fields, separated by ditches. The whole has, in fairly small doses, an attraction altogether its own, probably deriving from the intense and lonely openness.

There are, in fact, comparatively few such dead flat areas. Two other well-defined ones are Romney Marsh, an expanse some 15km (10 miles) square bounded by the Royal Military Canal linking the former ports of Hythe and Rye, and in the West Country, the attractive Kings Sedge, Queens Sedge, and other named moors, separated by the low Polden Hills, their flatness accentuated by the Isle of Avalon and the tower on Glastonbury Tor, 58m (189ft) above its surroundings. These moors, although threatened, have so far been left relatively undrained and uncultivated and are used as low pasture.

The 'Highlands' of the West Country

We shall have to abandon for the moment the geological subdivision to consider together the part of highland Britain which lies within the counties of Somerset, Devon and Cornwall. These comprise the granite bosses of Dartmoor and

Bodmin Moor, the mainly Red Sandstone masses of Exmoor and the Brendon Hills, and the Quantocks, and the Carboniferous Limestone bulk of the Mendip Hills. All of these ranges top the 300m (1000ft) contour, the highest point being High Willhays on northern Dartmoor, 621m (2039ft).

First, a word of caution. The south-western peninsula is almost certainly the most popular holiday area in the British Isles. In summer, from mid-June to mid-September, and at the main Bank Holiday weekends and school holidays it is very crowded indeed, and both accommodation and the capacity of the roads are very strained. It is nevertheless an attractive area and probably the best times of year to see it are in spring or October or even early November. It does enjoy a generally milder climate than the rest of Britain – although winter conditions on Dartmoor particularly can be very severe – and I have known very warm days even at that late season. It merits, however, quite a high rating in the rainfall stakes.

The igneous rock, granite, of which Dartmoor and Bodmin Moor are composed is characterised by being hard and impermeable. This, combined with the relatively flat top of Dartmoor and its high rainfall, leads to very boggy patches on the high parts, which lessens the usability of some of the crossing tracks. However, the same water where it runs off has created attractive wooded valleys, together with the inevitable accompaniment – steep hills. There are quite a number of small and attractive roads in the southern part of the Moor, but fewer in the northern part, to which access is restricted by its use for military training. One of the scenic features of the rolling high parts of the Moor is the 'tor' or outcrop of resistant rock some

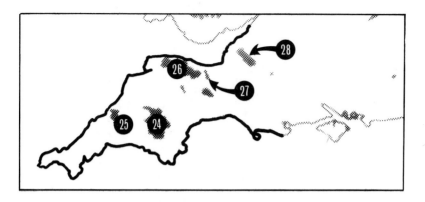

The West Country: 24 Dartmoor; 25 Bodmin Moor; 26 Exmoor; 27 Quantock Hills; 28 Mendip Hills.

20–30m (65–75ft) high standing exposed at the highest local points. Bodmin Moor resembles the more northerly, bleaker part of Dartmoor on a smaller scale.

The sandstone of Exmoor and the Brendons is a rich red and is interspersed with softer slates. Being softer than the granite of Dartmoor, these are more deeply dissected by river valleys, most of them attractively wooded, largely with oaks, at the lower levels. There are also larger areas of woodland on the northern slopes, and part of the top of the Brendons (which are divided from Exmoor by the valley of the River Exe but are continuous in structure with it) has been afforested. There are several high-level and ridge roads crossing both sets of hills. On the northern side, Exmoor reaches the coast with some spectacular cliff scenery.

The Quantock Hills are an attractive and miniature version of the previous two, the ridge – with the underlying rock mainly slate – running in a north-west to south-east direction for some 25km (15 miles) and attaining a maximum height of 384m (1261ft). They are quite heavily wooded, partially by hardwoods, partly by conifer plantations. Their attractiveness as a compact cycling area is enhanced by the large variety of roads and tracks along and crossing the hills. Some details of these are given in Chapter 13.

To the north-east of the Quantocks and about 25km (15 miles) distant, lies the rounded bulk of the Mendip Hills. Geologically and scenically, these limestone hills, with their westward prolongation to the sea just south of Weston-super-Mare, are quite different from the others. The top is relatively flat, open and in a way featureless with grey stone-walled fields, but there are several small roads and tracks following close to the main ridge. It is the valleys on the edges of the hills which are the main attraction: of these, Cheddar Gorge and Burrington Combe are the most spectacular and best known – Cheddar in particular is a very much commercialised spot. The western end of the hills and the outcrops of Wavering Down and Bleadon Hill are more wooded.

III

The clay vales

The first of these, intermediate in age between the chalk and the Oolitic Limestone of the Cotswolds, lies in a south-west to north-east band between the two ranges, running from about Melksham in Wiltshire until it disappears below the recent peaty deposits of the Fens somewhere near Cambridge. The other, much larger, corresponds roughly with the Lias and Keuper geological series – next older in sequence than the Oolite. On the ground this corresponds with a considerable proportion of Leicestershire, northern Gloucestershire, the Worcester part of Worcester and Hereford, western Staffordshire, eastern Salop, Cheshire, the largely built-up metropolitan county of West Midlands and, to the north and east, central Nottinghamshire.

The term vale does not mean that these are flat areas and the geological lumping-together does not bring with it a complete identity of scenery. The general type of countryside is comparable, however: generally agricultural, with a tendency more to stock-rearing and crops other than cereals, villages and towns with variations in architecture depending on the materials originally available – wood, brick or harder stone usable for building from local outcrops of limestone. The proportion of woodland varies from the ancient forests of Arden and the Dukeries to the almost treeless plain of north Bedfordshire. It is also through this part of England that the country's great rivers flow. This is quintessential rural England (outside the large towns and cities) and criss-crossed with ideal cycling lanes. It is possible to travel from the Thames valley to the Mersey seeing no more of a classified road than crossing it. This is not spectacular country but it can bring surprises of its own and this is one of the areas where quietness can be found at some place at all times. It is towards these vales that we would direct the wheels of the novice cycle-tourist before he or she turns to the hills, and several of the short day circuits given in Chapter 11 lie within them.

The Welsh Marches

The counties bordering Wales, Salop and the western part of Hereford and Worcester, are two which captivated me in my earliest cycling days. The geological detail becomes too complicated to go into here, with some of the oldest rocks in the country thrust to the surface by more recent earth movements. The result is a succession of ridges and isolated hills, separated by fertile and picturesque valleys, harbouring towns and villages bordering on chocolate-box prettiness.

From the south-east, as the cycle-tourist comes to the Cotswold escarpment edge above Cheltenham or Winchombe, he sees away on the horizon the humpbacked and worn-down mountain range of the Malvern Hills. These rise to a maximum height of 424m (1395ft) at their northern end, Worcester Beacon; in fact all the major Salop hills also reach about the same, somewhere in the 400–550m (1300–1800ft) range. To the traveller from the east the Malverns are the first mountain-shaped mountains to be seen: viewed end-on from the north they appear a perfect pyramid.

To the west of the Malverns lies a stretch of undulating country of orchards and hopfields, with isolated wooded hills, some 45km (28 miles or so) in extent and reaching to the Welsh border. The city of Hereford on the River Wye lies about in the middle. To the north of this lie ridge upon ridge of relatively low wooded hills for about 40km

Midland England: 29 Welsh borders; 30 Malvern Hills; 31 Hereford; 32 Ludlow. Diagonal shading – the clay vales. Although not strictly part of the Midlands, the three East Anglian counties of Norfolk (N), Suffolk (S) and Essex (E) also offer pleasant and not-too-strenuous touring.

(25 miles) to the town of Ludlow, which is the real centre of the area. East of Ludlow the Clee Hills rise impressively from the valley of the River Teme, followed by a succession of five great ridges, separated by attractive dales: Wenlock Edge (limestone), the very old Caer Caradoc-Wrekin range, the again very old Long Mynd, followed by the Stiperstones with their impressive jagged quartzite top and the Long Mountain. The whole area has an abundance of minor roads, some well-graded and some climbing steeply. The network of lanes east of the Clees and the ridge road and crossing of the Long Mynd are especially fine.

Wales

It is convenient, from the point of view of classification, to consider Wales under one heading, but in fact the Principality – in addition to being a separate country, and the nearest with its own language, giving a 'foreign' air to touring in some parts – offers a variety of scenic type. A large proportion of the country comes within our classification of 'highland' but there are in addition some pleasant parts at a lower level, particularly in the south and west. The country conveniently divides itself into three main blocks, south, mid and the north.

South Wales

'South Wales' probably brings to most minds a vision of mining valleys and the industrial parts of the counties now known as Gwent, and Mid, West and South Glamorgan. Within even these counties, however, there are some pleasánt areas of open country, such as parts of South Glamorgan and the Gower peninsula of West Glamorgan, and even the notorious 'valleys' are separated by ridges in many cases of little-spoiled upland. These valleys themselves, source of a great deal of Britain's wealth in the nineteenth century are not without their own interest. To the east, bordering England and partially in the English county of Gloucestershire is the very attractive Forest of Dean – which has been described as 'the pleasantest coal-mining area in the world' – bounded on the west by the deep-cut lower Wye Valley. From here to the north and west is a wide open, rolling and frequently wooded countryside. These rolling undulations, with their many border castles, give way, quite abruptly, after some 25–30km (15 or 20 miles), to what is probably the most attractive compact mountain region for the cyclist, the Black Mountains with, further to the west again, the Brecon Beacons extending to the Carmarthen Vans. These three chains of mountains, some 45km (28 miles or so) in extent are deeply dissected blocks of red sandstone, rising to a maximum of 811m (2660ft) at Waun Fawr, Black Mountains, 886m (2907ft) at Pen-y-Fan, Brecon Beacons, and 802m (2632ft) at Carmarthen Van itself, with quite a deal of high moorland above 600m

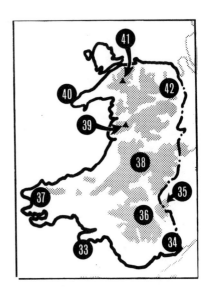

Wales: 33 Gower peninsula; 34 Forest of Dean; 35 Black Mountains; 36 Brecon Beacons; 37 Pembroke; 38 Mid-Wales; 39 Cader Idris; 40 Lleyn peninsula; 41 Snowdon; 42 Clwydians.

(2000ft). From the south and east these mountains appear as unspectacular rounded hills; from the north – there is a superb viewpoint on the Erwood to Brecon road – the impressive north face of the whole range is visible, some 600m (2000ft) above the valleys of the Wye and Usk.

Further west, in what is now the southern part of the county of Dyfed, is more rolling country as hills become lower – although many of the road climbs are steeper here than in the higher mountains. The countryside is a variety of cultivated valleys, some areas of higher moorland and woodland. In the westernmost part we reach what was once dubbed 'The Little England beyond Wales', western Pembrokeshire, largely cultivated apart from the Preseli hills. This area offers some of the finest cliff scenery on the British mainland, particularly between St David's Head and Cardigan. Once again the generally lower level of the terrain belies the steepness of some of the short sharp hills, particularly near the coast.

Mid Wales

Mid Wales offers some of the wildest, and in places some of the most remote, country within reasonable reach of the main centres of population. It can be considered somewhat arbitrarily as being bounded on the south by the valleys of the lower Wye and Usk and to the north by a great valley caused by a major geological movement, and which runs from south-west to north-east, from Barmouth and Dolgellau by Bala to Corwen and the English border near Chester. It is largely a raised and dissected plateau on the heights of which rise many of the major rivers: in fact the Severn and the Wye, which do not meet again until Chepstow, Gwent, after some 200km (120 miles) of wandering, rise within about 4km (2½ miles) of each other on the rounded slopes of Plynlimon. The underlying rock of much of the region is slate and altered shales, largely non-porous, so there is usually quite a lot of water about with boggy patches on top of some of the hills. Cyclable roads and paths, although not as numerous as in rural England, are more plentiful here than in the north of Wales, and the great open spaces, together with the works of man in the form of artificial lakes and forests, once more make for some very attractive cycling country. Refreshment, apart from major towns and the coastal strip, is fairly sparse, so that the cyclist has to be particularly self-sufficient in this region: many small villages boast neither shop nor pub! This lends some piquancy to the rather unkind title (not accorded for this reason) of the 'Desert of Wales'.

At the north-western extremity of our defined zone we begin to enter high mountain territory again, the highest and most jaggedly mountainous being the massif of Cader Idris, rearing up to 892m (2927ft) from the sea-level Mawddach estuary. The chain continues north-eastwards by the twin peaks of Aran Fawddwy (905m, 2970ft) and the slightly lower Aran Benllyn, and then becomes more rounded in the Berwyn range, where the highest point, Moel Sych, is nevertheless 827m (2713ft) high. Several more or less cyclable tracks cross this latter range.

North Wales

This region can be considered in three parts, the Lleyn peninsula which points a long finger towards Ireland, Snowdonia, and the eastern moorlands, culminating in the Clwydian and Eglwyseg ranges.

Although it is undoubtedly part of north Wales, the Lleyn peninsula, stretching some 45km (say 28 miles) out into Cardigan Bay, is in many ways reminiscent of Pembroke or Cornwall. It is generally undulating with mostly cultivated countryside, interspersed with rugged granite bosses, running down to attractive beaches and coves: these account for its popularity as a holiday area. There is quite a network of small roads and further inland it is dominated by the two granite peaks of Yr Eifl (564m, 1849ft, and mis-transliterated as 'The Rivals' on some maps) on the northern coast.

Travelling northeastwards, we enter Snowdonia, the best-known and most mountainous part of Wales. The high mountains, topped of course by Snowdon itself, 1085m (3560ft), are separated by deep and spectacular valleys, the whole being neatly divided into blocks. The principal disadvantage of the area for the cyclist is that the practicable through routes along these valleys, Nant Gwynant, Llanberis Pass, Nant Ffrancon, etc. with little alternative, are main, and sometimes trunk, roads, consequently carrying heavy traffic particularly at holiday times. Nevertheless, the grandeur of the mountains makes it an area worth visiting – preferably away from the main holiday season – but perhaps showing a little less than some other places the advantage of the bicycle. It must be added that the rainfall is relatively high.

Further east, say beyond the Conway valley, we pass into an area of mainly limestone moors and a veritable maze of small lanes, many of them climbing steeply from wooded valleys: in one single small patch about 5 × 3km east of Dolgarrog and near the little village of Eglwysbach there are on the 1:50 000 Ordnance Survey map no fewer than 14 sets of single arrows (denoting slopes greater than 1-in-7, 14%) and 6 sets of double arrows (steeper than 1-in-5, 20%)! There are some very attractive parts before the moors open out southwards into the rather bleak area around Pentrefoelas. The network of minor roads continues right across to the Vale of Clwyd, one of the most fertile areas in the country, bounded on the east by the Clwydian limestone range. These hills rise sharply from the vale, the highest point being Moel Famma, 554m (1818ft), and are crossed by several minor roads and one or two cyclable tracks. To the south the range continues as the limestone mountains above Llangollen, including among their attractions the well-known Horseshoe Pass and the perhaps less-known but superb

minor road from Minera to Llangollen by World's End, passing below the impressive cliffs of the Eglwyseg Mountain and the old hill fort of Caer Dinas Bran before dropping to the valley of the Dee.

The backbone of England

This is by far the largest feature we have considered so far in England – the great range of largely limestone and gritstone hills which extend northwards from just above Derby and Stoke-on-Trent to the Scottish border, a total distance, in a straight line, of some 240km (150 miles). Since they reach a width in places of over 40km (25 miles), it is obvious that the Peak District – in the south, the bleak moors separating industrial Lancashire from ditto Yorkshire, the magnificent Yorkshire and Durham Dales and the high gritstone moors up to and beyond the Roman Wall, between them comprise a major part of upland England. As the rock varies, so does the scenery. The limestone areas, rather bare in the uplands have fine valleys and gorges, while the gritstone areas and, further north those where the volcanic intrusion of the Great Whin Sill – a thick horizontal band of rock which has forced its way between other softer ones – helps shape the escarpments, are less well drained in the uplands and offer a more forbidding landscape.

The southern central part of the Peak District is one of the limestone areas, with some volcanic activity. This part covers the Matlock-Bakewell-Castleton area, with its deep dales, some of them – such as the notorious Winnats Pass climb above Castleton – collapsed former caverns with steep gorge-like sides. To either side the harder, and here tilted, Millstone Grit, a very hard coarse sandstone, forms more jagged 'edges': to the west Axe

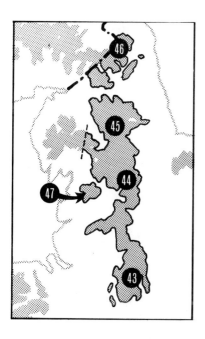

The backbone of England: 43 Peak District; 44 Yorkshire Dales; 45 Durham Dales; 46 Cheviot; 47 Bowland.

start here – certainly the Pennine Way long-distance path does, beginning its long course at Edale by climbing to the bleak peat moors of the Peak proper, going straight to its highest point, Kinder Scout 636m (2088ft). Except for the main trunk routes linking Yorkshire and Lancashire, roads become scarce and there are in fact no spinal or ridge routes, apart from the often ill-defined Pennine Way itself, until we begin the descent from the moors themselves to the valley of the River Aire near Skipton.

Here we are in limestone country again, with superbly attractive valleys forming the often-wooded dales and separated by striking upland scenery. Parts of the Pennine Way itself are ridable here, apart from which, although it would be stretching the truth to refer to it as a network, there are many delectable roads both along and between the dales. Here, too, are spectacular limestone features, particularly round Malham where the former waterfall of Malham Cove and the immense collapsed cavern of Goredale Scar dominate. There is perhaps 55km (35 miles) of this country, including the grit-capped 'Three Peaks' – Ingleborough, Whernside and Pen-y-Ghent – all topping 690m (2260ft), before the bleaker moors set in again.

Now we are in the country of the high roads and high fells, but with a cultivation and agriculture up to surprising heights. This is where the highest roads in England are to be found: the A689, formerly the B6293, from Alston to St John's Chapel rears up to 627m (2056ft), while the map credits the minor road from St John's Chapel to Langdon Beck with the same height. Certainly, in my experience, another road from Alston, the A686 to Penrith, offers in dropping from the 576m (1889ft) of Hartside Fell one of the most breathtaking descents

Edge and the Roaches, an almost lunar landscape unexpectedly rising above the Staffordshire plain, and to the east Stanage Edge between Hathersage and Sheffield. Small roads and a number of tracks abound – and, at popular times which includes most weekends, so do people, since some 12 million live within 80km (50 miles) of this attractive and famous area. Some of the better-known and more accessible beauty spots, such as the Goyt Valley west of Buxton, are subject to traffic regulation schemes at the busiest periods. The Millstone Grit moors begin north of Castleton and perhaps the Pennines proper may be considered to anywhere in these islands. For the record, the highest tarmac road in Britain is hereabouts and is that leading to a radar station on Great Dun Fell, reaching a height of 847m (2781ft); it is not generally open to the public. From here northwards, the country is mainly high moor and grassland, with some fertile and wooded valleys. Near the Border, however, some of the most extensive forests in the country have been planted, with Kielder Forest covering an area of some 300km² (nearly 114 square miles). There is still an appreciable number of small roads and tracks, although the number of through routes is limited. Like mid-Wales, this is high remote country and the cycling traveller has, above all, to be self-sufficient in food and drink.

While the sheer size of the whole Pennine Range ensures that there are always some uncrowded areas, some places are very popular, particularly on summer weekends and during holiday periods: note that many northern towns – and Scottish ones, since we are not far from the Border – have particular weeks or fortnights when virtually the whole town is on holiday. The local tourist boards – see Appendix 1 for the addresses of the national ones – can advise on dates likely to be heavily booked in particular places. The Matlock and Castleton areas of Derbyshire, the Goyt Valley on the Derbyshire-Cheshire border, the Malham area of the Yorkshire Dales and the central part of the Roman Wall, near the excavated fort of Housesteads, are all very busy at times.

Although it is not strictly part of the Pennines, it would be wrong to omit mention of Bowland Forest, lying to west of the Yorkshire Dales and separated from them by a spectacular geological fault, Giggleswick Scar. The Forest – a hunting rather than a wooded one, although there is some recent planting – continues the general characteristics of the Pennines to the east and is a mixture again of limestone and grits. There are several attractive small roads and tracks crossing it: the principal one, the Trough of Bowland, is quite a spectacular little pass, looking much more than its 305m (1000ft). It is another popular spot at weekends.

The Lake District

This, the most mountainous part of England with England's highest mountain, Scafell Pike (978m, 3210ft), has much the same good and bad points as North Wales for the cyclist – and they have relatively little to do with the steepness and length of the hills. The scenery is unsurpassed in its grandeur but the number of roads and *ridable* tracks is limited although greater than in Snowdonia: there are several paths over which a bicycle can be taken, but there will not be a great deal of riding involved in some of them. However, that said, a very enjoyable trip can be designed taking in some of the foothill country west of Kendal and the lower hills nearer the coast as well as some of the high passes. It is as also a good area to combine cycling with some walking, perhaps spending two or more nights at a suitable spot, and walking on one of the intervening days. For the record the principal road climbs are the Kirkstone Pass (454m, 1489ft) – a main road climb, A592; Wrynose (390m, 1281ft) and Hard Knott (3m, 10ft higher), climbing from the Duddon valley, the latter very hard from either side; Honister (358m, 1176ft) and very hard from the east, Borrowdale, direction; and Newlands (334m, 1096ft), hard from the west, Buttermere, end, from which it rises at an *average* of nearly 1-in-7 for a mile (13% over 1·6km); and Whinlatter,

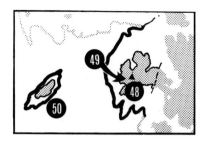

Lake District and the Isle of Man:
48 Lake District; 49 Scafell Pike;
50 Isle of Man.

(381m, 1043ft) on the B5292 west of Keswick, which is a much more graded climb. The steepness and length of some of these hills calls for a fair amount of discretion on the descents: you should make sure that you are using your brakes evenly to avoid overheating either rim, particularly the front one. There are few places in the centre of the area where you can let the bicycle have its head downhill. Many of the most attractive roads are 'dead-end' routes, at least without taking to paths, and either 'rough-stuff' of a toughness beyond the scope of this book or a degree of retracing will be necessary. The area is very popular indeed both with winter and summer visitors, particularly with other outdoor travellers on foot. Nevertheless, it is a 'must' for every cycle-tourist at some time in his or her career: if you can, try the spring after the Easter crowds have dispersed or October when the colouring is superb. The area, too, underlines the futility of false ambition: a daily journey of 50km (say 30 miles) can prove to be plenty!

The Isle of Man

The Isle of Man lies 130km (80 miles) from Liverpool, 70km (45 miles) from the Lake District, 30km (20 miles) from the nearest point in southern Scotland, and 55km (35 miles) from the nearest part of County Down. The character of the Kingdom of Man, with a strong Celtic and Norse overlay, roughly reflects its geographical position: the landscape, the nature of the light and much of the rural building is very reminiscent of Ireland, but the Manx are very proud of their own traditions, claiming among other things, the oldest parliament in the British Isles.

Within its quite small size, 45 × 16km (28 × 10 miles) it embraces a very wide range of scenery, from the dunes and flat pastures of the north, by way of the mountainous centre, dominated by Snaefell (620m, 2034ft), to the rolling hills and cliffs of the south. By comparison with the mainland, traffic is generally light and at most times even the main roads comprising the TT course are relatively quiet; other parts are almost somnolent. The minor roads are numerous and attractive and the Island provides an excellent centre for a tour of, say, a week or so for the beginner who has easy or tougher country readily available, to choice. An additional attraction for cyclists looking for an introduction to the competitive cycling world combined with their tour is the Isle of Man International Cycling Week, held around the middle of June.

Northumberland and the Border coast

To the east of the northern end of the Pennines, beginning at roughly the level of Morpeth, north of Newcastle-upon-Tyne, and continuing across the Scottish border to within sight of Edinburgh lies a strip some 25–40km (15–25 miles) wide and 120km (75 miles) from south to north. This strip, em-

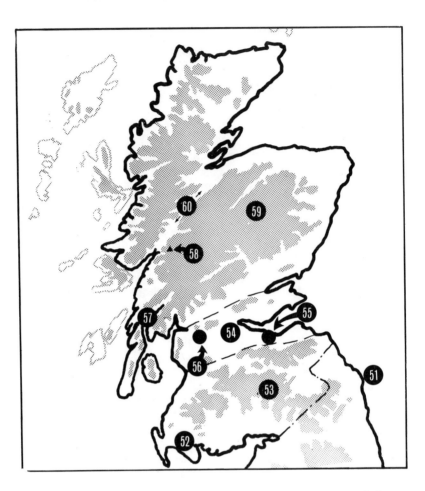

Scotland (and Northumberland): 51 Northumberland coast; 52 Galloway; 53 Southern Uplands; 54 The Central Valley; 55 Edinburgh; 56 Glasgow; 57 Argyll; 58 Ben Nevis; 59 Cairngorms; 60 Great Glen.

bracing the rounded bulk of the Cheviot (816m, 2676ft) and the rather lower Lammermuir hills in Scotland, offers ideal cycling with a blend of hill country, with some fine roads and tracks, river valleys and more gentle agricultural country, bounded on the east by a variety of coastal scenery, ranging from sandy beaches and the offshore island of Lindisfarne, approachable at low tide, to quite impressive cliffs at St Abbs Head. Numerous inlets house small fishing harbours and the coast is punctuated by solidly built border castles in varying states of preservation – and even habitation.

Scotland

It is on crossing the Scottish border, and above all after crossing the central valley containing Glasgow and Edinburgh, that we find ourselves in country of a scale approaching that of continental Europe. A would-be cycling record-breaker on the 'End-to-End' route from Land's End to John o'Groats will still face nearly 600km (over 360 miles) of the 1400km total when crossing the border at Gretna Green; in covering those 600km he (or she) will reach a northerly latitude approaching that of Sweden's capital, Stockholm – having started level with Prague.

As with Wales it is convenient to divide Scotland into three main areas, plus the Isles: the Borders and Galloway, the Central Valley, and the Highlands. The boundaries are less arbitrary, for geological features define the areas closely. The Central Valley is the outstanding British example of a rift valley, the block on which Glasgow, Edinburgh and most of the other large towns are situated having slipped downwards, probably some thousands of feet, relative to the regions south-east and north-west. The two 'faults' bounding this valley have a south-west to north-east trend, and this 'Caledonian Trend' is prominent throughout Scotland. If we deal a little briefly here with Scotland it is not to belittle its appeal for the cycle-tourist nor to insult the country's eight million inhabitants: it is rather that the scale of much of the Highlands in particular is so vast that it is impossible to deal with it in detail, in addition to which, there is so much of impressive grandeur and outstanding beauty, that the cyclist needs rather less guidance than in a smaller, more-readily missed region. In other words, apart from avoiding summer traffic, you can't go wrong!

The Borders and Galloway

The southern Uplands comprising the Border country and the western prolongation to the Clyde coast are often bypassed by the cycle-tourist and others making their way direct to the Highlands. This is a pity, for even if the hills do not reach the heights of those further north, they are quite considerable compared with some of those we have already dealt with, and there are many fine roads. Some of the major roads, particularly those leading from the south to Glasgow and the port of Stranraer carry very heavy traffic, but elsewhere even many of the A-roads are relatively quiet. There is a broad range of hills stretching south-west from the North Sea coast near Dunbar for some 200km (120 miles) to Stranraer, many over 600m (2000ft) and reaching their highest in Merrick (824m, 2764ft) in Galloway. Much of the lower-lying part is cultivated but there are large tracts of open, breezy moorland, and relatively recent afforestation and man-made lakes. This is, too, an area rich in literary associations – and don't forget the Dumfriesshire blacksmith, Kirkpatric Macmillan, who designed and built in 1839 in his smithy at Thornhill a rear-driven bicycle forty years ahead of its time.

The Central Valley

Just as midland England carries a large part of the country's industry, so does central Scotland, but – again parallelling England – there are some very pleasant cycling areas, particularly for the beginner, within easy reach of the main cities. Certainly most London cycle-tourists would not complain at having the Trossachs, the Campsie Fells, the Clyde coast and the eastern side of Loch Lomond all within 40km (25 miles) as their Glasgow colleagues have, and they would just as much envy the rider from Edinburgh who has the Pentland, Moorfoot and Lammermuir Hills equally close. In addition there are many less rugged but pleasant areas west of Edinburgh and across the Forth in the old Kingdom of Fife, while there is an interesting marshy area north-west of Stirling, Flanders Moss, with an atmosphere quite different from its surroundings. Besides, who could possibly resist going to have a look at a region which has places called the Offrins of Gartur, the Backside of Garden, Nether Easter Offerance, the Wards of Goodie and the Pendicles of Collymoon – all within a couple of miles of each other ?

The Highlands

The Highlands proper begin roughly at a line running from the foot of Loch Lomond through Dunblane to Perth, and embrace, because of the pronounced south-west to north-east trend such peninsulas as Kintyre and the area between Loch Long and Loch Fyne which actually lie south of parts of the Southern Uplands. These further extremities are often missed by the cycle-tourist – partly, I am sure, because the road distances to reach them are considerable. Campbeltown at the foot of Kintyre, for instance, is somewhere about 220km (135 miles) from Glasgow by road, although only 80km (50 miles) in a straight line. Here, as in the Isles we shall mention later, a close study of the ferry or even the air timetable is well worth while: Dunoon is 130km (79 miles) by road from Glasgow – and 40km (25 miles) via the Gourock ferry! It would be a pity to miss this south-western extremity of the Highlands, because the long sea lochs, particularly Loch Fyne and the Sound of Jura offer some very fine coastal riding. The classification given to a road in this part of

the world depends much more on its relative importance than its size, and the classified road along the eastern shore of Loch Fyne is in fact a very pleasant country lane.

The Highlands are sharply divided in two by the Great Glen, an enormous valley containing Loch Ness and following the lines of a geological dislocation (some authorities have suggested that the north-western Highlands have moved nearly 110km (68 miles) south-westwards relative to the more southerly part). Here is a region of high mountain, the highest as we have already seen being Ben Nevis at 1343m (4406ft), with a very large area over 1000m (3050ft).

There are relatively few roads, so that some do carry concentrated traffic during the summer months: most local complaints are of hold-ups caused by caravans. In general, although the roads go higher and the climbs are longer, they are more 'continental' in nature, with relatively easily graded slopes. Often, the only alternative to a classified road is rough-stuff of an heroic nature. North-west of the Great Glen is an area composed of the oldest rocks in Britain, and probably more of a cyclist's countryside than the sterner and more massive Cairngorm and Ben Nevis range. This is a country of steep-sided sea lochs, many meriting the title of fjord and offering superb views westwards over the outer isles. For the record once more, the longest climb in the country is here, from sea level near Kishorn to the summit of the Bealach na Ba, 626m (2054ft), in the space of about 9km (a little over 5½ miles), averaging 1-in-15·4 (6·5 %) – but going up to 1-in-4 (25 %) on two of the bends. As you move northwards – and to some extent eastwards – so the country becomes bleaker and more treeless, lending an austere grandeur to some of the most remarkable volcanic peaks such as Stac Polly and Suilven. Oddly enough, although the population is very sparse – only one person to every few square miles – the distribution is remarkably even, so that while you remain on a road you are rarely completely out of sight of habitation.

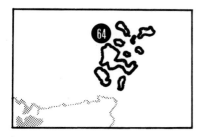

The Islands: 61 Skye; 62 Mull; 63 Harris and Lewis; 64 Orkneys.

One of the practical results of travelling so far north is to increase the length of summer days, and in fact at midsummer there is no true darkness, merely an extended period of twilight. At that time of year, sunset and sunrise are somewhere of the order of an hour to an hour and a half later and earlier, respectively, here than in southern England. Darkness is correspondingly longer in winter. Distances between sources of food can be quite large so that the wise cyclist stocks up adequately when he can. Under the impetus of the Highlands and Islands Development Board accommodation has become less scarce, if relatively rather dearer, than it used to be and food supplies are more frequent now that they generally arrive by road rather than by sea. Here – and in the Isles – Sunday is very strictly observed by many of the inhabitants and you are unlikely to find the chance small shop or indeed anything other than the large hotel open. Whether you agree with them or not, the religious convictions are deeply held and it is courteous to avoid giving offence to those who live in the country in which you are a visitor. Some ferries, although fewer than in the past, similarly do not operate on Sundays: the CTC *Handbook* is invaluable here. Scottish cyclists have long had the habit of cooking up their own meal and hot drink on their travels and it can be a habit worth copying.

The Isles

'The Earth's the Lord's, and all that it contains, except the Highlands and the Isles – and they're MacBrayne's' ran the old couplet in the days when that company, now Caledonian MacBrayne Limited, held the virtual monopoly of not only the ferries to the offshore islands but also the buses. Even now, a close perusal of the Caledonian MacBrayne timetable, obtainable from them at The Pier, Gourock PA19 1QP, is necessary for anyone contemplating visiting any of the islands except perhaps Skye, which has a frequent service from Kyle of Lochalsh. Many steamers make a round trip which means that they stop at a given island only on certain days of the week. Some of the air services, intended to allow inhabitants of some of the outer isles – Islay, Tiree, Benbecula and Lewis – to shop in Glasgow or Inverness, offer also a means of getting there. From the cyclist's point of view probably Mull and Skye are the most appealing with the greatest variety, although the Scandinavian nature of the Outer Hebrides – Lewis, Harris, Benbecula, North and South Uist, and Barra – and the Orkneys and Shetlands has its attraction for some, with its intimate mixture of stone, sky and sea. Beyond them, there is nothing but the ocean.

An often neglected corner of Scotland – a view from one of the many quiet roads which follow long sea lochs in Argyll. This is Loch Fyne.

10

Finding the way

The greatest silent friend the cycle-tourist has – after the faithful and necessary bicycle – is a map: it is the means by which unknown country is brought alive and its possibilities and pitfalls shown. To many experienced travellers an hour or two spent reading a map, of places known or with anticipation, is better than many other entertainments. It is, more practically, the means by which the cycle-tourist can determine how to get to the places he or she wants to visit, to avoid those he doesn't, and to make the best use of the superb network of minor roads. And it will be a very necessary tool as we press on to more adventurous riding away from metalled roads.

Maps for the cyclist

Traditionally the cyclist in Britain always favoured the Ordnance Survey 1in-to-the-mile or Bartholomew's ½in-to-the-mile maps. With the growth of motor traffic on the A and B-class roads, the more detailed information of the 'One-inch' was becoming more and more sought after. Metrication is proceeding, however, and the OS series has changed from 1in-to-the-mile, or a scale of 1:63 360, to 1:50 000, while the 'Barts' series – as it has affectionately been known to generations of cyclists – is being replaced by the 1:100 000 scale. The 1:63 360 scale is retained for some special sheets by the Ordnance Survey, covering particular 'tourist' areas. Two other scales of OS map can be of use to the cyclist: the 1:250 000, about four miles to the inch (or 2·5km to the cm) and the 1:25 000, about 2½in to the mile (0·25km to the cm).

Ordnance Survey 1:50 000

This map is the most generally useful for the exploring cycle-tourist since it is the smallest scale to show in detail every metalled road (although not always immediately distinguishable as such) and topographic feature of note, and the only one to show comprehensively which paths and tracks are rights of way. It will be recalled that cyclists are specifically permitted to use bridleways in England and Wales; the distinction between paths is not made in the same terms in Scotland. As far as following routes goes, in practice, these maps are superb. This is not to say that they have no disadvantages. The cyclist is very interested in topography, in hills and valleys, and these are shown by contour lines and spot heights; this means that more experience is necessary to appreciate relief compared with the green (low) becoming brown (high) layer colouring of some other maps – such as Bartholomew's – or the combination of layer tints and hill shading used on the Ordnance Survey's own 1:250 000. Each 1:50 000 sheet covers an area of 40 × 40km, say 25 × 25 miles, so a prolonged tour can demand a bulky and expensive load. The folded versions of the map (the one usually sold, in the lurid magenta covers) are rather large: at about 9 × 5¼in (23 × 13cm) they do not fit too easily into the pocket. The current method of folding is distinctly inconvenient for the cyclist, since two movements are needed to open up large and awkwardly-shaped 'portrait format' areas showing about 12 × 20km. The map can be bought (considerably more cheaply) from major suppliers flat, without covers, and more and more outdoor users are preferring to buy these and fold them to their own requirements. A large area of unfolded map is very vulnerable to damage by the wind: for cycling use, a fold which opens up to show an area about 11km square at a time, giving a folded size of about 8½ × 4¼in (say 22 × 11cm) is very convenient, and may be achieved by trimming off the excess margin of the map, folding the map back on itself twice across the vertical direction, to give a narrow horizontal strip, and then concertina-ing this into eight folds horizontally. By this means the top or bottom half of the map can be seen, in 11 × 11km sections, without further refolding. The fold can be made even more compact if the map is actually cut into top and bottom halves and each folded separately. The repeated folding and unfolding of the multiple folds of the usual cased map leads to its early wearing-out at the corners. I have dealt with this point at some length because of the great difference it can make to the ease of consulting a map: it should be added that many

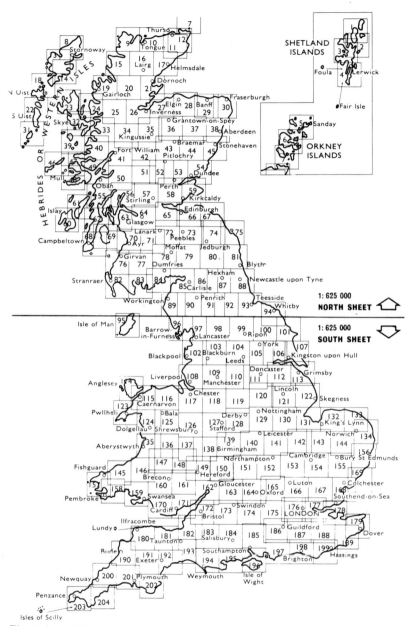

The index of Ordnance Survey 1:50 000 sheets covering England, Wales and Scotland.

other maps, including Bartholomew's, are open to similar criticism, whereas some continental map suppliers, such as Michelin, have obviously appreciated the point – and Michelin's main business isn't even maps!

Two series of the OS 1:50 000 are published. The interim First Series is a photographic enlargement of the older 'One-inch' map, partially revised and with some of the colour conventions altered. This is being progressively replaced by the Second Series, generally similar in overall appearance but with claimed improved clarity and a unified style. Both have similar sheet size and each Second Series sheet will be a direct replacement of the First Series, covering exactly the same piece of country.

Most of the art of practical map-reading is an appreciation of the distance and direction in which you have travelled, with this mental picture related to the map. The conventions by which particular features are shown are listed in the legend down the right-hand side of each map sheet: there is *no* short cut – they have to be learned. The colour conventions for roads of differing type are becoming universal: blue for motorways, from which bicycles are of course excluded, red for main, A-class roads, orangish-brown for B-class secondary roads, yellow for minor roads, tarred, and white for minor roads untarred and small streets, etc. in towns. Without going quite as far as the French cycle-touring writer Pierre Roques ('When you buy a map, begin by crossing out all the red roads'), I cannot stress too strongly that it is by the small yellow roads, with perhaps some less busy B-roads, that the cycle-tourist will travel, for comfort and quiet enjoyment. If it is necessary to follow an A-road, check – from the map, of course – whether there is a route parallelled by a motorway or major dual-carriageway which is likely to have funnelled off most of the heavy traffic. Although in general trunk roads, marked '(T)' after the road number on the map, take the heaviest traffic, in some cases even these are quite quiet where a motorway has taken over: for example, those parts of the A4 (the Bath road) which run close to the M4 are relatively peaceful, as are those stretches of the A40 (the Oxford road) bypassed by the M40.

'White' roads and paths need more caution, for they vary from easily ridable – slightly rough or even lightly tarred and metalled – to near quagmires, varying of course with the season, locality and geology. On both series of map these white roads abound. On the First Series there are two widths: 'wide' white roads, officially according to the

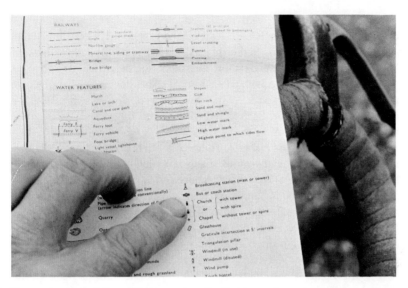

The explanation of the symbols used on the Ordnance Survey map is given down the right hand side of each sheet.

legend 'under 4·3 metres of metalling untarred', are nearly always perfectly good small roads, and it's often not clear why they don't appear as yellow ones; 'narrow' white roads, 'minor road in towns, drive or track (unmetalled)', cover all these categories, and may well not be public rights of way. (It is in practice safe to assume that yellow roads are public rights of way, although the Survey do not guarantee it.) On the Second Series, there is only one style of 'white' road, classified as 'minor road untarred and minor road in towns'. The main clue, from the map, as to whether a white road is likely to be physically cyclable is whether or not it links *two* settlements or habitations. If it links two yellow roads, say a mile apart, with a farm halfway along, it is quite probable that one end is the farm's major access and the other relatively disused, or mainly used by tractors and animals. If, however, it links two reasonable-sized settlements, it is likely to be used to get from one to the other.

The question as to whether or not a white road is a right of way is not easy to resolve. There are three types of right of way shown on the map in England and Wales: footpaths on which the cyclist can claim no right (but may well choose to chance his arm at his own risk); bridleways on which the cyclist may ride, giving way if necessary to horses and pedestrians; and the 'road used as public path or byway open to all traffic'. This 'RUPP' category is gradually being eliminated, such routes being reclassified either as footpaths, bridleways or byways – not necessarily maintained or metalled – open to all traffic. If a white road on the map is marked also as a bridleway (red dashes) or a road-used-as-public-path (First Series: red dashes with dots on alternate sides; Second Series: red dashes and dots alternating), then there is no problem. Also, if the map shows a white road coming to a stop and continuing as either of these two, then the implication is that the public has a right of way to reach the start of the path. However, beware – not all sheets of the map show rights of way over their whole area. There is a small pink square part-way down the legend which shows whether there is any part of the map for which right-of-way information was not available at the time of publication.

The other major immediate concern of the cyclist is how hilly the route is likely to be. Very steep hills are marked by chevrons or 'arrows' across the road; these point *downhill*. Two chevrons close together denote a hill steeper than 1-in-5 (20% or about 11°) which is pretty steep, and one chevron hills between 1-in-5 and 1-in-7 (between 14 and 20%, or from about 8–11°). These markings are given on 'yellow' or higher graded roads only. Otherwise, you have to judge the hilliness by noting how closely grouped the contour lines are and relating this to your own experience. You will probably find that it is less tiring, and dispiriting to go up a relatively short steep hill and down a long gradual one, than the other way round, and you should bear this in mind when choosing between alternative routes. The map will also give some clue as to how exposed or sheltered a road is likely to be. Roads in valleys, roads marked with a solid border – officially 'fenced', but more likely in practice to be hedged or walled, roads through woodland, and roads across generally undulating countryside are likely to be relatively sheltered. Unfenced roads across flat countryside or along the tops or ridges of hills will be exposed.

One other feature common to all Ordnance Survey maps is the system of coordinates for giving the position of an object, and known as the National Grid. The 1:50 000 and 1:25 000 maps are divided into kilometre squares and the legend at the side of the map shows how to quote the 'grid reference' of the 100m square within which a given point lies. The 1:250 000 map is divided into 10km squares, allowing a spot to be specified by its 1km square (or, approximately, to the nearest 500m). More and more organisations are specifying the location of places (Youth Hostels, for example) by means of their grid references, and some county authorities – for example Dorset – mark the six-figure grid reference, that is, the 100m square, on signposts.

This of course by no means exhausts the information given on the map, for in addition to natural features and villages a variety of what the Survey terms 'tourist information' is given, including the position of picnic sites, camp sites, beauty spots and ancient monuments, as well as the very practical position of public conveniences outside towns and villages. The more you use a map, the more you will appreciate the wealth of information it can convey and the more easily you will relate it to your own experience on the ground.

Ordnance Survey 1 : 250 000 or 'Quarter-inch'
The Fifth Series of this map, which covered the whole country in 17 sheets, was much improved over the earlier editions. It is now being progressively replaced by the Sixth Series in a generally similar style but which, by virtue of using back-to-back printing, covers the country in only 9 sheets. This format also requires less folding and unfolding. The Ordnance Survey describe it as 'the motoring map', but it can be useful to the cyclist for route planning or even for use on the road for relatively direct journeys. Not all roads are shown, which may lead to confusion where an apparent corner turns out to be a junction, but all those shown are cyclable. This map gives a particularly good impression of relief by means of layer tints from pale green to deep golden brown, combined in hilly areas with hill shading. Only classified M, A and B-class roads are coloured. Rights of way and other detailed information are not given.

Ordnance Survey 1 : 25 000
This is a very much more detailed map than the 1 : 50 000 and is again published in two series. The original First Series, each sheet 10km square, is being gradually replaced by the new-style Second Series sheets, each of which is 20km west-to-east by 10km south-to-north. The newer map also employs a wider range of colours. Both show detail down to field boundaries and small ponds, and indicate such features as farms with outbuildings at approximately their on-the-ground shape and scale. The First Series is now becoming somewhat dated, although major revisions are added at each reprinting; the Second Series replacement rate has been accelerated over the last few years and new sheets appear at regular intervals. Many of those already

By using a map to seek out small roads and byways it is possible to find quiet country even at popular times: this is in the Cotswolds at August Bank Holiday.

available cover mountain and hilly areas, notably north and west Scotland, the Northumberland coast, Exmoor and Dartmoor.

This scale, with a First or Second Series base map as appropriate, is also used for the relatively new Outdoor Leisure series, of which 17 sheets are now available, covering areas such as the Three Peaks, the Lake District, Malham and Upper Wharfedale, and the Brecon Beacons. Designed principally for walkers, these sheets show such items as camp sites, mountain rescue posts, land to which the public has access, and access paths, in addition to the information of the base map. These maps can be very useful for the type of cycling we shall deal with in Chapters 13 and 14.

Ordnance Survey 'One-inch'
This traditional scale lives on in the special 'Tourist Maps'. Most are similar in style to the old One-inch map – not too unlike the 1 : 50 000 – but give more tourist information and show relief by means of layer tints and hill shading. These maps are a very attractive buy for the cyclist and it is worth listing the sheets available. They are Exmoor, Dartmoor, New Forest, Peak District, Lake District, North York Moors, Loch Lomond and the Trossachs, Ben Nevis and Glen Coe, and the Cairngorms.

It is worth mentioning secondhand maps at this point. Although it is advisable to have maps which are as up to date as possible, many features do not change, particularly in remote and mountain areas. If you are offered any of them, One-inch Ordnance Survey Seventh Series or post-1950 'Barts' Half-inch are still perfectly adequate for most of the areas the cycle-tourist would naturally visit. The Sixth Series was not an easy map to read, nor particularly attractive; some older ones, while perhaps no longer usable are quite beautiful in their own right as examples of the map-maker's art – the Third Edition with its superb hachured hill-shading was perhaps the zenith of this type.

Bartholomew's 1 : 100 000
'Barts' Half-inch, the old cyclists' favourite – and at its best one of the most visually attractive maps produced of the British Isles – is being replaced by the 1 : 100 000 'National' map series. Like the First Series OS 1 : 50 000, this is effectively a partially revised photographic enlargement from the original 1 : 126 720. In the changeover, the opportunity has been taken to alter the style of some items, particularly noticeably the colouring of woodland areas and the employment of

rather paler layer tints. Additionally, and strangely, the detail shown has been slightly reduced, particularly as regards the contour interval and range of tints for showing relief and the marking of topographical details. The map now shows rather a (confusing, to my eye) mix of type faces, the rather attractive hand-lettering of the original clashing with the mechanically produced faces used for tourist information and antiquities. However, it remains quite a practical map for the cyclist, with two of the provisos which applied in some measure also to the OS 1:50 000. First, you have to be even more careful in interpreting a 'white' road on 'Barts': 'wide' white roads are nearly always all right – 'narrow' roads may range from quite good or even metalled roads right through tracks and paths down to scarcely visible traces on the ground. As a relatively small private company Bartholomew lack the revision and survey resources of the government body and so they depend in some measure on the goodwill of users for correction of detail of this kind: any information that you pass on will help to improve the map for the user of the next edition. The second caveat, as with the 1:50 000, concerns the increased folded size consequent upon the change of scale, while the double-unfolding movement to open is a difficult manoeuvre on a bicycle. The opened size, $10\frac{1}{2} \times 14\frac{1}{2}$in (27 × 37cm) is rather more manageable than the OS, however, and at the smaller scale covers quite a useful 26 × 33km of territory. Experience with foreign maps, particularly the French and Swiss national surveys, suggests that a good 1:100 000 map would be close to the cyclist's ideal scale.

One other Bartholomew product which can be unreservedly recommended for tour planning is their annually-revised 1:300 000 atlas. Showing virtually the same degree of detail as the OS 1:250 000 series, it covers the whole country for the price of about three sheets of the latter. The atlas form is not really appropriate for carrying by bicycle, but for planning it is excellent.

Lost?

You (and I!) will naturally make mistakes from time to time. The first thing is not to panic. If you remember passing a road junction a short way back, retrace, if not, stop or go gently on to the next. If, however, the road ahead goes steeply downhill, say off the ridge of a hill, it is obviously prudent to try to keep what height you have and to stop immediately and look for clues. You should know where you are within a mile or two, so you will not have to search too great an area of the map.

First, are there any signposts — if you are at a junction – which will suggest where you might be? Does the layout of the junction and the direction of the roads conform with the map? Are you at a prominent bend in the road? On top or at the foot of a hill? Is there a large farm or house nearby which might be named on the map? Are there any topographical features – valleys, streams, woods, orchards, quarries, end of an unfenced stretch of road – which fit in (caution: it is quite easy for an unfenced road to have become fenced since the map was made or, particularly in arable areas such as East Anglia, the reverse)? Are there any man-made features – railway bridges, level crossings, churches (with or without towers or spires), pubs, windmills, wind-pumps, overhead power lines, isolated telephone boxes, signposted footpaths or bridleways leaving the road, milestones, canals?

If you are in a town or village is there a street name which suggests which road you are on – 'Birmingham Road' or 'Leicester Street' (but don't be misled by noble families and their seats – 'Bedford Road', 'Sandringham Road', 'Wellington Street')? Telephone boxes and letter boxes usually indicate where they are, as do railway stations and hospitals. Finally, you can sink your pride and ask – in fact, the usual reaction to your opening a map within a hundred yards of a non-cyclist is for the latter to come over to ask whether you are lost!

Even the old dodges for determining the compass directions are worth remembering: the sun actually *is* somewhere towards the south at midday (or 1 p.m. Summer Time) and moves round from east to west at half the speed of the clock; lichen really does grow more readily on the shaded, north side of trees, posts, walls and buildings; churches lie roughly on a west-east line, some with great accuracy; at night the 'Pointers' of the Plough point to the Pole Star, which is very close to due north.

Carrying the map

It is desirable to have the map readily to hand, and my own personal preference is to carry it in a back pocket, from which it can easily be taken for reference, either while stopped or, briefly, while riding. You should only look at the map while riding when you are quite sure that there is no other traffic about and that it is safe to do so, and it should *never* be for more than a few seconds' confirmatory glance. It is possible to buy a special map carrier, the Pletscher, which fits beneath the head of the expander bolt of the handlebar stem and has a spring clip to hold the map. I find these carriers rather ugly and they cannot easily be used with an allen-key fitting expander bolt. Despite this some experienced riders swear by them; you should never attempt to read the map while riding if one of these carriers is being used.

Most handlebar bags have a transparent pocket on top to take and protect a map; it should be noted that those of continental origin are specifically designed to accommodate the $4\frac{1}{2} \times 10$in (11×25cm) of the Michelin $1:200\ 000$ map. British maps are now available only on unbacked paper, which needs some protection, particularly in wet weather. Probably the most satisfactory way is to use the map inside a transparent plastic envelope which will cover the folds in use. It will be necessary to take it out to turn over to the next folds. Specialist firms mount or laminate maps, at a price, but this – laminating particularly – inevitably makes them more bulky.

Typical rural midland England – cattle in lush water meadows, a winding stream and the spire of the church of the next village just visible over the hill.

11

First steps

This chapter gives, in the form of sketch maps and short notes, some suggestions for fairly easy days out in pleasant count. with total distances up to about 65km (40 miles) or so. They are *not* billiard-table flat – and some parts of the country are intrinsically hillier than others. The suggested starting points are towns or cities easily accessible by road or rail: they are mostly 'tourist centres' and the sort of place you might want to visit anyway. There is no compulsion, of course, to follow the whole of any route, and as they are complete circuits you can start and finish at any point, or if you are, say, leaving a car at a convenient spot you could avoid some of the urban bits. You can also use these ideas as models for similar routes based on other starting points.

In each case remember that the sketch map (and those in Chapters 12 and 13) is meant as no more than an indicator so that you can trace the route on a practical map such as the OS 1:50 000. The notes indicate which sheets are required and also give more detail of any tricky junctions or involved portions of the route. The roads chosen are as far as possible small unclassified ones; the sketch maps show where they cross or incorporate classified roads. All the maps in this section are reproduced to the same approximate scale, which is shown below:

Each of these circuits was compiled in one direction, indicated by one of the signs

on each map. The notes follow this direction, but you can go either way round.

The following abbreviations are used in Chapters 11, 12 and 13:

OS Ordnance Survey (1:50 000 sheet number unless otherwise stated); GR grid reference; L turn left (or fork or bear if specified); R turn right; SO straight on; N, S, E, W north, south, east, west (and combinations); uc unclassified road, i.e. not A, B or M-class; Br, Fm, Gn, Gt, Ho, Lt, St Bridge, Farm, Green, Great, House, Little and Saint, when used in place-names; PH public house; rly railway; SH spot height marked on map, in metres; stn station. All the sketch maps are reproduced to the same approximate scale:

Quite a number of instances of road numbers having been changed have come to light during the preparation of the routes in these chapters. Roads replaced by new bypasses, or roads which have acquired new local importance as feeder routes, may fall or rise in the hierarchy and there are inevitable delays before some of the changes appear on published maps. (And don't forget that your own maps are not automatically self-updating!) This type of change, together with other road alterations and realignments is continuous. Be prepared to follow the road which goes in the right direction from the right place even if the number differs from the one on your map.

Notes on the maps

CAMBRIDGE

OS maps: 154 and 153 Bartholomew: 20

①◇ Leave city by Newnham Road, which becomes Barton Road, A603. At GR 436 575, optional uc detour to Grantchester.

②◇ There is a whole network of exquisite lanes in Ashwell.

CHESTER

OS map: 117. Bartholomew: 28 and 23.

③◇ Chester has a quite involved one-way system. Leave Cathedral E by Foregate Street and Boughton on A51 to junction with A5115 (old A41) and B5130, Sandy Lane. Follow Holt signs.

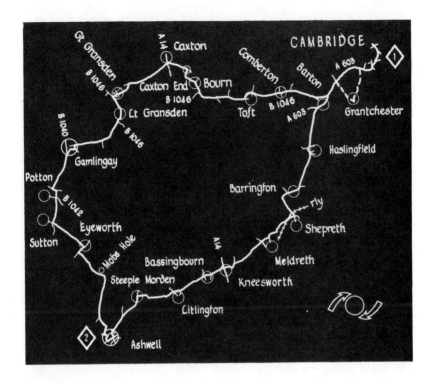

Map labels: Gt Gransden, B 1046, Caxton End, Ct Gransden, B 1046, B 1040, B 1046, Gamlingay, A14 Caxton, B 1046, Bourn, Toft, B 1046, Comberton, Barton, A 603, A 603, CAMBRIDGE, 1, Grantchester, Haslingfield, Potton, B 1042, Eyeworth, Barrington, rly, Shepreth, Sutton, Mobs Hole, Bassingbourn, A14, Meldreth, Steeple Morden, Kneesworth, 2, Litlington, Ashwell

GRANTHAM

OS map: 130. Bartholomew: 25.

4 Leave town centre S on B1174, old London Road, to SH 100m, 2km.

HERTFORD

OS map: 166. Bartholomew: 15.

NORWICH

OS map: 134. Bartholomew: 26.

5 From Cathedral E along Bishopsgate over River Wensum to inner ring road, Riverside, A1067. L on A1067 to first roundabout, second exit L on uc road up hill over Mousehold Heath.

OXFORD

OS map: 164. Bartholomew: 14.

6 From E end of 'The High' at Magdalen Br, GR 522 061, SE to roundabout 'The Plain', 200m. Fork L on old A40, A420, Headington road and take first major fork L after ½km, to Headington Hill and New Marston. L and R to A40 interchange at GR 533 088, 1km. Bear R over A40 and immediately fork L for Woodeaton.

7 L at Eynsham church to join bypass B4044, L over Swinford bridge.

STRATFORD-UPON-AVON

OS map: 151. Bartholomew: 19.

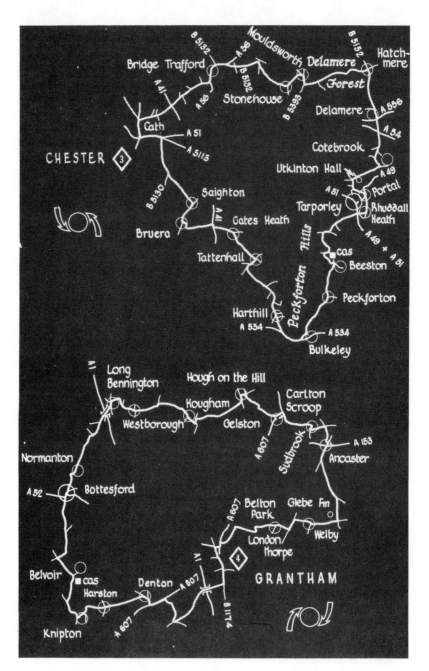

CHESTER 3

Bridge Trafford
B 5132
A 56
Mouldsworth
Delamere
Hatch-mere
B 5152
B 5132
Stonehouse
B 5393
Forest
Delamere
A 556
A 41
A 56
Cath
A 51
A 5115
A 54
Cotebrook
Utkinton Hall
A 49
B 5130
Saighton
A 51
Portal
Tarporley
Rhuddall Heath
Gates Heath
A 41
Bruera
A 49 × A 51
cas
Beeston
Tattenhall
Peckforton Hills
Peckforton
Harthill
A 534
A 534
Bulkeley

Long Bennington
M 1
Hough on the Hill
Hougham
Cartton Scroop
Westborough
Gelston
A 607
Sudbrook
A 153
Ancaster
Normanton
A 52
Bottesford
A 607
Belton Park
Glebe Fm
London Thorpe
Welby
Belvoir
cas
4
GRANTHAM
Harston
Denton
A 607
A 1
Knipton
A 607
B 1174

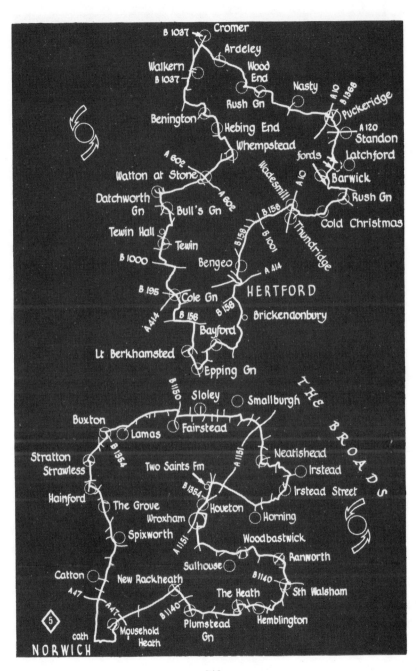

Cromer
B 1037
Ardeley
Walkern
B 1037
Wood End
Nasty
A 10
B 1368
Puckeridge
Rush Gn
Benington
A 120
Standon
Hebing End
Whempstead
Latchford
fords
A 602
Wadesmill
Barwick
Watton at Stone
A 10
Datchworth Gn
A 602
Rush Gn
Bull's Gn
B 158
Cold Christmas
Tewin Hall
B 158
Thundridge
Tewin
B 1000
B 1001
Bengeo
B 195
A 414
Cole Gn
HERTFORD
A 414
B 158
Brickendonbury
B 158
Bayford
Lt Berkhamsted
Epping Gn

B 1150
Sloley
Smallburgh
THE
Buxton
Fairstead
BROADS
Lamas
Stratton
Strawless
B 1354
Neatishead
A 1151
Two Saints Fm
Irstead
Hainford
B 1354
Irstead Street
The Grove
Houeton
Wroxham
Horning
Spixworth
A 1151
Woodbastwick
Catton
Ranworth
New Rackheath
Sulhouse
B 1140
A 47
The Heath
Sth Walsham
⑤
A 47
B 1140
cath
Mousehold
Plumstead Gn
Hemblington
NORWICH
Heath

141

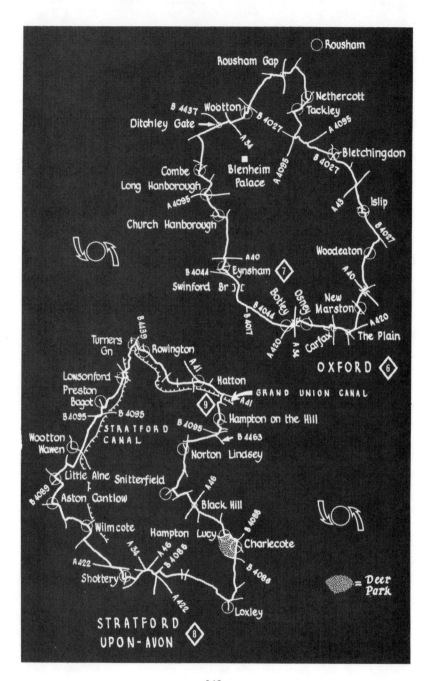

Rousham

Rousham Gap

B 4437 Wootton

Ditchley Gate →

Nethercott
Tackley

A 4095

B 4027

A 34

A 4095

Bletchingdon

B 4027

Combe

Long Hanborough

A 4095

Blenheim
Palace

A 43

Islip

B 4027

Church Hanborough

A 40

B 4044

Eynsham

Swinford Br

B 4044

B 4017

Woodeaton

A 40

New
Marston

Botley

Osney

A 420

A 34

Carfax

A 420

The Plain

7

OXFORD 6

Turners
Gn

B 4439

Rowington

A 41

Hatton

GRAND UNION CANAL

Lowsonford
Preston
Bagot

B 4095

B 4095

STRATFORD
CANAL

9

A 41

Hampton on the Hill

Wootton
Wawen

B 4089

Little Alne Snitterfield

Aston Cantlow

Wilmcote

Shottery

A 34

A 46

B 4089

A 422

B 4095

B 4463

Norton Lindsey

Black Hill

A 46

Hampton Lucy

B 4088

Charlecote

B 4086

A 422

Loxley

STRATFORD
UPON-AVON 8

= Deer
Park

142

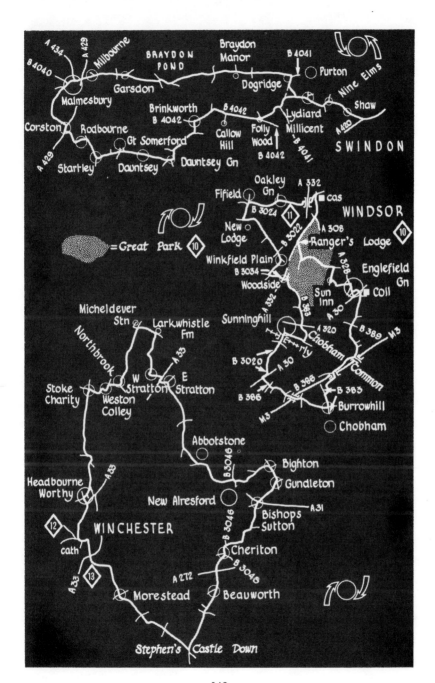

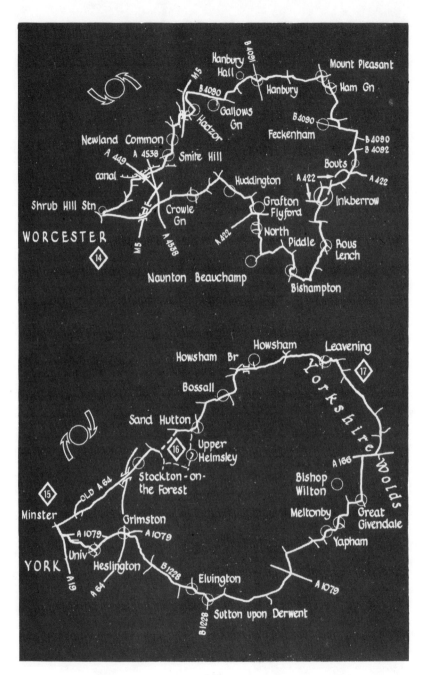

Map 14 (top):

TOJ

Hanbury
Hall
B 4091

Mount Pleasant

B 4090

Hanbury

Ham Gn

Gallows
Gn

Hadzor

Feckenham

B 4090

B 4090
B 4092

Newland Common

A 449

A 4538

Smite Hill

Bouts

canal

Huddington

A 422

Bouts

A 422

Shrub Hill Stn

Crowle
Gn

Grafton
Flyford

Inkberrow

WORCESTER

M5

A 4538

A 422

North
Piddle

Rous
Lench

14

Naunton Beauchamp

Bishampton

Map 16/17 (bottom):

Howsham

Leavening

Howsham Br

Bossall

17

Yorkshire Wolds

Sand Hutton

Upper
Helmsley

16

A 166

Stockton-on-
the Forest

Bishop
Wilton

OLD A 64

Meltonby

Great
Givendale

15

Minster

Grimston

Yapham

A 1079

A 1079

Univ

YORK

A 19

Heslington

B 1228

Elvington

A 1079

A 64

Sutton upon Derwent

B 1228

144

⟨8⟩ From Avon bridge 300m N of Shakespeare Memorial Theatre follow A34 SW to first roundabout, 300m. Take first exist L, B4086, and first R after 300m to Loxley.

⟨9⟩ It may be possible to follow the canal towpath to avoid A41. You should have a permit (valid for one year) from British Waterways Board, Willow Grange, Church Road, Watford, Herts. You have to walk at locks etc where marked.

SWINDON
OS map: 173. Bartholomew: 7 and 8.

WINDSOR
OS map: 175. Bartholomew: 9.

⟨10⟩ Leave Castle to join A332 at roundabout at GR 969 757, 1½km. Follow A332 to Rangers Lodge Gate, 3km. L through gate into fenced part of park: cycling permitted in small groups. Cars except residents prohibited. Fork L immediately after gate to T-junction, 1km. L past equestrian statue to crossroads at GR 967 722, another 2¼km. L leaving park to junction at GR 987 722, 1km.

⟨11⟩ From Oakley Green B3024 to junction with Parsonage Lane at GR 953 765. L on uc road crossing A308 to Clewer. R at Clewer church,

under A332 and rly bridges along river bank to Castle.

WINCHESTER
OS map: 185.
Bartholomew: 5 and 8.

⟨12⟩ From Cathedral take N (London) road for 3km towards Kings Worthy.

⟨13⟩ SO at ring road, A33, to city centre.

WORCESTER
OS map: 150.
Bartholomew: 18 and 19.

⟨14⟩ E from Shrub Hill Stn on uc road past hospitals over M5 to cross A4538 at SH 43m after 3½km.

YORK
OS maps: 100, 105 and 106.
Bartholomew: 33.

⟨15⟩ Leave York Minster by Monkgate and Heworth Green, old A64, to crossroads where old A64 bears L after 1½km; SO on uc road.

⟨16⟩ Marked route is gravel track; alternative shown is road route via Upper Helmsley.

⟨17⟩ SO in Leavening up steep hill to take first R after 1km, which climbs to join ridge road.

12

Further afield

With this chapter we move on to some more ambitious routes. The dozen examples link towns 200–300km (120–200 miles) apart, including five ports and London airport, so that they also serve to lead the visitor to Britain into the heart of the country – and beyond. Their principal object is to offer pleasantly cyclable alternatives to the all-too-obvious main roads. Some of the routes visit the towns or cities from which the short circuits of Chapter 11 start. In addition, some of them cross other routes so that parts of each may be combined, or even made up into extended circular tours. They also lead towards the areas of the more remote tours of Chapter 13.

There is nothing rigid about any of these routes – obviously you can plan your own detours if something on the map or a place you have read about attracts, and rejoin the main route later. As I said in the main introduction to this book, these are not the only ways between the starting and finishing points. They follow as far as possible minor metalled roads with occasional diversions onto easily followed and equally cyclable tracks.

It is not practicable, for reasons of space, to give an inch-by-inch description. The sketch maps are designed to allow you to trace the route on your own more detailed maps, and the notes to guide you past any difficult points. The routes will be easiest to follow on the OS 1:50 000 map, but you could manage with the Bartholomew 1:100 000 or even the OS 1:250 000. The sketch maps for these more or less linear routes have to be long and narrow: they are designed to be followed from bottom to top, left to right – or vice versa. To allow them to be fitted into the column space they are not usually aligned here with the north at the top in the way that conventional maps are: instead the north is indicated for each panel by means of an arrow marked N. They are all reproduced to the same approximate scale:

All the routes pass through or near places of interest of various types. I have made no attempt to catalogue them, although some are marked: one person's absorbing study is another's ultimate boredom! The 1 : 50 000 map is once more a very good indicator of what there is to be seen (smaller scales less so) or you can study specific guide books before setting out.

Notes on maps

ROUTE 1 – BATH to CHESTER
(p. 148, 149 left)

OS maps: 172, 171, 161, 148, 137, 126 and 117. Bartholomew: 7, 13, 18, 23 and 28. OS 1 : 250 000 (6th Series): 8 and 7.

1 Leave Bath by uc roads over Lansdown Hill, NW 5 km.

2 Free cycle path on Severn Bridge is reached by going round M4 roundabout, following Service Area signs, then 'Cycle Path Chepstow' sign along NE side of bridge. Path continues to A446/A48 roundabout at Chepstow, 6km.

3 At Church Stretton, Route 12 from Heathrow joins and Tour B starts.

ROUTE 2 – BATH to CAMBRIDGE via OXFORD   *(p. 149 right, 150)*

OS maps: 172, 173, 163, 164, 152, 153 and 154. Bartholomew: 7, 8, 14, 15 and 20. OS 1 : 250 000 (6th Series): 8 and 9.

4 Leave Bath on A4 to Bathford, NE 4km.

5 At Cumnor, R and then L on A420 for Oxford, E 5km. Swinford bridge on main route is toll-free to cyclists.

ROUTE 3 – SOUTHAMPTON to OXFORD   *(p. 151)*

OS maps: 196, 185, 174, 175 and 164. Bartholomew: 5, 6 and 14. OS 1 : 250 000 (6th Series): 9.

6 Leave Southampton by new Itchen bridge (still marked as 'Ferry' on most maps) and follow A3025 for 300m after bridge. L on uc roads through Bitterne (cross A334) and Harefield (cross A27) to West End, NE 6km.

7 At New Alresford R on A31 and L at top of High Street on B3046 for ¾km, then L on uc roads to East Stratton.

8 At Overton, Route 4 – Dover to Bath – crosses.

9 From Wheatley *either* follow uc roads via Horspath and Temple Cowley to city centre *or preferably* in fine weather follow road marked as 'No through road' over Shotover Plain (3km W of Wheatley) then down hill via uc roads to city centre, W 8km.

ROUTE – DOVER or FOLKESTONE to BATH   *(p. 152, 153 left)*

OS maps: 179 (just), 189, 199, 198, 197, 186, 185, 174, 173 and 172.

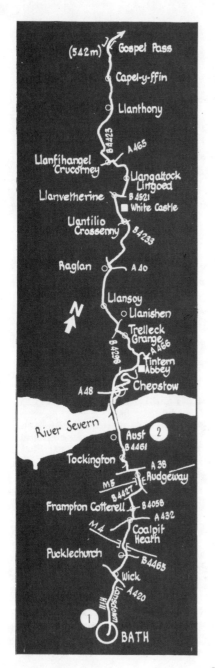

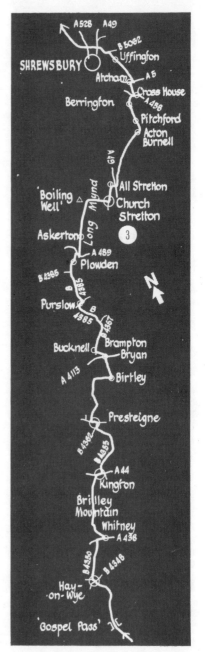

Map 1 (left panel):

(542m) Gospel Pass

Capel-y-ffin

Llanthony

B4423

A465

Llanfihangel Crucorney

Llangattock Lingoed

B4521

Llanvetherine

White Castle

Llantilio Crossenny

B4233

Raglan   A40

Llansoy

Llanishen

Trelleck Grange

B4293

A466

Tintern Abbey

A48   Chepstow

River Severn

Aust   ②

B4461

Tockington

A38

M5   Rudgeway

B4427

Frampton Cotterell   B4058

A432

M4   Coalpit Heath

Pucklechurch   B4465

Wick

A420

① BATH

Map 3 (right panel):

A528   A49

B5062   Uffington

SHREWSBURY   A5

Atcham

Cross House

Berrington   A458

Pitchford

Acton Burnell

A49

All Stretton

'Boiling Well'

Long Mynd

Church Stretton

Askerton   ③

A489

Plowden

B4385

B4385

Purslow

B4385   A4367

Bucknell   Brampton Bryan

A4113   Birtley

Presteigne

B4362   A4355

A44   Kington

Brilley Mountain

Whitney   A438

B4350   B4348

Hay-on-Wye

'Gospel Pass'

148

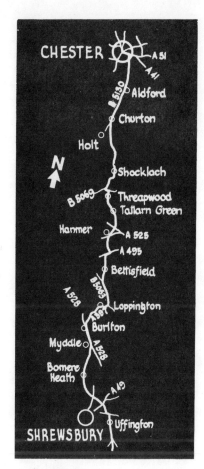

Bartholomew: 10, 6, 9, 8 and 7.
OS 1:250 000 (6th Series): 9 and 8.

10 Dover has an extensive one-way system designed to make it easy to leave and approach the car ferry terminal (Eastern Docks) or the train ferry (Western Docks). From either follow A2 signs for London (*not* A20) to Buckland, NW 2km. L on uc road parallel to A2 through Grabble and River to join B2060.

11 Route 10 – Newhaven to Cambridge crosses between Brightling and Plunnet's Town.

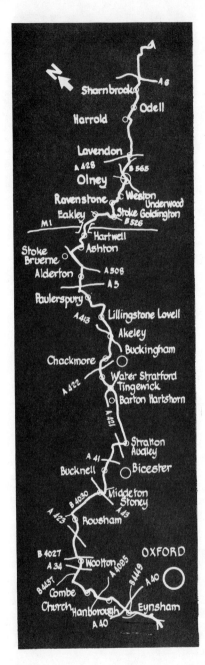

12 Route 3 – Southampton to Oxford crosses at Overton.

13 Leave Bradford-on-Avon on B3108 W to Winsley, over Kennet and Avon Canal and River Frome, under rly, then R to junction with A36, WNW 4½km. SO across A36, SO at next crossroads to enter Bath via Claverton Down. This is a very steep climb but offers superb views behind and in front.

ROUTE 5 – HARWICH to CHESTER via CAMBRIDGE (*p. 153 right*, *154, 155 left*)

OS maps: 169, 155, 154, 142, 141, 130, 129, 119, 118 and 117.
Bartholomew: 21, 20, 25, 24, 29 and 28. OS 1:250 000 (6th Series): 9, 6 and 7.

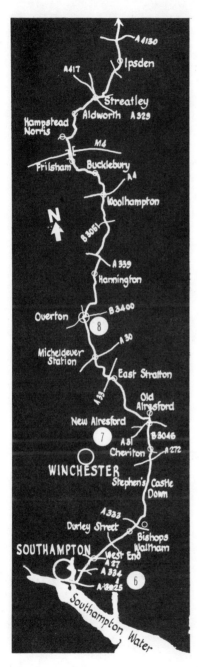

14 Leave Harwich W on A604 for 5km, then R on B1352 through Ramsey and Bradfield to Manningtree, W 15km.

15 At Cambridge, Route 2 – Bath to Cambridge – and Route 12 – London (Heathrow) to Cambridge – join.

16 At Flash Bar R on A53 for 2km and at sharp bend in road L on stony track to join uc road crossing Axe Edge; alternative road $\frac{1}{2}$km further along A53.

17 From Cat and Fiddle follow A537 then first L on uc road to Bottom-of-the-Oven; bear R to second R at T-junction, just S of W, 2½km. R down hill past lakes through Sutton Lane Ends to crossroads at GR 921 709; L to cross A523 and Macclesfield Canal at Oakgrove.

18 From Middlewich L on A530 to junction at GR 689 649 after 2km; R on uc roads to Winsford.

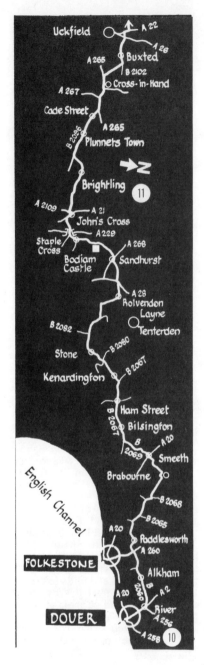
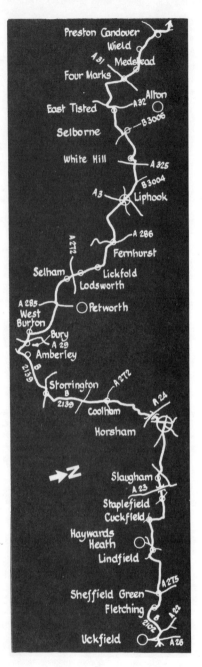

Left map:

Uckfield
A 22
A 26
A 265
Buxted
B 2102
Cross-in-Hand
A 267
Cade Street
A 265
B 2096
Plunnets Town
→ N
Brightling
(11)
A 2109
A 21
John's Cross
A 229
Staple Cross
A 268
Bodiam Castle
Sandhurst
A 28
Rolvenden Layne
B 2082
Tenterden
B 2080
Stone
B 2067
Kenardington
B 2067
Ham Street
Bilsington
B 2069
A 20
Smeeth
Brabourne
B 2068
B 2065
A 20
Paddlesworth
A 260
English Channel
Alkham
A 20
B 2060
A 2
FOLKESTONE
River
A 256
DOVER
A 258
(10)

Right map:

Preston Candover
Wield
A 31
Medstead
Four Marks
A 32
Alton
East Tisted
B 3006
Selborne
White Hill
A 325
B 3004
A 3
Liphook
A 286
A 272
Fernhurst
Selham
Lickfold
Lodsworth
A 285
Petworth
West Burton
Bury
A 29
Amberley
2139
Storrington
B
2139
Coolham
A 272
A 24
Horsham
→ N
Slaugham
A 23
Staplefield
Cuckfield
Haywards Heath
Lindfield
A 275
Sheffield Green
Fletching
B
2102
A 22
Uckfield
A 26

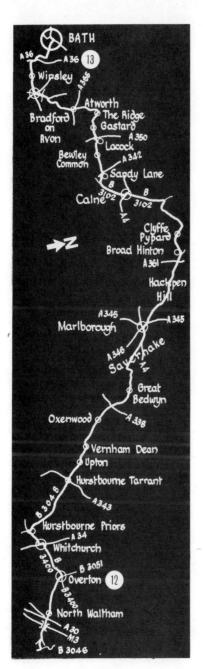

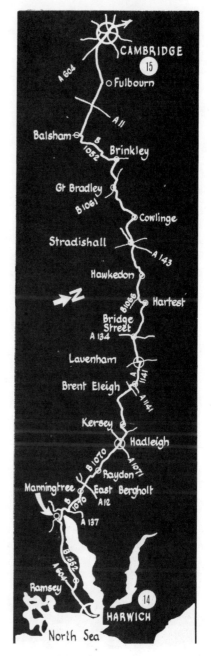

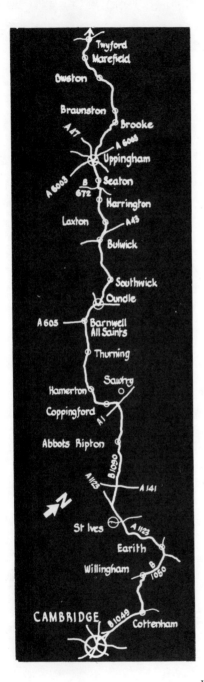

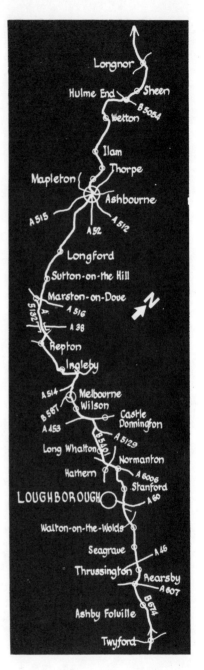

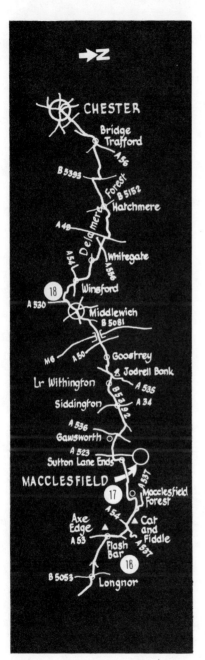

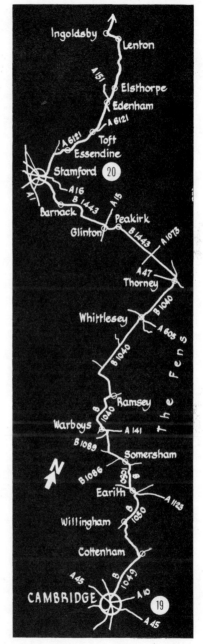

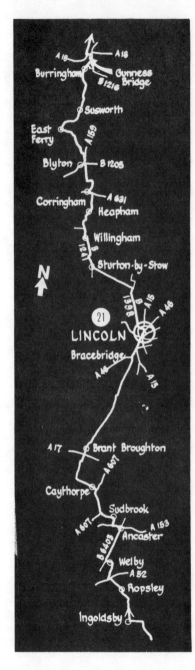

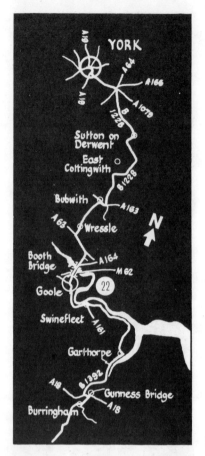

ROUTE 6 – CAMBRIDGE to YORK
(p. 155 right, 156)

OS maps: 154, 142, 141, 130, 121 and 106. Bartholomew: 20, 25, 30 and 33. OS 1:250 000 (6th Series): 9 and 6.

19 Leave Cambridge N on A604, Castle Street, then R on B1049 to Histon and Cottenham, N 9km.

20 Leave Stamford town centre E on A16 and after 1km L on A6121.

21 Leave Lincoln NNW by B1398 through Burton to crossroads just before RAF Scampton, NNW 7km.

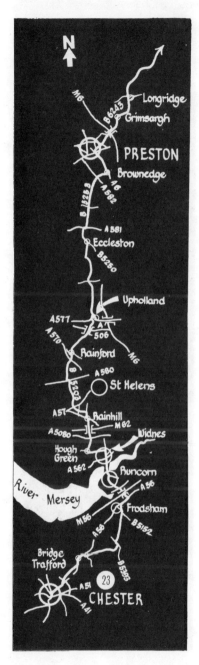

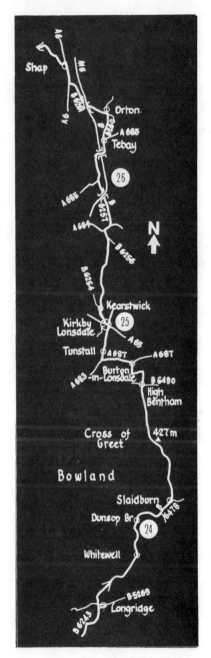

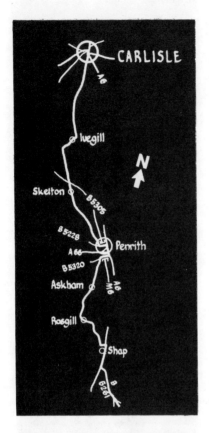

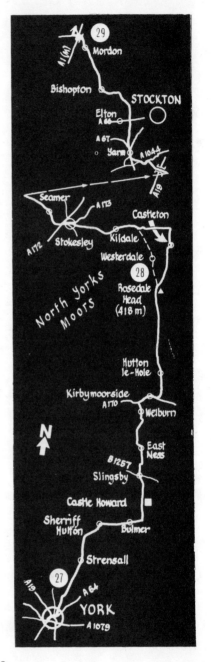

22 When the Humber Bridge from Barton-on-Humber to Hessle (with free cycle path) opens, this will offer spectacular alternative route.

ROUTE 7 – CHESTER to CARLISLE (p. 157, 158 left)

OS maps: 117, 108, 102, 103, 98, 90 and 85. Bartholomew: 28, 31, 34, 35 and 38. OS 1:250 000 (6th Series): 5.

23 Leave Chester by A5116, then just after rly br, R on uc road to join A56 at Bridge Trafford, NE 6km. L on A56 and after 2km fork R on uc road just after rly br to B5393 at Buckoak; L on B5393 and first R at Simmonds Hill on uc roads

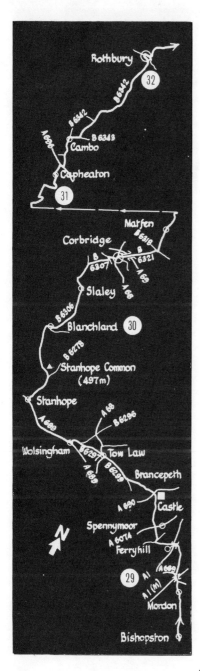

to join B5152 to A56 at NE end of Frodsham, NE 11km. R on A56; after crossing River Weaver and Weaver Navigation L to cross M56, then SO across Runcorn ring road, A557, to take old road to town centre, N 5km. Cross Manchester Ship Canal and River Mersey by bridge and take L exit at N end of bridge through Widnes to roundabout at junction with B5178, 2km from bridge. L on B5178 for 2km, then R on uc roads to Cronton, NNW 5½km. SO across A5080 over M62 to Rainhill, SO at A57 on B5413, then L on uc roads to cross A58 on B5203 to junction with A580, WNW 9km. L on A580 and R again on B5203 crossing A570 to Rainford, R on uc roads to Upholland, junction with A577, NE 10km. This section is quite complicated as well as being urban; I've done my best, but the 1:50 000 is pretty well essential for this bit.

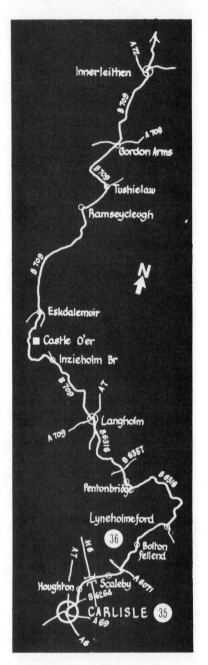

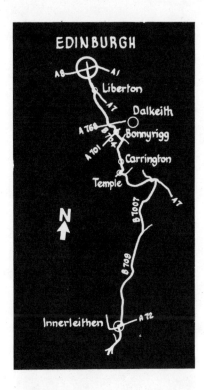

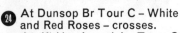

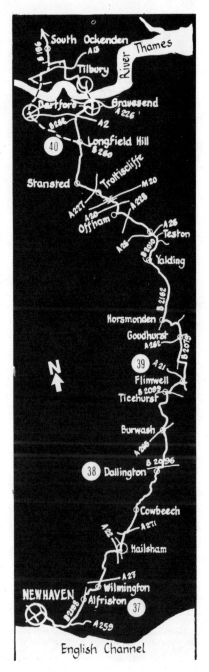

(24) At Dunsop Br Tour C – White and Red Roses – crosses.

(25) At Kirkby Lonsdale Tour C again crosses.

(26) Other, tougher, byroad alternatives to A685 are obvious on OS 1:50 000 map.

ROUTE 8 – YORK to EDINBURGH
(p. 138 right, 159, 160 left)

OS maps: 105, 100, 93, 92, 87, 80, 81, 74, 75, 67 and 66. Bartholomew: 33, 36, 35, 39, 42 and 46. OS 1:250 000 (6th Series): 5 and 4.

(27) Leave York by Gillygate and Clarence Street, B1363, then fork R into Haxby Road, uc road.

(28) From Rosedale Head marked alternative is through Westerdale and over Kildale Moor.

(29) From Mordon continue NW to join A689, L to cross A1(M),

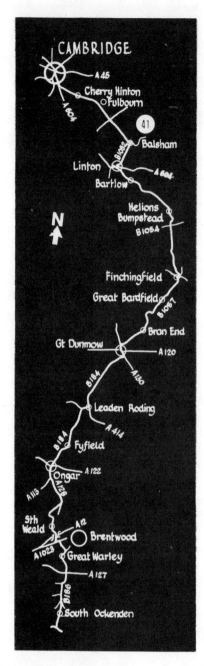

third exit L from roundabout on uc road through Chilton, then L to cross A1 at Ferryhill to join B6287 to Kirk Merrington, NW 14km from Bishopton. R on B6288, L on B6289 cross SO at A6074 on uc road over River Wear.

30 At Blanchland Tour D – Borders and the Wall – crosses.

31 Many uc road turnings between Matfen and Capheaton.

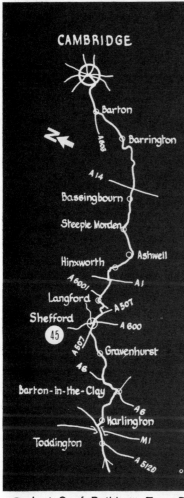

32 Just S of Rothbury Tour D crosses again.

33 From Norham cross River Tweed and Scottish/English border; 1km after border second R to join B6347, L through Whitsome then SO on uc road at end of village, via uc roads and B6460 to join A6105 to Duns.

34 Marked alternative from Duns is L on A6112, fork R after 1km on uc road through Longformacus.

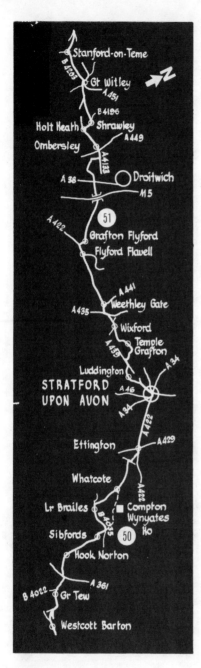

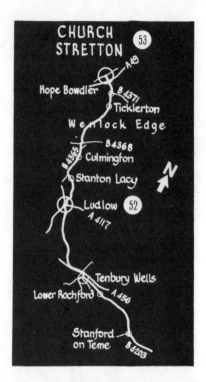

ROUTE 9 – CARLISLE to EDINBURGH *(p. 160)*

OS maps: 85, 86, 78, 79, 72, 73 and 66. Bartholomew: 38, 41 and 46. OS 1:250 000 (6th series): 3.

35 Leave Carlisle N on A7 across River Eden, immediately R on B6264 for 1¾km, then fork L on uc road to Houghton.

36 Numerous uc road alternatives between Scaleby and Pentonbridge.

ROUTE 10 – NEWHAVEN to CAMBRIDGE *(p. 161 right, 162 left)*

OS maps: 198, 199, 188, 177, 167 and 154. Bartholomew: 6, 10, 16, 24 and 20. OS 1:250 000 (6th series): 9.

37 At N end of Alfriston R on uc road, L to Milton Street, bear R in Milton Street on track to Wilmington road.

38 At Dallington Route 4 – Dover to Bath – crosses.

39 At Flimwell L on A21 for 400m, then fork R on bridleway into Bedgebury Forest; follow gravel road to T-junction of tracks after 2km, L on gravel road to join B2079.

40 Alternative to Gravesend-Tilbury ferry is by B260 to Dartford, follow Dartford Tunnel signs. No cycling in tunnel – bicycles are conveyed for a small charge by trailer. From tunnel N to A13 junction at roundabout, second exit L, E on A13, L after 1km to join B186. From ferry follow A126, L after 3km to Little Thurrock, still on A126; R opposite church on uc road, cross A13 then uc roads L to North Stifford, join B186 and tunnel route at GR 594 804. Rather urban, I'm afraid, until past Ockendon.

41 Alternative from Balsham is to follow B1052 for 2½km, then L on Roman Road (rough but ridable) for 10km over Gog Magog Hills.

ROUTE 11 – LONDON (HEATHROW AIRPORT) to CAMBRIDGE

OS maps: 176, 166, 165, 153 and 154. Bartholomew: 9, 15 and 20. OS 1:250 000 (6th Series): 9.

42 Leave air terminals by cycle tunnel to side of main tunnel to roundabout on N side of airport. First exit L from roundabout to join A4; L on A4 for 1¼km, R on A408 through Harmondsworth. Fork L after 1½km on uc road over M4 to rejoin A408 at West Drayton, 3½km N of airport terminals. Urban.

43 From Flaunden maze of uc roads to junction with B4505 at GR 006 034 near Bovingdon.

44 At Linslade R on A418, follow Hemel Hempstead (A4146) signs then L on uc road to Stanbridge.

45 At Shefford R at traffic lights on A600, fork L on A507, then L on uc roads through Clifton to join A6001 to Langford.

ROUTE 12 – LONDON (HEATHROW AIRPORT) to CHURCH STRETTON via OXFORD and STRATFORD-UPON-AVON
(p. 163 right, 164)

OS maps: 176, 175, 164, 151, 150, 138 and 137. Bartholomew: 9, 14, 16 and 18. OS 1:250 000 (6th series): 9 and 7.

46 Leave airport as note 42 to West Drayton. First L on uc road, L at T-junction to Richings Park, SO to junction with B470 at Langley. L on B470 to Datchet, R on B376, fork L after ¾km on B3026, L on B3022 to Eton and Windsor.

47 Route 3 – Southampton to Oxford joins just before Cuxham.

48 To leave Oxford follow Oxford circuit route (Chapter 11) through Woodeaton to Islip.

49 At Lower Heyford Route 2 – Bath to Cambridge – crosses.

50 Marked alternative is by uc roads from Sibford Heath to Whatcote past Compton Wynyates House.

51 From Grafton Flyford, follow uc roads through Huddington, to cross rly and Worcester and Birmingham Canal at Dunhampstead, GR 918 600. First L then R under M5, L after M5 on uc roads to cross A38 via Ladywood to join A4133 at Hadley.

52 Leave Ludlow on A4117, Cleobury Mortimer road, L immediately after rly br N on uc road, forking L and R through Stanton Lacy.

53 Tour B – Circuit of the New Welsh Lakes – joins at Church Stretton.

13

High adventure

Mountains and 'rough-stuff'

We now move on to some more ambitious riding in hilly and mountainous country, in the form of sample circular tours encompassing in
some cases rough tracks. The use of the 1 : 50 000 map is essential here,
and where necessary detailed grid references of turning-off points are
given.

In most cases any track recommended is ridable throughout:
certainly the major part of every one is; but there may be parts where
you have to wheel the bicycle, either because of gradient or surface.
Conditions will vary with the weather: streams in particular may
fluctuate from near dryness to torrents – in mountain areas almost
within a few minutes.

Fords and watersplashes seem to have a fascination for many cycle-
tourists but what is happy-go-lucky amusement under some conditions
needs care in others. As with all travel off the beaten track, risks which
are trivial within easy reach of civilisation, assistance, warmth and
dryness are not quite the same when you are in a very remote place.
Fords on metalled roads are usually ridable – and are often bypassed
by a footbridge over which you can wheel a bicycle. (Many are quite
slippery, however, and a ford with a green, slimy bottom can confer
similar properties on the uncautious cyclist.) Try to avoid having to
steer out of a straight line when passing through a ford and, if possible,
reconnoitre beforehand the shallowest, smoothest or firmest line to
follow. Try to avoid getting anything but the wheels and tyres under
water. Pedal bearings are particularly vulnerable and at their lowest
point are only about 10cm (4in) above the ground. If you do get water

Cycle tourists seem to find fords fascinating but in remote places they should
be treated with respect.

in them, lay the bicycle on its side to let the water drain out and lubricate with a thickish oil as soon as possible. If the ford is deeper than a very few inches, the safest course is to wade through – preferably minus socks (and shoes if there are no sharp stones) – and wheel or carry the bicycle. Many mountain streams are crossable by stepping from boulder to boulder in the manner of stepping stones.

I have tried as far as possible to avoid describing rough tracks or paths which involve any large degree of carrying the machine. For me at least, that's one of the points where enjoying cycling ends! Nevertheless, riders' abilities differ and some may prefer not to ride stretches that others would: without wishing to be a sobersided killjoy, I cannot overemphasise that prudence must come first. A buckled unridable wheel is expensive but no more than a nuisance a couple of miles from home: fifteen miles from civilisation on a mountain track, in deteriorating weather, it could be a disaster! It should go without saying that fragile and extra-light equipment is *not* suitable for this type of cycling.

When wheeling a bicycle over a rocky section take care to avoid hitting any vulnerable part, particularly gear mechanism, cranks, pedals or outer chainring, against rocks or stones. It is only too easy to wheel the machine over 15cm (6in) rock steps without being aware that those same steps are bouncing on the chainring. Some 'roughstuffers' avoid the possibility of damaging cranks, toeclips and pedals, if they expect to wheel the bicycle for any appreciable distance, by passing the left toestrap round the left chainstay – assuming a freewheel is fitted. The bicycle cannot be manoeuvred backwards when the crank is fixed.

Keep riding as far as possible if you are confronted by a muddy patch – using very low gears – but always keep an eye open for a dry spot to put your foot down if you are forced to a halt. Some surfaces – chalk is the worst – can become unbelievably slippery when wet: it's nearly always better to stay on the grass as far as you can.

Never overestimate your ability in this sort of country, particularly if you want to enjoy the experience. Daily mileages on roads are likely to be low and even more restricted when you take to unmetalled tracks. As a guide and example, the track from the Caban Côch reservoir following the Claerwen (part of the 'Circuit of the new Welsh lakes' tour) took us – a group of six experienced riders – about 4½ hours for the 16km (10 miles) from metalled road to metalled road. This included an hour's picnic lunch stop, a factor you should include in your calculations. About 40 miles (say 65km) covered mainly on metalled roads is a reasonable day's total for a moderately fit experienced rider in a tough area. You can always follow an interesting-looking detour at the end of the day if you have time on your hands.

Otherwise, the rules of riding on mountain roads and rough tracks and paths are those of common sense. In many cases, these routes (some of them roads of great antiquity) are the only ways of penetrating a particular piece of country, and the rewards can be great.

Six sample tours

The six sample tours that follow cover a mixture of popular and less well known areas of Britain. The Welsh and Yorkshire tours cover appreciable distances on 'rough-stuff' and for these parts at least the use on the ground of the 1:50 000 map is essential. The Cornish tour, although possible to follow on 'Barts' should preferably be checked against the OS map because of the complication of the maze of very small roads near, for example, Falmouth. Ironically, in the tougher and more remote countryside of the other tours, the lack of alternative routes allows you to get by with a less detailed map – although there are off-the-road points of interest shown on the larger-scale version.

The routes are specified as a series of place names, road types and directions with the *straight line* distance and direction from the previously specified point clearly given in the form 'NW 5km'. I have quoted distances in metric measurements throughout since the OS 1:50 000 map is marked with a 1km grid and the 1:250 000 with a 10km grid, while at the Bartholomew 1:100 000 scale you can conveniently use, say, a 15cm (6in) rule, since here 1cm represents 1km.* Since these routes are often circuitous, the actual riding distances are likely to be very much greater than the straight-line distances quoted. All the sketch maps are roughly to this scale.

* For the record and the Imperially minded, 1 mile = 1·6093km – in practical terms you can say 4km = 2½ miles, 5km = 3 miles, 8km = 5 miles, 10km = 6 miles.

TOUR A – CORNWALL

This tour uses OS sheets 191, 190, 200, 201, 203, 204. It may also be *followed* without too much difficulty on Bartholomew 1 and 2 provided the details have first been compared with the OS map. It is best enjoyed outside the main holiday months.

Leave LAUNCESTON N on A388, then L at church GR 328 852 on uc roads to Egloskerry, WNW 6km.

L in Egloskerry past Tresmeer to Three Hammers, GR 228 877. R on uc roads through Trelash by Otterham to Marshgate, junction with A39, WNW 13½km. SO on A39 for 1km, then L through Tresparrett and Hennett to junction with B3263. L on B3263 through Boscastle and Tintagel to Tregatta, WSW 11km. R on steep uc roads to join B3314; SW on B3314 for 5km to Pendoggett, L on uc roads via St Kew and Chapel Amble to Gutt Bridge, SW 14½km. L on B3314, then R on A39 to Wadebridge, SSE 3km.

Immediately after level crossing (disused) L on uc roads via Burlawn to Rosenannon, GR 955 660, R and L to join B3274 at Tremayne. L on B3274, first L on uc road to join A39 into St Columb Major, SW 12km.

At S end of town SO on uc road between A3059 and A39 to White Cross on A392. SO on uc roads crossing A3058 to Newlyn East, SW 11km.

R on uc roads crossing A3075 (R and L), first L to join B3285 to Perranporth. S on B3284, fork R after 4½km on uc road to join A3075, R on A3075 to cross A30 (necessary to walk because of odd layout of junction), SW 11½km.

Uc road SE to join B3277, immediately R on uc roads to cross A390, R and L, to Bissoe, SO 1km to junction just before viaduct GR 784 409, SSE 7km.

R across river and by complex of uc roads to junction with A39 at Perran Wharf. L on A39 and first R to Mylor Br, SSE 5km.

Cross bridge over Mylor Creek and *either* L to Flushing Ferry

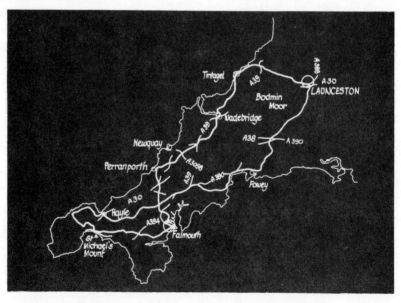

170

(summer service only) *or* R to bridge at Penryn and L through Falmouth to Pendennis Point, one-way circuit round castle, SSE 5km.

Leave W along shore road then follow choice of uc roads to Constantine, just S of W, 10km.

Leave village W to cross B3291 on uc roads through Trelothquithack, fork R to cross A394 to Wendron, WNW 5½km.

L on B3297, fork R through Coverack Bridges to Crowntown. L on B3303, first R to B3302, R on B3302 and second L to Godolphin Cross, W 7km.

SO on uc roads to join B3280 near Goldsithney, then A394 to Marazion, W 9km.

Leave Marazion N on uc road bearing L to cross A30, then B3309 through Ludgvan to junction with B3311. L on B3311 to Badger's Cross, GR 486 332, NW 4km.

R on uc roads to Treen, R on B3306 to Zennor, NW 6km.

SO on B3306 (several possible out-and-home detours from B3306 to coast) to junction with B3311, R on B3311 for 2km, then L on uc roads to Lelant Downs, L to junction with A3074, ESE 9km.

R on A3074, bear L to join A30 across creek into Hayle. R after first rly bridge on B3302 to Leedstown, L on B3280 through Praze-an-Beeble to Blackrock, E 9km.

L on B3280, then B3297 to Four Lanes, NE 5km.

R on uc roads through Penhalurick and Trethellan Water to cross A393 (R and L) through Frogpool to Bissoe, ENE 9km.

R and fork L to Truro, NE 6km.

Leave Truro Cathedral E to roundabout on A39. SO on uc road to rejoin A39 to Tresillian. Continue on A39, then A390 to Probus, ENE 8km.

R on uc roads to cross River Fal at Golden Mill. SO where road becomes gated track for ¾km. R at metalled road, L on B3287 to Fair Cross Stone, GR 955 474, E 5¼km.

R on B3287 then SO on uc roads to Pentewan, E 6km.

R across bridge, up steep hill to crossroads at GR 028 514, R to Charlestown, L and first R to join A3082, R on A3082 to Par, NE 9km.

R on A3082, fork L on B3269 to Bodinnick Ferry (possible detour to Fowey). L after ferry on uc roads through Lanteglos Highway to Pelynt, E 13km.

R on B3359, L after 300m on uc roads via Sowden's Bridge and Tredinnick to join B3254 through Duloe to fork with uc road at Polvean Cross, GR 233 588, NE 6km.

Fork L on uc roads to cross A38 at Dobwalls, SO on uc roads by Common Moor and Minions to Upton Cross, NNE 14km.

SO across B3254 on uc roads through Rilla Mill and Trebullett to LAUNCESTON; NNE 13km.

TOUR B – CIRCUIT OF THE NEW WELSH LAKES

This tour uses OS sheets 137, 136, 135, 147, 160, 148.

For following the tracks on this tour a map of at least 1:50 000 scale is essential. Villages and shops are rare in parts: keep well stocked with food.

It is convenient, although not essential, to begin this tour at CHURCH STRETTON, Salop, on routes 1 – Bath to Chester and 12 – London (Heathrow) to Church Stretton.

Leave CHURCH STRETTON W on uc road up Burway Hill, forking right at the top of the Long Mynd to Ratlinghope and Bridges, WNW 6½km.

L over River East Onny and R on gated road, forking L over the Stiperstones through Shelve to junction with A488, WNW 7km.

L on A488 for 2km then R on uc

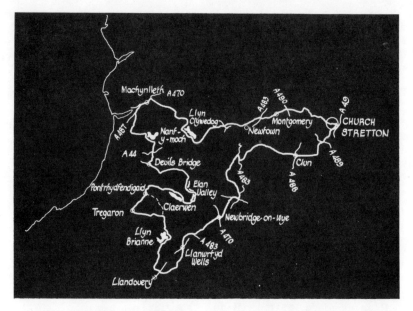

road at GR 319 979 through Priest-weston to Chirbury; R on A490 for 300m, then L on B4386 to Montgomery, WSW 11km.

R on B4385, L on B4385 at N end of town to join B4386 to A483 at Abermule, GR 163 951, WSW 6km.

SO on A483 for 2km, then R on B4389 over River Severn and Shropshire Union Canal to junction with B4568, L on B4568 along N side of River Severn to junction with B4569 at GR 038 932, WSW 13km. L on B4569, SO across A489 at Caersws to Trefeglwys; SO on B4569 to fork at Cerist, GR 963 882 (*not* fork at 963 885 to Van), SW 9km.

R on uc road to B4518, R on B4518, first L on uc road past Clywedog dam (GR 910 870) on very up-and-down road round W side of Llyn Clywedog to T-junction in forest at GR 867 893, just N of W, 9½km.

R through forest (L turn is attractive route back to Llanidloes) to rejoin B4518 at Staylittle; L on B4518 for 1½km, to junction at GR 883 938, NNE 5km.

L through Dylife on old coach road to Machynlleth, WNW 15km.

L on A470, L on A487 to Ysgubor-y-coed, SW 8½km.

L on uc road and after 600m at GR 687 947, very sharp R on gated road through Llwyn-gwyn. At Gwdr-cwm, GR 674 917, bear L to join Talybont road at SH 133m, GR 678 902, just W of S 5km.

L via forest and Nant-y-moch Reservoir to Ponterwyd, SSE 11½km.

Leave Ponterwyd S on A4120 to Devils Bridge. L on B4574 to Cwmystwyth, SSE 8km.

SO on old coach road to Pont-ar-Elan, GR 904 716, SSE 11km.

(Road works and new reservoir in prospect on this road: if road blocked L at Blaenycwm, GR 826 756 on track to Llangurig, then S on minor road on W side of River Wye to Rhayader, R on B4518 to bridge between Carreg Ddu and Caban Côch reservoirs, GR 910 639.)

R past reservoirs to bridge between Carreg Ddu and Caban Côch reservoirs, GR 910 639, S 8km

from Pont-ar-Elan.
Cross bridge and follow road on N side of Caban Côch reservoir to E side of Claerwen dam, GR 871 636, W 4km.

SO as road becomes track following N shore of Claerwen reservoir, crossing Afon Claerwen (footbridge) and Afon Claerddu (stepping stones) to rejoin metalled road at GR 794 680. SO on road N of 'Teifi Pools' (Llynau Egnant, Hir, Teifi) to Ffair Rhos, WNW 14 km.

L on B4343 to Pontrhydfendigaid. There are now two possible routes to the Towy valley, one rough and quite time-consuming, the other longer and hilly but metalled.

1 *rough* L at Pontrhydfendigaid through Strata Florida. Road becomes track – mostly ridable – at GR 755 646, but with many fords, depth depending on season; multiplicity of forest roads can be confusing at one or two points. Joins metalled road at GR 804 568, SE 13km from Ffair Rhos.

2 *metalled, hilly* SO on B4343 to Tregaron, L on uc road via steep climbs and descents to GR 804 568, where track from Strata Florida. joins, SE 13km from Ffair Rhos.

SE for 1km on metalled road to SH 351m, at GR 812 563, R on track which becomes metalled road after 3km, following E shore of Llyn Brianne to Rhandirmwyn, just W of S 13km.

SO for 5km to GR 771 399, L on uc road to A483 at Cynghordy, SSE 4½km.

R on A483, first L on uc road to Tirabad, L to Llangammarch Wells, ENE 14½km.

L over River Irfon to Cefn Glancamddwr, R to join A483 to Beulah, R on B4358 to Newbridge-on-Wye, NE 14km.

SO across A470 to rejoin B4358, then A4081 to Llanyre, GR 043 622. L on uc roads to A44 at SH 192m, GR 077 654. R on A44 to Crossgates, NE 10km.

L on A483 for 2¼km, then L on uc road through Abbeycwmhir, then R to Bwlch-y-Sarnau, GR 030 747, NW 11½km.

SO to rejoin A483 at GR 086 824, R on A483 for 1¼km, L on uc roads to join B4355 at GR 120 827, NE 12km.

R on B4355 for 4 km, then L on uc road to join B4368, R on B4368 to Anchor Inn, ENE 6km.

SO on B4368 to Clun, ESE 13km.

L on A488, R after 200m on B4368 through Clunton to Ashton-on-Clun, E 9km.

L on uc roads through Hopesay to A489 at Horderley. L on A489 for 300m, R on B4370 to Cwm Head, NNE 8km.

L on uc roads through Minton and to Little Stretton, where join B4370 to CHURCH STRETTON, NNE 5½km.

TOUR C – WHITE AND RED ROSES

This tour uses OS sheets 105, 104, 103, 97, 98, 99, 90, 91, 92 and may be followed without too much difficulty on Bartholomew 33, 32, 31, 35, 36.

Leave YORK NW on A59, fork L at GR 587 514 on B1224 through Acomb and Rufforth to Long Marston, W 10km.

R on uc roads through Tockwith and Cowthorpe to A1 at Ox Close Ho, just N of W 9½km.

Cross A1 (R and L) on uc road to junction with B6164, L to North Deighton, R to Spofforth on A661. R on uc road at S end of village keeping R to Follifoot, W 6km.

L on uc road to Spacey Houses, cross A61 through Pannal, L and L through Daw Cross to Bunkers Hill, R to junction with B6161, just S of W 9km.

L on B6161 through Leathley to Leathley Br, R on uc road across River Washburn to join B6451 to GR 200 460, SW 7½km.

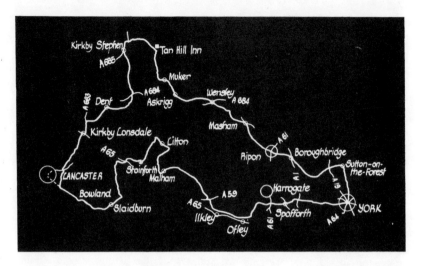

R on uc road and first L by Weston, Askwith and Nesfield on N side of River Wharfe to junction with A59 near Beamsley, NNW 14km.

Either R on A59 for 1½km then L on uc road *or* L on A59, R on B6160, both routes meeting at Barden Br, NNW 5km.

NW on B6160 through Burnsall and Threshfield to fork at NW end of village at GR 988 638, NW 9km.

Fork L on uc road which becomes grassy track at GR 947 655. SO on track to junction with Mastiles Lane, L to GR 930 655. Fork L by Goredale Bridge to Malham, W 9km.

R at W end of village by Malham Cove, to W of Malham Tarn on moorland road to Arncliffe, NNE 9½km.

L up Littondale through Litton to Halton Gill, L over pass (436m) to Stainforth, WSW 12km.

R on B6479 and L after 200m over Stainforth Bridge by Stainforth Force. R at T-junction to Swarth Moor, L at T-junction through Austwick to junction with A65 at Harden Bridge, W 6km.

L on A65 and immediately R on uc roads to cross roads at SH 176m,

GR 726 666. L over Bowland Knotts (summit about 420m) to B6478. R on B6478 to Slaidburn, S 14km. (*Crosses Route 7 – Chester to Carlisle*)

SO on B6478 to Newton, R on uc road to Dunsop Br, R over Trough of Bowland; by Lee Bridge to cross-roads at GR 520 590, WNW 20km. (SO to LANCASTER NW 5km if desired)

R on uc road through Quernmore to junction with A683 at Caton, L on A683 for 400m, first R on uc roads through Halton Green to junction at GR 515 659, 7km.

R on uc road to join B6254 through Arkholme and Whittington to Kirkby Lonsdale, NE 16km.

R on A65 over River Lune, first L on A683 through Casterton, to GR 624 804. Fork R on uc road to Barbon, NNE 4½km.

R on uc road up Barbondale to Gawthrop, R into Dent, NE 10½km.

Leave Dent E (choice of two roads) to Lea Yeat, L up very steep hill over fell road to Garsdale Head, junction with A684, ENE 9½km.

R on A683 to Moorcock Inn (burnt down and closed at time of writing), L on B6259 to Kirkby Stephen, NNE

174

20km.

R on A685 for 1km, R on uc roads through Winton and Oxenthwaite to Barras, ENE 8km.

R on fell road to Tan Hill Inn (highest inn in England, about 520m) GR 896 067, SE 7½km.

R down West Stones Dale to B6270, S 5km.

L on B6270 through Keld, Thwaite and Muker to SH 258m, GR 925 975. R up very steep pitch over Askrigg Common (summit 498m) to Askrigg, SE 12km.

L and L through Carperby to Redmire and Wensley, junction with A684, E 14½km.

R on A6108 for ¾km over River Ure, first L on uc roads to Coverham, L to East Witton, SE 6½km.

SO on A6108 past Jervaulx Abbey, R at SW end of park, where A6108 bears L, past Ellingstring and through Fearby to Masham. R on A6108 and second R to Grewelthorpe, SE 13km.

L (choice of uc roads) to Ripon, SE 10km.

Leave Ripon E on B6265 through Boroughbridge to SH 28m, GR 431 626, SE 14½km.

L through Great Ouseburn, cross River Ouse at Aldwark to Tollerton, L to cross A19 to Huby and Sutton-on-the-Forest, just N of E, 15½km.

R on B1363 to YORK, SSE 13km.

TOUR D – BORDER AND THE WALL

This route uses OS sheets 85, 86, 87, 79, 80, 81, 91, 92 or Bartholomew 38, 41, 42, 39, 35, 34. In the latter case it is desirable to check the status of 'white' roads against the OS map.

Most of the first part of this tour passes through very sparsely populated countryside with few villages – buy food when you can rather than run out!

Leave CARLISLE N on A6, then

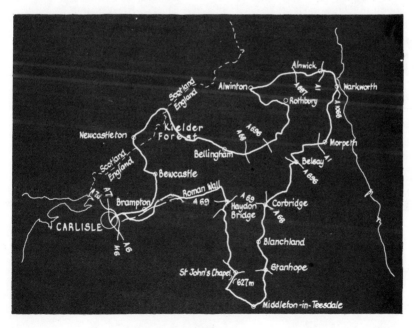

175

R after crossing River Eden on B6264 to Brampton, ENE 12km.

SO on A69 for 1km, then L on uc roads via Bridge End, Lanercost and Banks to junction with B6318 at GR 550 675, NNE 7km.

SO on uc road to Bewcastle, L to junction with B6318 for 300m, then SO on uc road, where B6318 bears L, through Blackpool Gate, and Kershope Forest to Newcastleton, NNW 21km.

R on B6357 to Saughtree, NE 13km.

R on uc road through Kielder Forest to junction at GR 721 869, just short of Stannersburn, SE 19km. (There may be road alterations in this area caused by reservoir construction.)

L to Falstone, R through Lanehead to Bellingham, ESE 13½km.

SO on B6320 then R in Bellingham village on uc road through Redesmouth, cross A68 at GR 908 819, SO on uc road to cross A696 at Knowesgate, SO on uc road to junction with B6342, 2km N of Cambo, just N of E 19km.

L on B6342 to junction at GR 060 977, NNE 10km.

SO on uc road where B6342 bears R, to Gt Tosson, L through Allerdene and Lt Tosson to join B6341 for ¾km, R on uc road through Holystone and Harbottle to Alwinton Bridge, WNW 16km.

R through Netherton and Whittingham to junction with A697, ENE 17½km.

SO on uc roads to join B6341 to Alnwick, E 10km.

Leave Alnwick S on old A1 then fork L on A1068 through Hipsburn to Warkworth, SE 9km. (alternative uc roads)

Leave Warkworth S on A1068, then after ¼km SO on uc road where A1068 bears L, by Morwick Hall to Acklington. R on B6345 to junction at GR 205 996, SSW 8km.

L on uc road through Chevington Moor to Ulgham, R on B1337 through

Longhirst to Morpeth, S 13km.

Leave Morpeth W on B6343 to Dyke Neuk, W 8km.

L on uc roads through Meldon, R and R to Bolam, L and L to junction at GR 098 795, SSW 6½km.

R on uc road to cross A696 obliquely onto B6309 through Stamfordham. SO across B6318, still on B6309 to junction at GR 059 675, SSW 12½km.

SO on uc road to join B6321 to Corbridge, cross River Tyne and follow uc road S up Prospect Hill, then via uc roads to Slaley, junction with B6306, SW 13km.

L on B6306 to Blanchland, S 7½km.

SO on uc road over River Derwent, bear L over Edmundbyers Common to join B6278, to Stanhope, SSE 11km.

R then fork L over River Wear, still on B6278 over Bollihope Common to junction at GR 992 288, S 10km.

R on uc road to Middleton-in-Teesdale, R on B6271 to junction at GR 849 317, NNW 14½km.

R over Harthope Moor (equal highest road in England, 627m) to St John's Chapel, L on A689 to junction with B6295, N 9km.

R on B6295 through Allenheads and Allendale Town, N 20km.

Keep R over Dryburn Moor to junction with B6303 at Thornley Gate, SO on B6303 to Langley, junction with A686, N 13km.

R on A686, L on A6078 to cross River South Tyne at Haydon Bridge. SO past church on uc road to junction with B6318, N 9km.

L on B6318 (optional out-and-home detours to N to Hadrian's Wall) to Greenhead (road busy in summer), WSW 17km.

R on A69, R after 200m on B6318 through Gilsland to Kiln Hill, WNW 4½km.

L on uc road along line of Hadrian's Wall to Banks. L to Lanercost, L up hill after Lanercost Bridge to cross A69 to Beck, junction with A689, SW 8km.

SO on A689, R after 300m on uc roads through Kirkhouse Farlam, and Talkin to Warwick Bridge, junction with A69, WSW 9½km.

SO across A69 to Newby East, L to Low Crosby, L on B6264 to CARLISLE, W 8km.

TOUR E - ARGYLL AND THE TROSSACHS

This tour uses OS sheets 57, 56, 55, 63, 62, or Bartholomew 45, 44, 47, 48.

Leave STIRLING SW on uc road crossing M9 at GR 784 921 through North Third to junction with B818, R on B818 to Fintry, SSW 20km.

SO on B818, then R on uc roads to Balfron (cross A875), Balfron Stn (cross A81) to join A811 to Drymen, just N of W, 14km.

R on B837, becoming uc road along E shore of Loch Lomond to Rowardennan Pier, NW 15km.

Take ferry (every day in season, otherwise weekends) to Inverbeg.

Cross A82 on uc road up Glen Douglas to join A814, W 10km.

R on A814 to Arrochar, L on A83 to Rest and be thankful, NW 8km.

L on B828, R on B839 to A815, L on A815 to Strachur, WSW 15km.

R on A886 for 6km, then R on B8000 to Otter Ferry, SW 24km.

L on B8000, fork L after 1km to join A886, R on A886, L B836 to join A815, E 22km. (*Alternatively*, continue on B8000 to Millhouse, SO on uc roads via Ardlamont Point to Tighnabruaich, return on A8003, B836 and A815 to Strachur.)

L on A815 to Strachur, WNW 20km.

R on A815 to Glen Kinglas, L on A83 to Inveraray, N 8km.

R on A819 to Cladich, N 14km.

L on B840 to Ford, SW 30km.

R on uc road on NW shore of Loch Awe to Barnaline Lodge, NE 15km.

L on uc road just after River Avich bridge to Kilmelford, W 13km.

R on A816 to Cleigh, just E of N 13km.

R on uc road (or continue on A816 if it is desired to visit Oban, in which case leave Oban E on uc

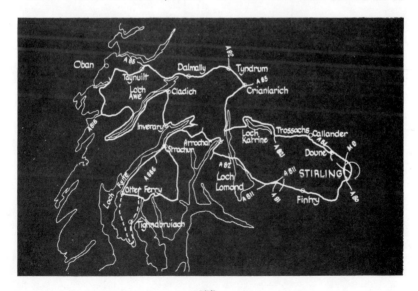

road past golf course) to junction at GR 890 292, R on uc road through Glen Lonan to Taynuilt, ENE 14km.

R on A85 through Dalmally to Tyndrum, E 33km.

R on A82 through Crianlarich to Inveruglas, S 22km.

Take ferry (seasonal service) across Loch Lomond to Inversnaid. Follow uc road to Stronalachar. *Either* R on B829 to Aberfoyle, then L on A821 over Dukes Pass to Trossachs Hotel *or* L to follow the metalled track round Loch Katrine to Trossachs Hotel *or* take ferry (seasonal) down Loch Katrine to Trossachs Pier. Trossachs Pier is 16km E of Inversnaid, Trossachs Hotel 18km. Follow A821 through Brig o' Turk, R on A892, R on A81 over Braes of Greenock, just S of E 12½km.

SO on B822 and left after 200m on B8032 to join A84 to Doune, ESE 10km.

R on A820, then after 1½km R on B824 to junction with A9/M9. SO on A9 at roundabout for 2km, then R in Bridge of Allan on B823 to STIRLING, SE 11km.

TOUR F – NORTH-WEST HIGHLANDS

This tour uses OS sheets 15, 16, 19, 20, 21, 24, 25, 26, 32, 33, 34, 35, 40, 41 or Bartholomew 55, 59, 58, 54, 50, 51.

Leave INVERNESS N on B9161 to take ferry across Beauly Firth to North Kessock, then follow B9162 to Tore, NW 9km.

L on A832 then fork R after 100m on B9162 to join A9 at Conon Bridge, R on A9 to Dingwall, NW 8½km.

Follow A9 through town and 200m after level crossing L on uc road to T-junction, R on uc road parallel to A9 to rejoin A9 at Evanton to junction with A836, NE 14km. (Note: roadworks projected in this area will eventually provide direct link to this junction from Inverness)

Fork L on A836 to rejoin A9 at Fearn Lodge, N 20km.

L on A9 to Bonar Bridge Stn. L on A837 up Strath Oykell to junction with A835 at Ledmore, NW 49km.

R on A837 through Inchnadamph, R at Skiag Bridge on A894 to junction with B869, NNW 20km.

L on B869 on very up-and-down road through Drumbeg and Stoer to rejoin A837 near Lochinver, W 13½km.

R on A837 through Lochinver and at S end of village SO on uc road through Strathan and Inverkirkaig to junction at GR 063 113, SSW 13km.

L on uc road to join A835 at Drumrunie, R on A835 to Ullapool, SSW 19km.

Continue on A835 to junction with A832, R on A832 to Dundonnell, S 8½km.

(Seasonal Monday-Saturday ferry operates across Loch Broom to join uc road to Dundonnell: enquire at Tourist Information Office in Ullapool.)

Continue on A832 by Gruinard Bay and Aultbea to Poolewe, just S of W 27km.

Continue on A832 beside Loch Maree to Kinlochewe SSE 26km.

R on A896 to Shieldaig, WSW 23km.

1km S of Shieldaig, R on uc road via coast to Applecross, L to summit of Bealach-na-Ba, 626m (2054ft), SSW 12km.

Descend pass to Tornapress, R on A896 to Lochcarron, E 14km.

L still on A896 to junction with A890. R over new bridge on A890 to Achmore, SSW 7½km.

R after bridge on uc roads through Duirinish to Kyle of Lochalsh, SSW 12km.

Cross ferry to Kyleakin on Skye. Continue on A850 through Breakish to junction with A851, L on A851 to Armadale (optional detour NW to Tokavaig), SW 25km.

(Note: this is just a lightning visit

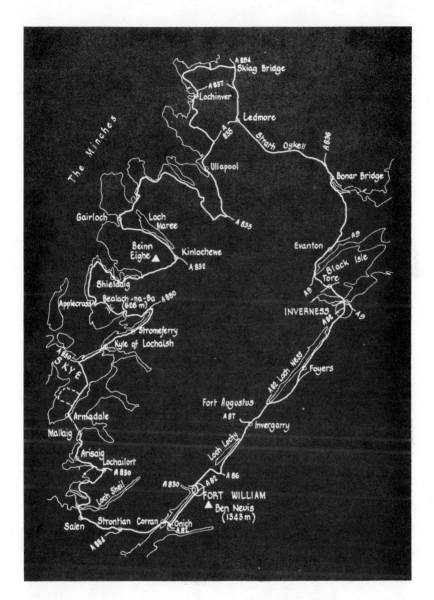

to Skye. There are many more very rewarding roads further N and W on the island.)

Take ferry from Armadale to Mallaig (seasonal service, Monday to Saturday) SSE 9km.

Follow A830 S to Arisaig and then E to Lochailort, SE 18km.

R on A861 through Kinlochmoidart to Salen, SSW 15km.

L on A861 through Strontian to Ardgour, E 34km.

Take ferry to Corran, L on A82 to FORT WILLIAM, NE 14km.

(To return to INVERNESS take A82, then L on A830 towards Corpach, R on B8004 to Commando Memorial, L on A82 to Fort Augus-tus, R on A862 to Whitebridge, L on B852 through Foyers to Dores, L on A862 to Inverness (or follow upper 'General Wade's Military Road' (uc) from Inverfarigaig, on shore of Loch Ness 4km beyond Foyers, to Inverness.) Inverness is 91km (straight line distance) NE of Fort William.

Some (mainly) ridable tracks

This short listing of off-the-road routes is given so that you can incorporate them in any tour you may be making. The full Grid Reference (incorporating the 100km square Grid Letters) of start and finishing points is given, together with any salient intermediate ones. The state of repair of these roads is constantly changing, and parts may even be being metalled as I write. Most are passable at most seasons. Not all are 'high' adventure in the sense of being a long way above sea level: a sprinkling of lowland routes is included, which tend to be muddier in very wet weather or to set hard into ridges in very dry, particularly if used by horses. The tracks here are grouped by area and are listed in order of their grid reference with the number(s) of the OS sheet(s) on which they appear; distances are approximate actual lengths. More detailed information on rough-stuff routes is disseminated by the Rough-Stuff Fellowship and the Touring Department of the CTC, which keeps a continuously-revised register of the surface condition of a number of bridleways (information available to members): see Appendix 1.

Southern England

ST 181 338 to ST 149 378, then either to ST 110 417 (Stape) or ST 155 410 (Holford); also from 110 417 to 155 410 (Stape to Holford) (OS sheet 181, Quantock Hills) Ridge track with varying surface, ridable in general, commanding views E, W and N; total SE-NW 12km.

ST 933 240 to SU 134 283 (OS sheet 184, Salisbury) Chalk-based Salisbury Downs ridge track, best spring and autumn; can be taken in sections, as it crosses metalled uc roads at 964 250, 003 267, 082 287 and 093 285; total 27km.

SU 118 681 (near Marlborough, OS sheet 173) to SU 589 815 (Goring, OS sheet 174) The Ridgeway, an extremely ancient chalk-based track along the western and northern ridge of the Wiltshire and Berkshire Downs. Surface varies with use and the season but most is ridable, if rather muddy after prolonged wet. As with most chalk tracks it is probably best during a dry spell after a wet one: the surface is then firm without being set into concrete-hard ridges. This route can be taken in sections, since it crosses eleven metalled roads including A419, B4000, B4001, A338, B4494, A34. There are various alternatives at the W and E ends, where the route departs a little from the true Ridgeway. Total length about 67km (17km on OS 173, 50 on OS 174) including about 9km of metalled stretches near Swindon. A detailed guide to the track is *The Oldest Road* by J. R. L. Anderson and Fay Godwin, Wildwood House, London, 1975; ISBN 0 7045 0167 8 (hardback) or 0 7045 0168 6 (paperback).

SU 179 129 to SU 232 142 (OS sheet 196, New Forest) Compacted gravel heathland and forest road with broad views on the open parts; 6km.

SZ 350 858 to SZ 458 837 (OS sheet 197, Isle of Wight) Grassy ridge track, chalk-based – ridability as other chalk-based tracks. Can be taken in sections as it crosses B3399 at 395 851 and uc road at 420 845; total 14km.

Wales

SH 657 134 to SH 610 060 (OS sheet 124, Dolgellau) Steep grass track up over shoulder of Cader Idris, ridable grass and stony track going down in direction quoted; 10km.

SJ 052 405 to SJ 136 347 (OS sheet 125, Berwyns) The 'Wayfarer' track, so known to cyclists because the memorial tablet to cycling writer W. M. Robinson, pen-name Wayfarer, is let into the

rock at the top. This track was one of his favourites. A little muddy in wet on NW side but generally ridable, boggy patches on SE side, best done in direction quoted; 12km.

SJ 043 385 to SJ 118 308 (OS sheet 125, Berwyns) Bwlch-maen-Gwynedd; indistinct in places on ascent – aim to right of stone circle – with tendency to boggy patches; 15km.

SN 925 184 to SN 988 275 (OS sheet 160, Brecon Beacons) Hill track, muddy in parts; 11km.

SO 034 174 to SO 040 246 (OS sheet 160, Brecon Beacons) Roman road, grassy track on S part, stony on N; 8km.

SO 186 289 or SO 191 270 to SO 204 286 then to SO 230 248 (OS sheet 161. Black Mountains) Bwlch Rhiw Trumau and Grwyne Fechan valley; Steep pull up from W side by either route, slippery in wet, superb descent to SE, best done in direction quoted; 7 to 8km.

SO 194 592 to SO 147 657 (OS sheet 148, Radnor Forest) Surface varies from compacted gravel to grass, extensive views to W, detour to waterfall Water-break-its-neck; 10km.

SO 250 288 to SO 188 334 (OS sheet 161, Black Mountains) Grwyne Fawr valley; grass track becoming indistinct near summit, cairn indicates position, mostly ridable. Descent to NW is stony down side of gully, sticky at the bottom; 9km.

A book covering some Welsh tracks, not from the cyclist's viewpoint but detailing some cyclable routes, is *The Drovers' Roads of*

Wales by Fay Godwin and Shirley Toulson, Wildwood House, London, 1977; ISBN 0 7045 0251 8.

Peak District

SK 227 842 to SK 202 873 (OS sheet 110) Stanage Edge Roman road; Steady climb from W along clearly defined track, paved track to Redmires reservoirs, becoming road to 268 858, then L along wooded track to A57; 8km, including reservoir road.

SK 183 825 or SK 203 827 to SK 198 798 (OS sheets 110, 119) Climb S from Hope Valley; compacted stony track ridable but steep, both routes meet at 190 802; 5km.

SK 263 806 to SK 262 830 (OS sheet 110) Burbage Rocks; grassy track, easily ridable, 2½km.

SK 261 747 to SK 254 776 (OS sheet 119) Curbar Edge and Froggatt Edge; sandy ridge track, easily ridable; 3½km.

SK 003 682 to SK 018 680 (OS sheet 119, Buxton) Short but attractive track passing Three Shire Heads, the meeting point of Cheshire, Staffordshire and Derbyshire, at 009 686. Ridable stone-based track; 3½km.

In addition some of the disused railway lines in the Peak District and part of the Cromford Canal towpath have been made into 'trails', most of which are available to cyclists: details from the National Park Information Centre, Aldern House, Bakewell, Derbyshire.

Not a rough route and a little south of the Peak District, it is worth

I have tried to avoid describing routes which involve too much carrying of the bicycle.

noting that the following is cyclable:

SK 522 097 to SK 543 114 (OS sheets 129, 140, Leicester) Metalled road through Bradgate Deer Park, closed to motor traffic and hence an ideal route for teaching very young children – to say nothing of the attraction of the deer and peacocks. Car park at W end by Newton Linford church; about 3km total.

Pennines

SD 903 657 to SD 885 675 (OS sheet 98, Craven) Track round N side of Malham Tarn; compacted stony surface, easily ridable; 3½km.

SD 903 657 to SD 975 678 (OS sheet 98, Craven) Mastiles Lane; mainly grassy track with one ford, fairly well drained, easily ridable; 8km.

SD 598 661 to SD 685 561 (OS sheet 97 and 103, Bowland) Salter Fell; begins – starting from NW as specified – as metalled farm road, tarmac ends at GR 603 632; rough concrete begins at 685 561 and lasts about 2km before tarmac road begins; rough stretch is about 10km total.

SD 925 895 to SD 863 853 (OS sheet 98, Wensleydale) Roman road from Bainbridge to summit of Fleet Moss; compacted stone road in lower NE part, grassy on solid rock at top end; generally ridable; 9km.

NY 693 248 to NY 853 312 (OS sheet 91, Appleby) High Cup Nick pass; one of the classic rough-stuff passes, but quite strenuous – allow about 5 hours and do not attempt it alone or in mist. Description is from W (Dufton) to E (Langdon Beck); this direction is easiest to follow, the opposite leaves the surprise opening up of the tremendous cleft of the 'Nick' to the end. Fairly ill-defined on descent with fords. From W tough climb up obvious path on N edge of Nick. Choice of L (i.e. N) or R bank of Maize Beck on descent. Footbridge at 749 270 tempts you to cross Beck but several deep sikes or peat hags on N bank; S bank is probably better. Tricky and, depending on weather, muddy descent past Moss Shop Mine. (Cauldron Snout waterfall not quite on route but, when water – now controlled by Cow Green dam – is high, is worth detour.) Easy from Birkdale to start of tarmac road.

Scotland (Southern and Central)

NN 938 387 to NN 987 341 (OS sheet 52, Loch Tay) Glen Shee track; 9km.

NT 102 628 to NT 126 548 (OS sheet 65, West Lothian) Old Drove Road from West Linton to Little Vantage; total unmetalled about 7km.

NT 688 629 to NT 698 722 (OS sheet 67, Duns and Dunbar) Lammermuir Hills crossing from Cranshaws to Elmscleugh; 13km.

NT 508 534 to NT 544 653 (OS sheet 66, East Lothian) Lammer Law crossing from Carfraemill to Longyester; 16km including 6km metalled at SW end.

14

Winter and night riding

Riding at night and in the winter have quite a lot in common: for one thing many people wouldn't expect you to do either from choice, but there are very rewarding experiences to be found in both.

Winter cycling

Why cycle in winter anyway? Certainly, for those planning to be active for the rest of the year, carrying on riding regularly throughout the winter months helps to retain a general level of fitness and suppleness even if winter mileages are considerably less. But there are rewards in winter cycling itself. Other traffic is generally lighter, places overcrowded in summer, such as parts of the West Country, become quiet again, and the very range of weather shows the countryside in a new light, with the leafless trees no longer obscuring the view.

The main winter problems to be overcome are those of keeping warm and dry, of weatherproofing the bicycle, and – in common with summer night riding – of lighting. When you adventure out into mountainous country or lower down in very cold weather, there are new riding techniques on potentially treacherous surfaces to be learned.

Keeping warm
People feel the cold to different extents, with people complaining variously of cold hands, feet (the commonest) or heads.

One highly developed winter activity is skiing, and some items are also very good for cycling, particularly ski mitts and gloves. They come in varying types and price ranges. The essential, as always, is that they should offer windproofing and insulation combined with enough porosity to allow the hands to 'breathe' – some of the plastic covered ones do not. The insulation may well not be enough on its own, and my personal preference is to have a pair of mitts inside which woollen gloves can be worn, that is to say a size larger than if they were to be worn alone. Both skiers and cyclists require to be able to use their fingers, so that flexibility is rarely a problem.

Before ski mitts became generally available on the British market and after a lot of experimenting, I devised a form of bag mitt to go over up to three (yes, three!) pairs of woollen gloves or mitts. Two materials proved to be satisfactory: chamois leather and a double thickness of wool/terylene worsted. The latter dries more quickly. They are made up into a simple bag form, cut to leave the thumb separate from the four fingers, with an extended woollen cuff. The leather or worsted bit comes down to the base of the thumb: experience suggests that a combination of chamois palm and worsted back might well prove to be the most effective and hard-wearing. They are not of themselves particularly warm since they offer little insulation – this comes from the woollen gloves worn inside.

All sorts of dodges can be tried for keeping the feet warm. First and foremost, winter shoes should be unperforated with sound soles, and should be larger than the summer ones by enough to allow you to use two pairs of socks. I have found a combination of the thick off-white Norwegian-style sock and a thinner closer-woven one to be very satisfactory. Some riders use, as in wet weather, polyethylene bags between socks to give some extra wind and waterproofing. Several proprietary footcovers, fitting on or around the toeclip are available. The only real remedy for extremely cold feet is to walk or, preferably, run for a short spell until they get warm again. Make sure that toeclips do not exert undue pressure and keep straps fairly loose.

It is possible to lose a great deal of body heat from the head. The areas most likely to feel the cold are the forehead and ears, and the most popular remedy is the knitted woollen hat which covers both. Suffering frost-'nipped' ears when cycling to work in a very hard winter a few years ago taught me, painfully, the severity of the conditions that a cyclist can generate: the act of travelling at, say, 20mph (32kph) into a 15mph (24kph) wind at a temperature of $-10°C$ (14°F) as it was on that occasion, produces private weather very close to an Arctic gale.

Similar provisions apply for the rest of the body: a layer of wool next to the skin, provided it can be tolerated without itchiness, otherwise use cotton, with enough porous layers over to keep warm. It is advisable to keep clothing as porous as possible without sacrificing windproofing, since the thing to avoid is excessive retention of sweat by the clothing. Metabolisms vary and some swear *by* proofed poplin or similar jackets, others *at* them. Certainly several fairly close-woven pullovers seem to fill the bill adequately. A light plastic unlined anorak is very handy for long descents, or for when you stop in the open, but builds up far too much moisture inside to be recommended for use for any distance while riding at anything above the slightest effort. It is in very cold conditions that a pair of woollen racing shorts worn under trousers, possibly with leg warmers as well, can offer great comfort. Finally, should you discover that you are becoming chilled, put on your cape. This turns its usual disadvantage – of making you too hot – into an asset.

The winter bicycle

The bicycle is essentially a simple mechanism and one of the best things you can do in winter is to simplify it further. Mud, water, and salt spray from treated roads, are the enemies of the more delicate parts such as chains, bearings and gear mechanisms. I would advocate strongly the use of a single gear for winter use. First, of course, it offers several less pieces of delicate mechanism to get damaged. It is also less critical as regards the condition of the chain (but *more* critical on chain line, below) so that a part-worn chain can be used, shortened, on the single sprocket without problems. Finally, the discipline of a single gear, particularly a single fixed gear, forces you to push a little harder than you might choose at times and to pedal a little faster at others, building up a reserve of strength and suppleness for the rest of the year.

The maintenance of the correct chain line is desirable with a free-wheel to within about $\frac{1}{4}$in (6mm) and rather closer on fixed, preferably to within $\frac{1}{8}$in (3mm). It is not generally satisfactory to use the same rear wheel as for gears, even if the hub is threaded both sides. I would strongly advise a separate rear wheel, single or double threaded and built symmetrically over the hub flanges, which should themselves be centred by locknuts and packing pieces (derailleur gear wheels are built asymmetrically to accommodate the five sprockets). The single freewheel or fixed sprocket – the latter with its flange towards the hub's – is screwed onto the hub and the wheel then placed in the machine without the chain on. The chain-line is then readily checked by placing a straight-edge across the chainwheel towards the rear sprocket and seeing how closely it matches the sprocket position. The latter can be varied to some degree by ringing the changes on the thickness of the spacers between the hub locknuts. If you have been using a double chainring with the gear you can either leave it on and use the *inner* ring or use a single ring; the latter may need a shorter bottom-bracket axle. (To avoid this complication, and also to avoid exposing expensive equipment to unpleasant conditions, many experienced riders prefer to have an older or cheaply equipped bicycle for winter riding.) The gear should be 60 to 65in, at least as a starting point. A hub intended for fixed-wheel use has two sets of threads on one or both sides of the hub, a larger diameter right-hand threaded portion onto which the sprocket screws and a *left-hand* threaded section for a special lockring, which is screwed by means of a peg spanner back against the sprocket, to prevent it unscrewing when backward pressure is applied whilst riding. A single freewheel merely screws onto the right-hand threaded portion with no need for a lockring. If you use a derailleur-size chain, the sprocket will be for $\frac{1}{2} \times \frac{3}{32}$in ($12 \cdot 7 \times 2 \cdot 38$mm); if you are using the chain from a bicycle supplied originally with a single gear or hub gear, it will probably be $\frac{1}{2} \times \frac{1}{8}$in ($12 \cdot 7 \times 3 \cdot 17$mm). I would advise not confusing things by sticking to the $\frac{3}{32}$in width if at all possible. The tightness of the chain is regulated by moving the wheel forward or backward in the rear fork end slot. When correctly adjusted it should be possible just to move the lower run of the chain up and down at its mid-point by about $\frac{1}{2}$in (say 15mm). Many cheap chainwheels are eccentric and it is desirable that the chain should be no slacker than this at the loosest point of the chainwheel revolution.

Riding a fixed wheel calls for a little practice before you no longer attempt inadvertently to freewheel round corners, but once learned is never forgotten. The principal advantages for winter riding are that it establishes a brisk rhythm and pedalling cadence – which helps to keep you warm – and that the subtle increase or relaxation of pressure on the pedals regulates your speed, say in a group, very precisely. Back pressure slows the bicycle and can do this much more gently than any brake – useful in wet or slippery conditions.

This is the time of year to ensure that the front mudflap is really doing its job and to grease wheel, head, pedal and bottom bracket bearings to keep water out. Frequent lubrication is essential. Pedal bearings in particular are very exposed and few pedals, except the very expensive Campagnolo, are effectively sealed. Various dodges have been mooted for sealing bearings against the weather – bottle caps to cover wheel bearings, narrow strips of stocking or tights material wound round the cones and oil-impregnated, felt washers and bushes similarly impregnated – but I have yet to find a really effective way of protecting pedal bearings, in particular those at the crank end.

Winter in wild country

The most rewarding of winter experiences is to get out into the snow-covered hills on a crisp bright day. It does, however, call for one or two special techniques and some cautions. Thin, soft, virgin snow, up about an inch (say 3cm), is very pleasant to ride through and offers no problem. Riding becomes pretty well impossible by the time the pedals touch the surface at the foot of the stroke, a depth of some 4in (10cm). It is quite possible to push a bicycle through soft snow up to 6in (15cm)

Many normally crowded areas are deserted in winter but can still provide very attractive cycling, particularly with an inch or two of snow. This is on Mastiles Lane near Malham in North Yorkshire.

deep, but after this even walking becomes a little hard. If the snow has been beaten down by traffic, or has melted and refrozen, or if the surface is smooth ice, then it is ridable with caution. In fact, it can be a very reasonable ride in the absence of other traffic – but it is undoubtedly slippery. It may be of help to let the tyres down in these conditions, say to one-third pressure – 20–35psi (about 1·5–2·5kg/cm²). Beaten down and ridged ice and snow, particularly in combination with slush, are abominable and require more than ordinary care. Always on ice or snow you should make every move gently – starting, cornering, braking – and as far as possible relaxed. Falling off on snow is not particularly uncomfortable, on ice not particularly comfortable, but both can be accomplished on deserted roads in relative safety. The possibility of falling is always there, so it is wise not to carry fragile items in the saddlebag side-pockets.

Do not overestimate your own abilities, or those of your companions. A mountain road over which you could average, say, 9mph (14kph) in summer may bring you down to 1mph (1·5kph) in snow. Better to have time to spare than to be caught out by darkness. Have adequate

One way of carrying a hot drink: a vacuum flask inner is taped into a cut-down plastic feeding bottle so that it fits into a standard bottle cage. As described in the text the fragile glass part is packed out with plastic foam.

spare clothing with you, some high-energy food such as chocolate or Kendal mint cake, and good maps. It is possible to carry a hot drink in a vacuum flask – but bear in mind that these are fragile. An old dodge here is to buy the glass replacement inner for a small flask and to cut the top off a normal plastic cycle feeding bottle so that the vacuum inner can be fitted inside, padded out with plastic foam. Most of the top of the plastic bottle can then be replaced, suitably trimmed and held in place with plastic insulating tape, leaving a neat bottle-cage sized padded vacuum flask of about $\frac{1}{3}$ pint (200ml) capacity – and low enough in price for it not to be a tragedy if it gets broken.

Observe the same guidelines in remote country as the hill walker. If there is any possibility of the way becoming uncertain, you should have and know how to use a compass as well as a map of at least 1:50 000 scale. Do not forget that the steel parts of the bicycle (and the magnets of dynamos and camera exposure meters) can affect the accuracy of any compass used near them. Do not travel alone and be sure that somebody knows where you are aiming to get and when. If in doubt, get down to low ground as quickly as possible.

Lighting

During official darkness – from half an hour after local sunset time to half an hour before sunrise – you will need lights, and it is prudent to use them in bad visibility at other times. They may be battery or dynamo powered.

There appears to be no fully satisfactory dry-battery lamp available. all have a multiplicity of low voltage contacts and their main dis-advantage is not that they refuse to work at all but they may flicker on and off or go off completely – often in street lighting or in the case of the rear lamp, undetected. (Glance round say every two miles or look at your shop-window reflection to check.) Fixing is rarely secure and they usually need to be strapped to the lamp-bracket with a toestrap for safety. Battery life is short – say three hours' continuous use, less in severe weather, when they are also susceptible to battery leakage. They last longer with intermittent use, say up to half an hour per day, which I would consider their limit.

Recently a more robust type of battery-powered lighting, making use of compact rechargeable batteries originally developed for space purposes has been put on the market under the name Nightfarer by

Billington. The smaller model with a frame-mounted cylindrical battery gives some three hours' light before recharging is necessary; versions with greater battery capacity can be used to give either a more powerful light or be used for longer periods continuously. Their use has not been sufficiently widespread at the time of going to press for full reports based on long-term testing to be available.

The dynamo – or strictly speaking, alternator – gives considerably more light, works at a higher voltage and is less prone to the defects of battery lamps. It does require, however, a slight but noticeable amount of extra effort – which is psychologically doubled or trebled – and it does not stay alight when you stop. The law provides for this by allowing you to stop unlighted or wheel your machine at the extreme left of the road. Various methods of switching in standby batteries automatically by electronic means have been proposed, but very few have been put forward as commercial propositions, and none on a large scale. On balance, even so, a good dynamo is cheaper, more effective, more reliable and lighter in weight than battery lamps, in addition to which it is ready for use all the year round and does not deteriorate while unemployed. The best compromise is to carry a small hand torch for those occasions when you need a light while stopped.

Dynamo sets are of two types, tyre-driven – by far the commonest – and built into the hub. The output of the tyre-driven type is about 3·3W. The advantages of the tyre-driven type are low cost, lightness and light output, its disadvantages the effort required to drive it and the liability of the driving pulley to slip on the tyre surface in very wet, icy or snowy conditions. The Sturmey-Archer Dynohub, despite being lower-powered (2W), heavier, lop-sided and requiring to be built into a wheel of its own, offers near to absolute reliability in all riding conditions, and is my personal choice for winter and riding-to-work use, and the lighter tyre-driven type for summer touring.

It is advisable to carry two spares of both front, usually 6V 0·45 or 0·5A for tyre-driven dynamos, 6V 0·25A for Dynohubs, and rear, 6V 0·1A, bulbs. Check that the fitting is suitable for your particular set: the standard is MES but some makers fit their own pattern of push-in bulb, particularly the Dynohub rear light.

There do not appear to be any legal restrictions on where you place the front light: some bicycles are provided with a lamp bracket boss on the front fork blade, usually on the right, while some small tyre-driven dynamos have the front lamp built into the dynamo generator, which is then usually fitted to the left-hand front fork, where the light then illuminates the near road edge without the distracting shadow of the front tyre. It should be fitted in such a position that it is not obscured by a cape when it is raining.

The rear light must be fitted to the centre line or offside of the bicycle: one of the best positions is at the centre or right of the rear of the bag carrier, where it cannot be obscured by bag straps and is visible through an angle of over 200°. This position comes well within the height range prescribed by law.

A word on lighting faults. Most tyre-driven dynamos have a single 'live' wire to the lamps, the circuit being completed by the frame of the bicycle to which the lamps and the dynamo are, theoretically at least, earthed. This arrangement is not always too reliable in practice and if you are in any doubt, or if your lights work intermittently, use a second return wire. I, personally, prefer to solder wire connexions where possible, either direct to the fitting or to solder tags. Intermittent failure can also result from a loose bulb or – more difficult to detect – one in which the filament has broken but where the broken ends remain in contact for part of the time. Most bulbs fail in time from vibration; if they fail frequently and are very blackened on removal, fit a replacement 0·05A higher, say a 0·5 in place of a 0·45A, at the first opportunity. The wiring should follow a neat path along the frame; most riders secure it with tape. I have experimented on a 'winter' bicycle with sticking the wire to the inside of the fork blade, the lower side of the down tube and bottom bracket and inside the rear mudguard, with an epoxy resin, such as Araldite Rapid, and the result seems both neat and successful. Some makers drill the frame tubes with small guides to carry the lighting wiring inside the tubes.

Night-riding

An all-night ride in summer is an experience that every cycle-tourist should try once. Night in June and July is relatively short, no more than about five hours of darkness, and the whole new world of scents and sounds an ample reward – with the dawn a bonus.

It is surprising how cold it can get on a summer's night, however, particularly under clear skies. If the darkest hour precedes the dawn, then the coldest one follows it. You will need gloves, some form of leg covering and an extra couple of pullovers. You will find that you need

It can get very cold around dawn even in mid-summer. Here, although it is June, the riders are using gloves and several pullovers.

to eat at about the same times as in daylight, with a midnight (or slightly later) 'lunch' bridging the gap between the normal evening meal and breakfast. Again, a hot drink is very acceptable, either by means of a vacuum flask or small stove. There is a sprinkling of all-night cafés up and down the country, and those motorway service areas accessible from other roads – e.g. Severn Bridge – are always open.

If you are using dynamo lighting, you will need a small torch for map-reading and sorting out food. If you are using battery lamps then you will need a spare set of batteries. It seems, in practice, that riding speed overall in the dark is about three-quarters that in daylight, so plan your route accordingly. Whereas many smaller main roads and B-roads are very quiet at night, some of the principal trunk roads carry very heavy traffic, much of it commercial, throughout the night, and in certain directions – such as towards the West Country on A30 and A303 – holiday traffic on summer weekends is considerable, particularly on Friday nights. Adequate maps are essential – pre-knowledge of the more complicated bits of the route even better.

Remaining awake all night affects different people in different ways. Some prefer to snatch a half hour's sleep after their night 'lunch', others (me included) prefer to stay awake all the time. Most people experience one or two stretches of drowsiness – the standard remedy is to strike up an animated conversation (even argument has been advocated!) with a companion. Almost certainly you will ride through these bad patches, usually quite quickly. If, however, you are one of the few who just cannot stay awake, there is no remedy but to stop and take a little sleep, however short.

We have found it particularly rewarding to combine a Friday-night to Saturday-morning night-ride with a Saturday night spent away from home, permitting a long weekend and avoiding having to retrace the outward route on the way back. A reasonable distance for experienced riders is about 150 to 200 miles (240–320km) for the combined night-ride and Saturday ride, ending up say 80 miles (130km) from home, leaving this distance to be covered on the Sunday. It's surprising how much can be crammed into a weekend if you really try!

The cleanliness of the air around dawn and the wonders of the waking world will, I am sure, compensate you for any slight discomfort on the journey. And you will have earned your breakfast!

15

The Journey

It had been a long journey and now it was nearly over. Ahead of them the coarse granite of the road wound gently down over the open moor towards the thin strip of blue that they knew was the final sea.

They had left their home in the city, so many miles away, days before on a grey nondescript morning, with no more than the odd grey nondescript figure on the damp dawn pavements. The main road, constrained between its kerbstones pointed away in the direction they were to take. Steadily the gardens of the tightly-packed houses had become larger, the spaces between them greater until at last there seemed to be more space than building and they were in the open country.

With relief, for the traffic had been growing as the workaday world awoke, they had turned away from the main road down the first of what were to be numberless lanes. The continuous pageant of moving tree and hedgerow, of wall and field had begun, undulating its varied profile as they passed by.

Subtly the nature of the land had changed. The soil of the cultivated fields became grey, and black, and red and then grey again. The villages had gone from brick to whitewashed plaster, to golden stone, to brick again and deep brown ironstone, and at last to grey slate. The houses themselves had become shorter and squatter as they moved north, rooting themselves deeper into the earth against the winters they remembered and knew must come again.

The roads beneath their wheels had changed in colour, in texture, in gradient, and the weather had changed as well. The sounds of the people had changed, the accents in the village shop or market town where they had bought their daily needs; the casual word passed on

Fording the sea – well almost. At low tide you can cross The Gannel at Newquay, Cornwall, by this rather slippery footbridge.

the road had seemed another language for even the words were changed, too. And they had lost count of the days.

They had climbed through beechwoods heavy with summer green and had sought the liquid shade from the noon sun as they climbed. Teasingly he had challenged her to be first to the top of the hill and she had seen him look back at the distant view and with a laugh had given him the slip. Together they had swooped down the open escarpment with the rush of the wind in their ears, through the poppy-flecked corn in the chalk-white fields and the children in the village school had called out as they flew by. They had stopped at an anonymous crossroads of minuscule lanes to look at the map and the noise of the insect world in the roadside grass had silenced them for a minute.

They had taken a wrong turning at another corner and the road, already narrow, had grown less and less in front of them until there were only two tyre-wide bands and tufts of grass between. Realising their mistake they had not turned back but in curiosity had followed the track across the lawn of rabbit-cropped turf over the open down until it had brought them to the top of the ridge with the blue plain of the middle country spread at their feet.

On one hazy day their road had followed the lazy loops of a slow-moving river, winding its way through geometrical tall poplars and willows, every turn of the road bringing a momentary new alignment of the withy plantations, a new glint of the placid water. The indolent mood of the river had infected them and they had slowed to match its pace.

They had eaten their midday meal on mole-pocked banks by the road when the sun shone, or in the dark oak bar of a small inn when the day was grey. They had dined in a clearing of unbelievably soft grass in a larch forest on the hottest day and in discomfort beneath a bridge in the mountains, when a sudden shower had caught them far from other shelter. And because the thoughts of cyclists are never far from food and drink, every meal had been memorable.

They had stopped for the night where the day ended or where their sudden impulse took them. A night here in a hostel, for company, there in a village cottage that had tempted with 'Bed and Breakfast' painted painstakingly on the simple gate, yet somewhere else at the inn in the small town whose name had so intrigued them. They had stopped on some days early in the afternoon to look round a mellow stone town or climb breathless to the top of an old earthwork, on others they had ridden far into the dusk and the sounds and scents of the evening had crowded in on them.

One night they had not slept at all but had ridden the night through under a silver moon, alone in the pool of their own lamplight. They had felt the day breeze die away and had shivered at the sudden cold at the bottom of the narrow valley and then marvelled at the equally sudden warmth of the small clearing in a wood. They had sat for a while with a flask of coffee in a remote and seemingly purposeless stone shelter and she had shown him where the warmth of the day's sunshine lingered in the heavy stone. They had cooked their midnight meal just below the crest of the down and had frozen momentarily as a lone rabbit had loped past, ignoring their presence. And they had all but frozen literally as the grey false dawn lightened the sky, until they had taken all the extra clothes from their bags. Then they had marvelled again at the waking world and the warmth of the risen sun.

197

They had remarked the changing smells of the country, the resin of the pine forest at high noon and the sudden smell of the earth after the shower, and they had resisted with difficulty and regret the tempting evening call of onion soup from an isolated cottage as they passed noiselessly by.

But they themselves were changing. They had become perhaps a little leaner, certainly a great deal browner. The vanquished miles had lent them more strength and the uplands were to test it. Now the lowland lanes and hedgerows had gone and there were grey mortarless stone walls about them. The road just around the corner no longer held any surprise for there was no corner. Visible above them, far above, was the cleft – minute at this distance – that the road took over the pass. And the road itself was an etched grey line on the purple of the heather and the green of the bracken. There was a new acid sharp scent in the air, the tang of bracken and sheep and woodsmoke, the smell of the mountains.

They moved more slowly now but the mountain was no enemy but a yardstick for measuring their own new strength. A flock of birds, to him without names but a pattern of black shapes weaving overhead, passed by and he idly asked her what they were called and she surprised him by knowing.

The sun had not shone all the time for it is only in stories and distant lands that it does. There had been the day they had woken in the upland village, with its grey slaty buildings huddled in on themselves as though not wishing to share their gossip with the immensity of the hills, to see the slates metallic and wet under a featureless cloud. That day they had climbed steadily again beside a stream and the mist had narrowed their world to the grey ribbon of road and the sodden tufts of reeds, with the black stream laughing at the two yellow-caped figures that dared to follow its course as it hurried back the way they had come.

As happens on such days, towards evening the greyness had cleared and the great hills were outreached by tall clouds that glowed in the setting sun. They had paused for some minutes at the top of the last hill to watch the sun sink and the topmost cloud turn to rose over the indigo landscape, before they had swept down to their night's rest at the hamlet below as the few lights came on one by one.

They had spent days in the mountains, climbing and descending, on one triumphant day finding themselves at the summit of the pass that the map said was the highest in the country and they had shared the knowledge that they had reached it unaided and that no-one could go higher. Below them, from the bank at the roadside they could see the twists of the road they had laboured up and the turns of the one they would go down from the open heather of the uplands, through the rocky gorge into the green fields of the model farm beside the toy village, where miniature cattle grazed. Above them, he pointed out to her the shaded hollow corrie in the flank of the great mountain, where the patch of snow still lay, even at this season. It was a milestone in their journey north.

Later, on a morning where the unbroken blue dome above promised a cloudless day, they had forsaken the hard road for an older one, a road of unbound pebbles and stone that traced its lonely line across the rounded hills. That day they had lunched, shoeless after fording a peat-coloured burn, in an intimate upland silence broken only by the soft tinkle of the water and the thin call of curlews.

They had not been entirely alone for the whole journey. They had met other cyclists, singly, couples like themselves, occasionally a small group. With one couple they had spent a whole day since their evening destinations lay in roughly the same direction. On one occasion they had caught an older cyclist not far from the top of a hill and had slowed to his pace while they spoke, as cyclists will, of the way they had come and of mutual friends and of where they were going. As they shared a drink at the top she had asked the ageless figure how old he was and he had said seventy-two and that he wasn't as sprightly as he used to be, and they had all laughed. But he was going westwards and would only come with them down the hill to the next fork, where the valleys met. Later they met a young girl on her first long journey, her eyes bright with the new sights at every turn. Neither voiced it, but they envied her that joy of discovery.

Their moods changed too, in the way that the weather will in the mountains. There was one day of long and steady but gentle climbing, but the north wind was in their faces and they rode for nearly three hours without a word. And on some climbs where he was the stronger they agreed each to ride at their own pace and to meet at the top, for they had come near to reproaching each other before, he her for her slowness and she him for his lack of caring. But at the top when she arrived she had found that he had prepared their simple meal as a kind of peace offering and they had laughed again.

It had been a long journey and now it was nearly over. As they freewheeled gently down the last hill the blue line of the great northern

sea grew wider and wider until it stretched across the whole horizon, while the road itself plunged through a few last bends to the shore. They leaned the bicycles that had brought them so far gently against the rocky wall at the edge of the road and walked out onto the deserted strand. She had taken her shoes off and was wriggling her toes in the surf at the tide's edge; he had picked up a shell and was looking at its wave-burnished whorls and lustre. The sun was lower in the sky now and they looked out over the water flecked with gold, to where there was no land any more between them and Atlantis and Tir-nan-Og and Valhalla.

And then they looked at each other, and smiled, for they alone knew the pleasures they had shared. It had been a long journey and now it was over. But there would be other journeys yet to come.

16

And next...

That brings us to the end, as it were, of the beginning – but by no means to the beginning of the end. I have deliberately restricted the scope of this book to the three countries of England, Wales and Scotland because that is where you will begin. But for the cycle-tourist, as for any other traveller, the world does not stop at the North Sea, the English Channel or St George's Channel. I have said nothing of the quiet and the limpid light of the west of Ireland, with hills of a blue so unlikely that strangers think there is something wrong with the colour film when you come back. I have not mentioned the rugged grandeur of the north of that island, with certainly the highest, and probably the finest, cliffs in Europe. I have restrained myself from extolling the delights of sleepy Provençal villages perched on im-probable hilltops, of green valleys rising from the cleft of the Dordogne, of the almost tangible cleanness of the thin air high in the Alps on a summer morning, of the nearly British cosiness of Normandy. I have written of rough tracks but not of the little paved roads that wind between ranks of trees that take up different alignments as you pass through northern Flanders, nor of the even rougher paving that leads through birch and pine to the Polish Baltic coast. But then, they are yours too, for the discovering. And they might make another story.

Appendix 1

Organisations connected with cycle-touring

CYCLISTS' TOURING CLUB   Cotterell House, 69 Meadrow, Godalming, Surrey (telephone: 04868 7217)

Founded in 1878 as the Bicycle Touring Club, the CTC was the first touring club – of any kind – in the world. Membership benefits include: bimonthly magazine *Cycletouring*, dealing with news, cycletouring and travel information, and technical matters; access to Touring Department, offering a comprehensive network of routes in Britain and Europe; specialist leaflets on technical matters and on specific topics such as cycle-camping; facility for purchasing the annual *CTC Handbook* (available only to members), listing recommended 'bed and breakfast' houses, caterers and repairers, together with information on such items as British Isles ferries and major estuary bridges, plus some technical information; third-party insurance (currently £300 000, but periodically updated) against claims resulting from the use of a cycle; legal aid if necessary; automatic entitlement to take part in local activities organised by District Associations of the Club or their 200 sections. Reduced subscription rates for categories of riders under 21, for married couples and other members of the same family: membership runs for one year from the end of the month of joining. In addition to its direct promotion of cycle-touring the CTC spends a large proportion of its time and resources in defending the rights of cyclists in general; it is the principal cycling body consulted when legislation or traffic orders concerning cyclists are contemplated. It is also the representative of cycling interests on a number of safety, amenity and technical bodies.

YOUTH HOSTELS ASSOCIATION (ENGLAND AND WALES)   Trevelyan House, 8 St Stephen's Hill, St Albans, Herts AL1 2DY (telephone: 0727 55215)

SCOTTISH YOUTH HOSTELS ASSOCIATION   7 Glebe Crescent, Stirling FK8 2JA (telephone: 0786 2821)

Between them, the YHA and the SYHA run a chain of over 330 youth hostels in Great Britain. To use a youth hostel you must be a member of the Association covering the country in which you are normally resident (that is to say, the YHA if you live in England, Wales or the Isle of Man, SYHA if you live in Scotland, and so on) *or* have an International Youth Hostel Federation membership card, which is considerably dearer. You can join by post to the addresses given, at regional offices and shops or, by means of a temporary pass valid for a shorter period but exchangeable for a full card, at a hostel. Membership runs for a calendar year, but subscriptions taken out after 1 October are valid until the end of the following year. There are reduced rates both for subscriptions and overnight stops for members from 5 (the minimum) to 21, and free membership for children from 5 to 15 whose parents are members. Hostels are graded according to the facilities available and different charges are levied for a night's stay for each grade. Accommodation is normally in segregated male and female dormitories, but some hostels have family rooms in which families with young children may stay. Blankets or duvets are provided and the use of a special sheet sleeping bag is obligatory; such bags may be bought from the YHA or SYHA or hired for the length of the stay at most hostels. Some hostels provide meals; nearly all have kitchens where members may prepare their own. Cooking utensils, crockery and cutlery are provided at YHA hostels; cutlery and tea-towels are not provided in Scottish ones. Members are expected to carry out simple duties connected with the running and maintenance of the hostel during their stay. Advance booking is advisable at popular hostels and busy times: detailed advice is given in the annual *Handbooks* issued by each organisation.

CTC TRAVEL LTD 13 Spring Street, London W2 3RA (telephone: 01–723 8407)

This company is a commercial travel agency with particular experience in making reservations and supplying tickets for rail or air travel with bicycles. They do not supply specialised routes nor organise tours: these services are supplied to their members by the CTC. CTC Travel Ltd are, however, agents for many tour and package holiday operators and can generally advise on combining these with a cycling holiday.

THE ROUGH-STUFF FELLOWSHIP (Hon Secretary: F. G. Dunster, 1 Thornfield Road, Cottington, Bury, Lancs (telephone: Cottington

4044); details and sample magazine from H. G. Robson, 23 Spring Terrace, North Shields, Tyne and Wear)

The amateur-run organisation is devoted entirely to encouraging the use of cycles on unmetalled tracks and paths. Information is disseminated by means of the *Rough-Stuff Journal*, a bi-monthly publication: the routes covered range from the gently pastoral to the hair-raising! In addition a number of local runs are held, and there is a traditional Easter Meet.

THE TANDEM CLUB   (General Secretary: Roger Allen, 8 Coachways, Mapperley, Derbyshire DE7 6DB; Membership Secretary and enquiries to: Peter Hallowell, 25 Hendred Way, Abingdon, Oxon OX14 2AN)

Formed as recently as 1971, originally to allow enthusiasts to have difficultly replaceable spares manufactured in economic quantities, the Club now has several hundred members. The spares service continues and the Club in addition publishes bi-monthly *The Tandem Club Journal* to keep members in touch with the tandem world. Individual members organise Sunday outings and weekends. Membership is either on an individual or, understandably, a couple basis.

BRITISH TOURIST AUTHORITY   Tourist Information Centre, 64 St James's Street, London SW1 (telephone: 01–629 9191)

ENGLISH TOURIST BOARD   4 Grosvenor Gardens, London SW1 (telephone: 01–730 3400)

WALES TOURIST BOARD   Welcome House, High Street, Llandaff, Cardiff (telephone: 0222 567701)

ISLE OF MAN TOURIST BOARD   13 Victoria Street, Douglas (telephone: 0624 4323)

SCOTTISH TOURIST BOARD   23 Ravelston Terrace, Edinburgh 4 (telephone: 031 332 2433)

These official tourist boards and their regional offices supply general information on touring in Great Britain, including brochures, accommodation lists etc. In addition to the 23 regional offices, there are now tourist information centres – signposted with a stylised italic white letter *i* on a blue background – in many towns, cities and tourist areas.

BRITISH CYCLING BUREAU   Stanhope House, Stanhope Place, London W2 2H

The BCB – the public relations organisation of the British cycle manufacturers' body, the Bicycle Association of Great Britain – has as its aim the encouragement of cycling in all forms. The bureau has available a wide variety of information on cycling topics.

Cycling clubs

In addition to the local activities of CTC sections, there are also many independent cycling clubs, some of which offer non-competitive activities, such as Sunday runs, weekends and longer tours. Some are affiliated to the CTC and these are probably those most interested in touring; a list is available on application with stamped addressed envelope to the CTC. Most such clubs are also affiliated to the BRITISH CYCLING FEDERATION, the body principally concerned with road and track racing; the BCF national headquarters is in the offices of the Sports Council, 70 Brompton Road, London SW3 1EN (telephone: 01–584 6706), and they can similarly supply a list of affiliated clubs. Alternatively your local library information section, youth service or Regional Sports Council may be able to advise you.

Camping

THE ASSOCIATION OF CYCLE AND LIGHTWEIGHT CAMPERS was born in 1901 as the Association of Cycle Campers, the first organised form of camping and the organisation which grew into the Camping Club of Great Britain and Ireland. The AC & LC now exists as a section of the Camping Club and membership (on a family basis for both the Club and the Association) is open only to Camping Club members, for a nominal fee. The Association has five regional sections and issues a bimonthly *Bulletin* which carries site, social and technical information. Details of membership may be obtained from the Camping Club of Great Britain and Ireland Ltd, 11 Lower Grosvenor Place, London SW1W 0EY, mentioning your interest in the Association of Cycle and Lightweight Campers.

Practical information on camping by bicycle is also available to members from the Touring Department of the Cyclists' Touring Club, who have prepared a regularly revised technical booklet on the topic. Further information may be found in the book *Cycle Touring in Europe* and from occasional articles in *Cycling* and *Cycletouring* (see Appendix 2).

Appendix 2

Select Bibliography

Naturally enough, there have been a great many books dealing with cycling, particularly competitive cycling, over the past 100 years. Listed here are a few which are likely to be of use and interest to the readers of this book. Both the Cyclists' Touring Club (see Appendix 1) and Selpress Books Ltd, 16 Berkeley Street, London W1, have much more extensive lists; note that the CTC can sell only to members.

General

Richard's Bicycle Book (ISBN 0 330 24203 2)
By Richard Ballantine; published by Pan Books Ltd, London, 1972, revised 1976.

Enthusiasm just this side of fanaticism runs through the pages – no doubts about the author's opinions! Quite good on maintenance, but takes some tricky steering to avoid the author's idiosyncrasies on, for example, gearing. The three pages devoted to dogs (to deter from attacking cyclists not to their welfare) almost left me sympathetic to the poor dumb brutes, but the book is great on the ecological and health justifications for cycling. Only partially translated from the American – beware of different usages – but racy and eminently readable.

Cycle Touring in Europe (ISBN 0 09 460840 7)
By Peter Knottley; published by Constable and Company Ltd, London, 1975.

A useful guide with tabulated information on the countries of Europe and the Mediterranean, with in addition valuable advice on cycle-camping, for which the author is a well-known enthusiast.

Albina et la bicyclette
Albina roule en tête (ISBN 2–7021–0178–X)
By Jacques Faizant; published by Calmann-Levy, Paris, 1968 and 1977 (in French)

In these two books Jacques Faizant, political cartoonist for *Le Figaro* and member of the Council of the Fédération Française de Cyclo-tourisme, introduces us to Albina, an (initially, at least) innocent young American girl living in Paris, who is persuaded to take up cycle-touring. In the sequel Albina leads a very mixed group on a voyage of discovery, by bicycle of course, culminating in the crossing of the famous Pyrennean pass, the Col du Tourmalet. For those who read French, these books are a source of sheer delight – and as a cyclist you'll see both sides of the joke. Probably the best exposition of the sheer joy of cycle-touring in any language.

Handbooks: CTC, YHA and SYHA
See under respective organisations in Appendix 1: these are supplied only to members.

Equipment and maintenance

Fix Your Bicycle
By Eric Jorgensen and Joe G. Bergman; published by Clymer Publications, Los Angeles, 1972.

Not translated from the American at all but one of the best books available on cycle maintenance. Ignore the ugh! cover because the technical drawings and explanations inside are first-rate and easy to follow. Although the words are entirely American, the illustrations make it completely clear what is being dealt with and most of the equipment, as in Britain, is Japanese, French or Italian anyhow. The authors are not afraid to point out when a repair is likely to be beyond what they consider to be the average reader's ability – though that's not often.

Richard's Bicycle Book (above) also covers general maintenance. For detailed listings of equipment handled by major importers, see the appropriate catalogues. Some of these may be bought through cycle dealers, some direct from the importers – try your dealer first. More extensive and worth noting are: *Everything Cycling*, published by Ron

Kitching (Wholesalers) Ltd, Hookstone Park, Harrogate, West Yorkshire, which includes tables of weights of equipment, dimensions of accessories, metric equivalents, etc., plus a self-explanatory section called 'Useful Advice'; and *Bike-riders' Aids*, published at intervals by The Holdsworthy Co Ltd, 1 Oakfield Road, London SE20, which lists a wide range of equipment and includes maintenance and riding tips from leading members of the Holdsworth racing team.

The Past

The current surge of interest in Victoriana has not passed cycling by, and there are quite a few recent books on cycling history and historical machines. One authentic volume from the past which is not too rare is:

The Badminton Library of Sports and Pastimes: Cycling
By Viscount Bury and G. Lacy Hillier; published by Longmans, Green and Co, London; various editions from 1887 onwards.

Now, of course, available only on the second-hand market, but a mine of entertaining information of a period when the bicycle was undergoing change as never before or since. I quote from the introductory chapter: 'The volume now in the reader's hand is designed . . . to form a useful handbook for all who are interested in any of the various ramifications of cycling. The intending purchaser may consult it . . . before concluding his bargain. The racing man will find his prowess recorded, and be able to fight his battles over again; the tourist will discover all that can help him to prepare for his intended outing, the advice given being founded on the accumulated experience of many predecessors.' Would that I could have done so much!

Cycles in Colour (ISBN 0 7137 0853 0)
By Robert Wilkinson-Latham; published by Blandford Press, Poole, 1978.

A very fully illustrated presentation – 64 pages of colour plates – of the bicycle from the earliest to the present day.

Maps

For those who would like to learn more of the art of the British official mapmakers the definitive work is

Ordnance Survey Maps: A Descriptive Manual
By J. B. Harley; published by the Ordnance Survey, Southampton, 1975.
A comprehensive and technical survey of all the series of maps produced by the Ordnance Survey from the 1:1250 plans, through the ones discussed in Chapter 10 to the 1:625 000 and specialised archaeological and historical maps. Includes a discussion on the accuracy of the various scales and an outline of modern mapping methods.

Details of the maps themselves are given in Chapter 10, and stockists are listed in Appendix 3.

The bicycle in fiction

Despite the large number of literary figures who have been notable cyclists over the last hundred years – Bernard Shaw, for example, was a life member of the CTC – the bicycle has figured relatively little in fiction. Two diversions from near the turn of the century which still ring true to today's cycle-tourist are H.G. Wells's *The Wheels of Chance* which describes Mr Hoopdriver's escape from his everyday tedium, and Jerome K. Jerome's *Three Men on the Bummel*, the story of a fairly impromptu tour in Germany. Neither book is now in print. Some further references appear in *The Bicycle in Life, Love, War and Literature* by Seamus McGonagle (London, Pelham Books; 1968), also now out of print.

Library services

Your local library may stock cycling and travel books, and they can certainly obtain them for you – this may be the only way of getting titles which are out of print. Libraries arrange books in numerical order according to the Dewey Decimal Classification. Bicycle books are not all in the same section and the following numbers cover the main categories, should you wish to browse along the shelves:

629.2272	Bicycles
.231	Bicycles, design, etc.
.28872	Bicycles, maintenance and repair
658.91	Bicycle hiring services

790.09423	Recreation facilities (includes use of national and country parks for recreation)
796.01960941	Sport for physically handicapped persons
796.6	Cycling
.609	History of cycling
912.04	Map reading
914.1	Great Britain
.104857	description, travel and guides
914.11	Scotland
.12 to	
.14	Scottish regions
914.2	England
.21 to	
.28	English regions
914.29	Wales
.291 to	
.299	Welsh regions

Most reference libraries also have a complete set of OS 1:50 000 maps.

Periodicals

Cycletouring
Published bi-monthly (even months) by Cyclists' Touring Club, 69 Meadrow, Godalming, Surrey.

The official organ of the CTC but also available on subscription to non-members. Covers general cycle-touring and travel news, some technical and book reviews, local and national CTC activities. Carries in addition feature articles on cycle-touring and allied activities. Classified sales and wants: frequently the best source of odd items, particularly connected with family cycling or old – usable and vintage, not veteran – equipment. Also medium for updating current *CTC Handbook*.

Cycling
Published weekly (Wednesday, dated for following Saturday) by IPC Specialist and Professional Press Ltd, Surrey House, 1 Throwley

Way, Sutton, Surrey SM1 4QQ (Postal subscription or much more cheaply through newsagents).

The only weekly cycling publication – very much news-orientated, hence devotes a great deal of space during the racing season to coverage of events. Some touring articles, and advertising features giving comprehensive coverage of cycle frames, components and accessories, as well as clothing. From time to time reviews of complete bicycles or market novelties. Occasional features on topics such as cycle-camping. Classified sales and want columns and buyers' guide to specialist services.

Rough-Stuff Journal
Official organ of the Rough-Stuff Fellowship – see Appendix 1.

Tandem Club Journal
Official organ of the Tandem Club – see Appendix 1.

Appendix 3

British suppliers of specialised equipment

This listing includes British suppliers of specialised equipment and services likely to be of use to the cycle-tourist. It includes, in general, only British manufacturers known to the author to supply the material or service specified: inclusion must not be taken as a personal endorsement nor exclusion as a criticism of any product. Items of overseas manufacture mentioned by brand name in the text are available through cycle dealers, whereas some of those given here are obtainable only from the source given. The following letter codes are used: M denotes a manufacturer and in the absence of any other code implies that they deal only through the trade but may supply information on their products to enquirers; P indicates that the item may be obtained direct by post; R indicates that the item is available for sale to personal callers at the address given.

Accessories (specified)

Barelli Ltd, Viking Way, Bar Hill, Cambridge (M) (pedals and pedal spares).

Bikit, Hollybush Lane, off Government Road, Aldershot, Hants GU11 2PX (M) (cable clips and repair outfits and materials).

N. Billington, 46 Arundel Road, Bromsgrove B60 2HN (MP) (lighting systems using rechargeable batteries).

Bluemel Bros Ltd, Wolston, Coventry CV8 3FU (M) (mudguards, pumps and dynamo lighting sets and reflectors).

Cyclo Gear Co Ltd, Crown Works, Baltimore Road, Birmingham B42 1DP (M) (accessories and tools, especially chain riveter).

GB Cycle Components, Hanworth Trading Estate, Feltham, Middx (M) (handlebar bends and stems, cable clips).

A.E. Griffiths, Airport View, Coventry Road, Elmdon, Birmingham B26 3QS (P) (Pletscher map carriers).

Andrew Hague Cycle Engineering, 1 Kipling Grove, Anstey Lane, Leicester LE4 0PF (MP) (adaptors for using saddlebags on loopless saddles, saddle treatment compounds, handlebar tape, allen key seat bolts, junior pedalling attachments).

H. Miller and Co, Newhouse Industrial Estate, Motherwell, Lanarkshire (M) (dynamo lighting sets).

E. Nicklin and Sons Ltd, Field Street, Willenhall, West Midlands (M) (steel chainwheel sets and cranks, chainrings including small sizes).

Nightfarer Lighting Systems—see Billington above.

Pearsons, 126 High Street, Sutton, Surrey (MR) (trailers).

Sturmey-Archer Ltd, Lenton Boulevard, Nottingham (M) (Brooks saddles, Dynohub hub dynamo lighting sets, Sturmey-Archer hub gears).

Bags and carriers

Carradice of Nelson Ltd, North Street, Nelson, Lancs BB9 7NF (M) (saddlebags, panniers and handlebar bags in nylon and proofed duck, leather straps).

Andrew Hague Cycling Engineering – see Accessories above – (adaptors for fitting saddlebags to saddles without bag loops).

Karrimor International Ltd, 19 Avenue Parade, Accrington, Lancs (M) (saddlebags, panniers, handlebar bags, carriers).

Pennine Boats, Hard Knott, Holmbridge, Huddersfield, Yorks (PR) (proofed nylon and similar 'outdoor materials' for bag and tent making or repair).

Tonard Brazing Co Ltd, 29 Leslie Park Road, Croydon, Surrey CRO 6TN (M) (carriers – front and rear).

Bicycles and frames

The manufacturers of bicycles and frames are far too numerous to list here and the reader is advised to consult either a local lightweight cycle dealer or current issues of *Cycling* and *Cycletouring*.

Clothing (except shoes and waterproof capes)

Been Bag Cycle Clothing Ltd, Crookhill Terrace, Crookhill, Ryton, Tyne and Wear (M) (clothing including shorts fitted with chamois leather substitute).

Bertram Dudley and Son Ltd, Commercial House, 1 Foundry Terrace, Bradford Road, Cleckheaton, Yorks (MP) (proofed poplin jackets).

Gibbsport, 45–47 Oldfield Road, Salford, Manchester M5 4NH (M) (racing-style shorts and jerseys, tracksuits).

Hebden Cord Co Ltd, Hebden Bridge, Yorkshire HX7 6EN (MP) (off-the-peg and made-to-measure shorts and 'plusses').

H. Hurley (Sportswear), 323 Whitehall Road, Wyke, Bradford, Yorks (MP) (proofed poplin jackets).

Lutz Ltd, 8 Lee Bank House, Holloway Head, Birmingham B1 1HP (M) (racing-style shorts and jerseys, tracksuits).

Sartor Ltd, Sartor House, Derby Street, Manchester 8 (MPR) (proofed poplin jackets).

Family cycling requisites

Andrew Hague Cycle Engineering – see Accessories above (junior pedalling attachments, handlebar fitting for rear of tandem).

Pearsons – see Accessories above (trailers possibly adaptable for child-carrying).

Ken Rogers, 71 Berkeley Avenue, Cranford, Hounslow, Middx TW4 6LF (MP) (junior pedalling attachment).

Dave Russell, 16–18 Chalvey Road East, Slough, Berks (MPR) (small high-grade frames to special requirements).

Maps and carriers

John Bartholomew and Son Ltd, The Edinburgh Geographical Institute, Duncan Street, Edinburgh (M) (map-makers).

Cook, Hammond and Kell Ltd, 22–24 Caxton Street, London SW1H 0QU (PR) (official OS Main Agents for England and Wales).

A.E. Griffiths – see Accessories above (Pletscher map carriers).

Thomas Nelson and Sons Ltd, 18 Dalkeith Road, Edinburgh EH16 5BS (official OS Main Agents for Scotland).

Ordnance Survey, Romsey Road, Maybush, Southampton (M) (official national map-makers).

Edward Stanford Ltd, 12–14 Long Acre, London WC2E 9LP (PR) (major stockists of British and foreign maps).

Ordnance Survey 1:50 000 and 1:250 000 and Bartholomew ½-inch and 1:100 000 maps may be obtained through booksellers, and most good ones stock the local sheets.

Miscellaneous

Bridgeport Brass Ltd, Ballinderry Road, Lisburn, Co Down (M) (repair outfits and tapered-edge patches).

DEB Chemical Proprietaries, Belper, Derbyshire (M) (Swarfega hand-cleaning jelly – obtainable from most hardware shops and general stores).

Metprotek, Station Parade, Virginia Water, Surrey (M) (weather-proof lubricants).

Roof racks

D. and P. Dixon, 29 Marine Close, Leigh-on-Sea, Essex SS9 2RE (MP) (roof racks to carry three or four bicycles upright with front wheel removed).

Shoes

Reynolds Cycles, 159–161 Wellingborough Road, Northampton NN1 4DX (MPR).

Pete Salisbury, 7 Pyghtles Terrace, Rushden, Northants (M).

Shaw Mills Chrome Leather Co, 20 Windsor Court, Lime Tree Avenue, Street Lane, Leeds LS17 6SL (M).

Specialised services

The following three lightweight manufacturers are prepared to discuss the building of special frames or other 'one-off' jobs:

Andrew Hague Cycle Engineering – see Accessories above.

Ken Rogers – see Family cycling above.

Dave Russell – see Family cycling above.

The following company includes among its products tricycles for the partially disabled.

George Fitt Engineering Ltd, Westmead Road, Whitstable, Kent (M).

Tandems

JRJ (Bob Jackson) Cycles Ltd, 148 Harehills Lane, Leeds LS8 5BD (MR).

Ken Rogers – see Family cycling above (tandems and tricycles).

The Tandem Centre, 281 Old Kent Road, London SE1 (R) (tandems and spares).

Jack Taylor, Church Road, Stockton-on-Tees, Cleveland (MR) (tandems and spares).

Waterproof capes

Bowden Weather Wear, 39 Boswell Road, Sutton Coldfield B74 2NQ (M).

Lillywhite-Lewis Ltd, St Johns House, Church Street, Princes Risborough, Bucks (M).

RF Developments Ltd, St Neots, Cambs (M).

Appendix 4

Tables and check-lists

TYRE SIZES

English size	ISO	European
none	28–541	600 × 28A
24 × 1⅜	37–540 ⎱† 37–541 ⎰	600A, 600 × 32A
24 × 1⅜ × 1½	40–540 ⎱† 40–541 ⎰	600B
26 × 1¼*	32–597	none
26 × 1⅜*	37–590	650 × 35A, 650A
none	28–590	650 × 28A
(26 × 1⅜ × 1¼)	32–590	650 × 32A
26 × 1½	40–584	650B*
none	35–584	650 × 35B
27 × 1¼*	32–630	none
27 × 1¼ (Elan)	28–630	Elan, Module E
28 × 1⅜	37–642	700 × 35A
28 × 1½	40–635	700 × 35B
none	28–635	700B
none	32–622	700C*

British sizes are nominal overall diameters and cross-sections in inches; European sizes are nominal overall diameters in mm – cross-section letters run from A to C. ISO figures are *nominal* cross-section and *actual* bead seat diameter, both in mm: tyres of identical bead seat diameter (e.g. 590) and comparable section can be interchanged. 28– and 32– may be used on the same rim (nominal for 32– is 20mm internal width); 32–, 35– and 37– may be used on the same rim (nominal for 37– is 22mm).

† Are compatible with care: if possible try several samples since manufacturing tolerances may allow some to fit better than others.

* Sizes most widely used.

REPLACEMENT BEARING BALL SIZES

Ball diameter (in)	Where used
$\frac{1}{8}$	Some headsets (usually older types); freewheels; some pedals (older types)
$\frac{5}{32}$	Most headsets; most pedals
$\frac{3}{16}$	Most front hubs; some pedals (older types)
$\frac{1}{4}$	Most rear hubs; most bottom brackets
$\frac{5}{16}$	Some older type and tandem bottom brackets (e.g. Chater-Lea)

TOURING CHECKLIST

This is intended to be as far as possible a complete list: you should not expect necessarily to take everything listed – it is an aide-memoire to make sure that things are not left out (see Chapter 7 for more detail and explanation). Tools and first-aid equipment are listed separately.

Clothing (according to season)

Underwear
Handkerchiefs
Shirts/tee-shirts/thin polos
Pullovers
Tracksuit top/jacket
Shorts and ankle socks
'Plusses'/training trousers and long socks
Change of trousers/jeans/skirt for evening
Slippers or sandals
Sleeping wear
Sheet sleeping bag (if hostelling)
Headgear (to choice)
Scarf
Gloves/track mitts/ski mitts
Racing shorts/leg-warmers/long skiing underwear
Cape/anorak

Washing kit

Soap/towel
Razor/blades
Toothbrush/toothpaste
Small nailbrush

Sundries

Housewife (needle, thread, etc.)/safety pins
Stuff sacks/polythene bags
Stretch straps/spare toestraps/'bonk bag'
Padlock/keys
Money/cheque book/bank and credit cards/travellers' cheques/member-
  ship cards (YHA, CTC, etc.)

Maps/handbooks

Addresses of accommodation and telephone numbers/2p and 10p
  pieces for telephones
Camera/film/lenses/notebook/sketch pad/pocket recorder/other hobby
  materials

Eating

Knife/fork/dessert spoon/teaspoon/sharp knife (for bread) – all wrapped
  in tea towel
Can-opener/crown cork remover/corkscrew
Primus stove/fuel/gas stove/cartridge/camping kettle or pan/holder/
  matches/lighter
Drinking bottle/cup/vacuum flask
Food/emergency high-calorie food – Kendal mint cake/chocolate
  glucose tablets/sweet biscuits

TOOLS AND SPARES CHECKLIST

You should generally have with you at all times the items marked
with an asterisk.* The more extensive spares are required for longer
rides when you expect to be further both from home and civilisation.
See Chapter 8 for pre-tour machine checks.

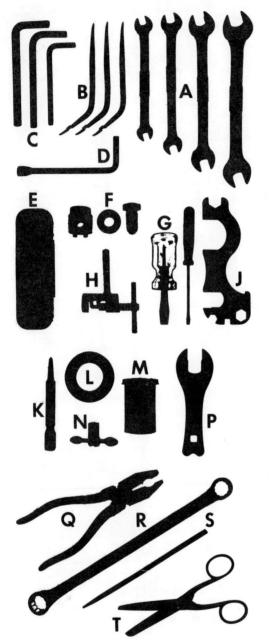

A spanners to fit every nut on the bicycle (the bulges round the middle of these is where I have put a strip of tape on the metric ones to distinguish them rapidly); *B set of three tyre levers; C allen keys to fit every socket screw on the bicycle; D a useful combined 6mm allen key and 8mm socket spanner, by Zeus or Campagnolo; *E puncture repair outfit containing rubber solution, sandpaper, patches, canvas, needle and thread, dusting chalk; F cotterless bottom bracket fitting tools for crank tightening or removal; G screwdrivers; H chain bearing pin extractor; J multiple spanner: not always as useful as it looks but the big opening by the letter J fits bottom bracket lockrings and the smaller opening opposite will remove pedals, although it is usually too thick for cones; K punch, in this case a retired and softened centre punch; L freewheel remover for use in conjunction with track nut to hold it on and a vice or large spanner to turn it: different types are needed for different makes of freewheel; *M small film tin containing Swarfega, or it could equally well house spare lamp bulbs cradled in cotton wool; P thin spanner for wheel cones, usually too flimsy for pedals; Q pliers, for manipulating wire, etc. *not* nuts; could equally well be long-nosed type although they don't usually have the wire-cutting facility; *R $\frac{5}{16} \times \frac{3}{8}$in ring spanner, particularly useful for solid centre (non quick-release) wheel hub nuts; S small triangular file; T small pair of scissors.

SPARES etc.

* Airtight inner tube of right size.
Rear brake inner wire
Rear cable inner wire
Spokes (right length for wheel less $\frac{1}{8}$in will avoid chance of piercing inner tube during replacement)
Front and rear lamp bulbs (in cotton wool in small tin)/front and rear batteries
Brake blocks
Rear hub spindle (especially tandems)
Nuts and bolts (suggest 2BA $\times$ 1in), possibly socket head
Plastic insulating tape (e.g. Lassotape)
Freewheel pawl-springs or lengths of old brake cable
Soft iron or copper wire 18–20SWG
Oil/grease
Chainring bolts/mudguard stay nuts
Cotter pin (ready filed to fit) if cottered set used
A few links of chain
Single freewheel $\frac{1}{2} \times \frac{3}{32}$in (or, less conveniently, fixed sprocket) for emergency use on spare hub threading (if hub is suitable)
Swarfega (in small tin)

FIRST-AID CHECK LIST*

Triangular bandage
Crepe bandage 5cm (2in) wide
Gauze or lint
Self-adhesive strip dressing (e.g. Elastoplast or Band-Aid) 5cm (2in) wide
Antiseptic (e.g. TCP)
Cotton wool
Safety pins (about four or five, 5cm or so long)
Cutting instrument: stiff-backed razor blade (e.g. Ever Ready or Star), scalpel blade or even sharp small penknife
Clean needle

* Courtesy R. McL. ('Mac') Crombie.

Index to Routes

Keys to routes index map

○1, ○2, etc. are the short day circuits given in Chapter 11:
1 Cambridge; 2 Chester; 3 Grantham; 4 Hertford; 5
Norwich; 6 Oxford; 7 Stratford-upon-Avon; 8 Swindon;
9 Winchester; 10 Windsor; 11 Worcester; 12 York.

❶, ❷, etc. and the associated lines ending at the black dots indicate
the place-to-place routes given in Chapter 12:

1 Bath–Church Stretton–Chester; 2 Bath–Cambridge;
3 Southampton–Oxford; 4 Dover–Bath; 5 Harwich–
Cambridge–Peak District–Chester; 6 Cambridge–Lincoln–York;
7 Chester–Preston–Carlisle; 8 York–Northumberland–Edinburgh; 9 Carlisle–Edinburgh; 10 Newhaven–Tilbury–Cambridge; 11 London (Heathrow)–Cambridge; 12 London
(Heathrow)–Windsor–Oxford–Stratford–Church Stretton. D=Dover;
F = Folkestone; H = Harwich; HR = London Airport (Heathrow);
N = Newhaven; S = Southampton.

A , B , etc. are the more extended tours in remote country given in
Chapter 13: A Cornwall, starting and finishing at Launceston;
B Circuit of the new Welsh lakes, starting and finishing at Church
Stretton; C White and Red Roses, a tour of the Yorkshire Dales
and Lancashire Pennines, starting and finishing at York and incorporating a York–to–Lancaster route; D The Border and the Wall,
starting and finishing at Carlisle and incorporating a link between the
place-to-place routes 7, 8 and 9; E Argyll and the Trossachs,
starting and finishing at Stirling; F The North-west Highlands,
starting at Inverness and finishing either at Fort William or Inverness.

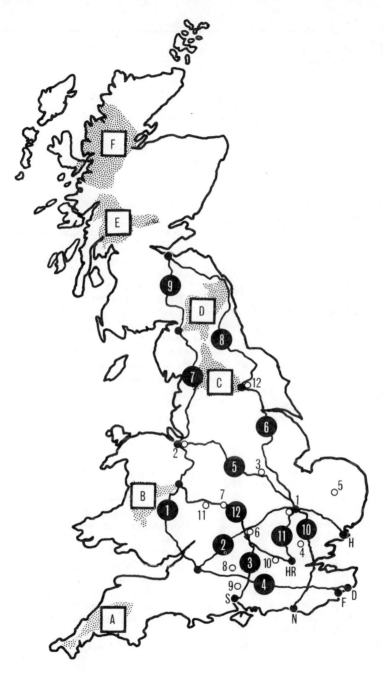

Index